THE NEVER-ENDING LIVES OF LIVER-EATING JOHNSON

THE NEVER-ENDING LIVES
OF LIVER-EATING JOHNSON

D. J. HERDA

TWODOT®

ESSEX, CONNECTICUT
HELENA, MONTANA

A · TWODOT® · BOOK

An imprint of Globe Pequot, the trade division of
The Rowman & Littlefield Publishing Group, Inc.
4501 Forbes Blvd., Ste. 200
Lanham, MD 20706
www.rowman.com

Distributed by NATIONAL BOOK NETWORK

British Library Cataloguing in Publication Information available

Library of Congress Cataloging-in-Publication Data

The previous edition was catalogued by the Library of Congress as follows:

Names: Herda, D. J., 1948– author.
Title: The never-ending lives of Liver-Eating Johnson / D. J. Herda.
Description: Helena, Montana : TwoDot, [2019] | Includes bibliographical references and index. |
Identifiers: LCCN 2018054017 (print) | LCCN 2018054697 (ebook)
Subjects: LCSH: Johnston, John, 1824?–1900. | Pioneers—Montana—Biography. | Trappers—
   Montana—Biography. | Frontier and pioneer life—Montana. | Indians of North America—
   Crimes against. | Montana—Biography.
Classification: LCC F731.J64 (ebook) | LCC F731.J64 H47 2019 (print) | DDC 978.6/02092
   [B] —dc23
LC record available at https://lccn.loc.gov/2018054017

ISBN: 978-1-4930-3825-1 (cloth : alk. paper)
ISBN: 978-1-4930-7442-6 (pbk. : alk. paper)
ISBN: 978-1-4930-3826-8 (ebook)

Contents

Liver-Eating Johnson around the time he scouted for General Miles in the Indian Wars, 1876–77.

INTRODUCTION

Up the edge of the lake a quarter of a mile nearer the enemy a small outfit of volunteer scouts were cooking the choice cuts from the hump of a buffalo shot that day, and . . . a long, dark browed man with a big telescope rifle over his shoulder strolled along the lake shore and sauntered up to the scouts' fire. This was Liver-Eating Johnson . . . a well-known frontier character who was said to have been . . . standing off the enemy when one of the warriors dashed in upon him where he was holed up in some rocks. He killed the warrior, cut out his liver, and ate it in sight of the Indians. This so filled the red men with superstition that they withdrew.
—GREAT FALLS (MT) TRIBUNE, SATURDAY, NOVEMBER 21, 1885

SO WAS BORN TO HISTORY THE LEGEND OF JOHN "LIVER-EATING" JOHN-son. More than mere fictionalized character, Johnson (he had dropped the *t* from his family name of Johnston in early adulthood) soon proved himself to be the kind of flesh-and-bones fighting man who helped open the West when it was still America's last frontier. He lived his many lives to the fullest—first as a farmer and then as a sailor, enlisted man, naval deserter, army scout, Union soldier, Indian fighter, teamster, gold miner, hunter, trapper, whiskey smuggler, woodsman, guide, deputy, trader, constable, log cabin builder, and whatever else he could think of to do to survive within the arms of the rugged and brutally unforgiving last western frontier known as the Rocky Mountains.

A massive man for his day at over six feet tall and weighing more than 250 pounds, Johnson was a gentle giant and a wailing banshee, meek as a lamb and mean as a cougar. He was an enigma for his time, the best of a disappearing breed—Jim Bridger, Jedediah Smith, Grizzly Adams, and Kit Carson all rolled into one. He dared to help tame the West and civilize a nation. Wherever he traveled, his .56-caliber Hawken rifle, along with his Wade & Butcher bowie knife and Walker Colt revolver, was never far from reach. Along his western travails, he dodged arrows, bullets, fists, severe weather, and wild animals until the frailty of old age finally brought him down—but not before he had avenged the murders of his Flathead Indian wife and unborn daughter, savage acts of butchery that sent Johnson on a quarter-century vendetta against the entire Crow Nation, the tribe responsible for the deaths.

Born in 1824, Johnson lived until just shy of the twentieth century. The times back then were more relaxed and yet more intense—simpler days that morphed into shorter, more violent nights where a single mistake could be a man's last. It was an era sprawling with some of America's most notorious western pioneers: Wild Bill Hickok, Calamity Jane, Buffalo Bill Cody, Doc Holliday, the Earp brothers, Belle Starr, and more. Indeed, Johnson most likely brushed shoulders with some of them—certainly, he knew "Calam" since he had appeared in a Wild West show with her, after which his notoriety spiked, and he had briefly traveled with Cody. Still, his later recollections consisted mostly of his relationships with fellow mountain men and women rather than with the "prairie-chickens," flatlanders, and citified gamblers plying the plains.

"I came to Montana in 1862," Johnson once told a reporter. "I was born in New Jersey 76 years ago, and came here from California. Yes, I used to chum with many famous frontier characters. There was 'Wild Cat Bill,' whose real name was Bill Hamilton. Then there was 'Skookum Joe,' and 'Yankee Jim,' and 'Hobble,' whose right name was Hubble. Several of them still live up in the Yellowstone canyon. The only time that I have been East since 1862 was when I enlisted in the civil war. Yes, I have ridden horseback all over the West, from Fort Beauford [sic] to Puget Sound."[1]

From east coast to west, from the Jersey shores to the craggy cliffs of northern California and southern Oregon, his travels rivaled those of any American before or since—all the more extraordinary because they were undertaken mostly on foot and some on horseback, with less frequent sojourns via coach, rail, and sail. To say that Johnson swelled with wanderlust is a miscarriage of the language.

Yet, wanderlust made up only a small part of the anxiety that roiled within the man, forcing him to search the horizon continually for new lines of work and new places in which to pursue them—and new ways to sidestep trouble.

Nevertheless, to his final days, he saw himself in one particular light: He was a fighter for justice pure and simple. A killer of the dreaded savage *Red Man*. A righter of wrongs, a salver of souls, a leveler of the least level of all playing fields—the Rocky Mountain West.

His love for his fellow man was vast and unyielding; yet, he rarely had a positive word for his mortal foe. How could he have had after the loss he sustained in the murder of his wife and unborn child? At the very peak of his roaring, whoring manhood, Johnson opened his arms to embrace his young wife—the meekest of lambs—who helped lift the veil of seclusion from his shoulders. Not long after, she was gone.

Asked later in life about his attitude toward Indians, he replied, "Do I admire 'the noble red man?' Not on your life! They can't fight, and you can't make them work. One white man is as good a fighter as five Indians. If they can get you to running, then they are all right. But to stand up and face a white man, they will never do it.

"The only thing where an Indian is better than a white man is at eating and stealing. The government had better make them work more and take some of the charity they are giving to the Indians and help out the poor white man with large families."

Johnson went on to address his singlehanded eradication of hundreds of Crow braves from the plains throughout his lifetime.

"Why did I kill so many Indians? Why, during the early days out here, somebody had to be licked all of the time, and after the fight was over somebody had to be dead. An Indian will not even wear the clothes that the government gives him if he can sell them. I have seen them sell such clothes time and time again right here in Billings. Sixteen of us scouts killed and put to rout 350 Indians once near the mouth of the Musselshell river. We just laid in ambush in several directions and plucked them off every way they tried to turn."[2]

That sounds today like a jaded reaction toward his fellow human beings by any account of political correctness and ethnic accommodation. But his feelings were reflective of the times—and *never* politically correct. They stemmed from the days when Native Americans found themselves at the mercy of an advancing nation of privileged white citizens, and whites felt themselves at the hands of an ever-ruthless band of marauding savages. Somewhere in between lay the truth. One day, it would touch home, both for red men and white men—as well as for blacks, Hispanics, Asians, and others who followed. But until that time arrived, open warfare was the mantra of the day. And Liver-Eating Johnson was one of its proudest and most successful practitioners.

If all this backstory sounds vaguely familiar, it should. In 1972, a film by director Sydney Pollack made box-office history. It starred Robert Redford portraying the life of Liver-Eating Johnson—*sort* of. The film contained some incidents so cannily reminiscent of the real Johnson's life that watching it is like staring at yourself in a mirror. Had Johnson been alive to see it, he would most likely have approved, although the character Redford played in *Jeremiah Johnson* bore little physical and even less spiritual resemblance to the real-life man of the mountains.

Some of the film's cherry-picked highlights of Liver-Eating Johnson's biography tease us as to the reality versus the fantasy—the smoke and the mirrors that have fueled Hollywood for more than a century. *Jeremiah Johnson*'s sharper, more focused reflections of Liver-Eating Johnson's life echo just enough reality to make the film palpable, with enough dramatic deviance from the truth to keep the audience mesmerized. A synopsis of the Pollack film encapsulates the real Liver-Eating Johnson's life:

Jeremiah Johnson departs the East, escaping the war with Mexico, to try his hand at trapping and hunting in the roiling Rocky Mountains out West. A former soldier, he flees civilization, equips himself with the best gear he can afford, and rounds up all the food, equipment, and staples he can load on a solitary pack mule before setting off on horseback to live the life of a mountain man.

Before long, Johnson finds himself lacking both food and basic survival skills and, in time, stumbles across a dead mountain man, frozen against a tree, his Hawken rifle clutched in icy hands and a note attached to his coat. The man, Hatchet Jack, explains in the note that he was mauled and disabled by a grizzly bear, so he bequeaths his prized .50-caliber rifle to whoever finds him. With it, Jeremiah takes down his first deer and turns the corner from wilderness failure to backwoods legend.

After his horse dies and Johnson is forced to face the waist-deep snow on foot, he is discovered by a venerable mountain man named Bear Claw (Will Geer), who takes him in and teaches him the ways of the mountains.

Eventually parting company with his mentor, Johnson saves another mountain man named Del Gue (Stefan Gierash) from certain death, and the two take up together, along with a young boy Jeremiah had rescued following an Indian attack on the boy's home. Endearing themselves to a tribe of Flathead Indians—the sworn enemies of the Crow—Jeremiah is honored by the Flathead chief with the gift of his daughter's hand in marriage in exchange for Johnson's pelts and several ponies he and Gue had appropriated in an attack against a Crow raiding party. Gue returns to the wilderness alone while Johnson builds a new cabin and a new life for himself and his Flathead wife and mute "stepson."

Despite having a family with whom he can't communicate verbally, Johnson finds fulfillment in his new life. When a cavalry detail arrives in search of a guide to help rescue some stranded pioneers from a wintery mountain pass, Johnson reluctantly takes the job. After leading the soldiers nearly to their goal, he returns to his wife and cabin only to find the Crow had brutally murdered her and his stepson. In response, Johnson immolates the corpses by setting the cabin afire before heading off on a vendetta against the Crow.

Finding the handful of warriors responsible for the deaths, Johnson races in like a madman and kills the entire group. The act triggers an endless series of solitary Crow attacks as Johnson travels the wilderness. One by one, the warriors ambush him, and one by one, they die. Johnson becomes a living legend among Indians and whites alike. Crossing paths once more with Gue, they share a meal before once again going their separate ways.

It's interesting that, early in Liver-Eating Johnson's interview with the newspaper reporter above, he called out some of the other mountain men with whom he'd been acquainted and whom he apparently held in high regard, particularly Skookum Joe and Hubble.

In a January 1889 article in the *St. Louis Globe-Democrat* on Johnson, which the *Billings Gazette* republished on November 10, 1940, the mountain man's exploits were highlighted once again. Following that article, the *Gazette* included excerpts from a memoir of Colonel J. T. Allen. It told of how men such as Johnson were constantly threatened by the Indians hostile to them. In one incident on the Pryor River, three trappers went up against three hundred Sioux warriors and emerged nearly unscathed. Mentioned prominently in the article describing life in the mountainous wilderness were none other than Johnson's acquaintances, Skookum Joe and Hubble.

The early spring of 1877 found Charley Cox and a companion, Hubble, on the lower Prior [Pryor] creek engaged in their chosen vocation—trapping beaver. It seemed to make little difference to these brave and fearless old pioneers of this western country, whether they trapped in the territory of the friendly or hostile Indians. They went where they knew game was in abundance, and for that reason their lives were often in great danger. As usual their camp was an ideal one, secluded and at the same time giving them protection in time of peril. They had a number of horses with them.

Chief Crazy Horse with his camp of hostile Sioux were located on the Little Big Horn river, where they had passed the winter. About the time of which I write, they had broke camp and were determined to return to their agency at Pine Ridge, Dakota. A small war party left their village with the intention of stealing ponies from the Crows and if necessary take a few scalps. They traveled westward until they came to Prior creek, where they expected to find a village of Crows, but in this they were disappointed.

So they pursued their way down that stream and finally ran into a small band of horses that belonged to the trappers. They rounded these animals up and after firing a few shots into the thick brush, where they thought the trappers were located, and in this they were quite certain, as they could see smoke rising from the campfire and left the country. At the time Hubble was away from the camp and after hearing the first shots listened for more. He saw the Sioux making away with their horses and listened in vain for a return shot from Cox's rifle, but the report came not to his ears, and he concluded that the savage Sioux had killed his comrade. Hubble did not return to camp, but started at once for the Yellowstone river, where he met some trappers and told them what had happened.

After a week or two they accompanied Hubble to the camp on Prior creek, to learn what had become of Cox. When they reached their destination a gruesome sight met their gaze. There was poor Cox kneeling erect with his rifle pointing, a bullet hole in his forehead between the eyes and five cartridges in his hand told a silent story. He never moved after he received that stray shot. However, it was lucky for the treacherous Sioux, for Cox was a dead shot. The trappers wrapped him in his blankets and buried him near the spot where he was found.

"Skookum Joe" censured Hubble for leaving camp and not going to see whether Cox was alive, dead or wounded. Whether Hubble did the right thing or not, and Joe might have done just what Hubble did, I know not.

It was in March when Lieutenant Done of the second cavalry received orders to take charge of the Crow nation during the year 1877 and came to the Crow Agency with a squad of soldiers. He enlisted interpreters, scouts and others to go with his command. W. H. White of Columbus, was one of his soldiers, also Sergeant Server, who recently died at the Crow Agency, was another. The lieutenant left orders with me to remain, as a courier from Port Ellis *would arrive with orders for him and when he came for me to come on with him. Early the next morning we were off on our mission. The trail was rough and we made slow progress until we reached Clark Ford at sundown. We were compelled to swim that stream and seven or eight miles down we camped at the Crow camp, wet and hungry and turned the dispatches over to Lieutenant Done. By the way, the soldier's name whom I had been traveling with was "Brigham Young." Then, like the war party who got away with the trapper's horses and killed Cox, we arrived at the gap on Prior creek. We followed it down and during a fierce rainstorm came upon the trappers' camp. They told us of the Sioux war party and what they had done. We went into camp then and remained some weeks, the trappers trading with the Indians for whatever they needed. Later the Crow camp moved on down the creek, then left it, crossing the country to the mouth of the Little Big Horn river. At this point during the summer, Fort Custer was built with General Buell in command.*

In the film *Jeremiah Johnson*, we never do learn what became of Redford's character, a tribute to Hollywood's filmmaking credo: *Always leave them wanting more.* The Jeremiah Johnson legend, we're led to believe, lives past him even to this day.

But real life rarely functions as dramatically as make believe. In the case of Liver-Eating Johnson, not even he, Skookum Joe, or Hubble—with all their experience and legendary success in fighting their way through the mendacity of everyday life—could endure forever. As one editor writing in Montana's *Red Lodge Picket* on January 22, 1900, said about Johnson when the mountain man neared his final days, "Liver Eating Johnson has certainly had a great career, according to all accounts, but the old shell will never be able to put up any more fights, unless it will be the final roundup and the fight with the grim reaper, for he is now on his way to the [Old] Soldiers Home in California."

Liver-Eating Johnson was destined to remain there for less than two months before he took his last breath, uttered his last word, and dreamt his final dream. A representative from the home wrote the editor of the *Red Lodge (MT) Picket* on Jan. 22, 1900:

Dear Sir: Thinking some of his friends might be interested and like to know, I write to inform you and them that John Johnston, better known there as "Liver-Eating Johnson," died at this home yesterday and was buried here today.

And just as simply as that, the most celebrated mountain man in the history of the American West was gone—along with more than a dozen kindred spirits—departed from his mortal bonds so uncharacteristically with a whimper . . . and not a *bang*.

CHAPTER ONE

The Legend Begins

FROM THE DUSTY RESERVOIR OF TIME, HISTORIANS FIND THE TASK OF separating legend and lore from reality and reason difficult. The fantastic voyage of John "Liver-Eating" Johnson is no exception. A violent, drunken mountain of a man who was cursed with less than a laudable reputation, his fame as a fearless fighter burst into legend. His physical stature only helped his repute blossom and flourish. He was a granite wall towering over most other mortals of his time. He weighed anywhere between 250 and 280 pounds, not an ounce of which, according to those who knew him, was fat.

Throughout his life, Johnston was known by several names, but most famously he came to be called "Crow Killer" and "Liver-Eating Johnson" (or "Liver-Eater" for short), names he earned through his penchant for killing Crow Indians before cutting out and eating their livers—a symbol to the Crow of the loss of their sacred afterlife. Johnson's habit, according to rumor, was born out of revenge for the Crow's killing of his wife and unborn child in 1847. Extracting his pound of flesh was his methodic means of righting an unforgivable wrong—and it left its mark on the Crow Nation in the form of a new and frighteningly all-too-real legend.

Numerous people contributed to the beginnings of the Johnson lore. Some contributions were justified, while others were not. Some skirted the issue of *reality* versus *fantasy* altogether, allowing truth to morph into something intangible, varying from one person to the next. One reporter, writing for Montana's *Great Falls Tribune* on May 16, 1905, recalled one citizen's account:

George Powell, proprietor of a restaurant at Harlem, is one of the pioneers of this state, having made his home in Montana for 41 years, and he has had many thrilling experiences as a pioneer of the west. He bears the scars of several bullet wounds, received in encounters with Indians, but he is hale and hearty and expects to spend many years more in Montana, which he considers the best place on earth. While in a reminiscent mood the other day, Mr. Powell talked in an interesting way of some of his experiences, saying:

"I was born in 1854 and when 10 years of age I came to Montana to grow up with the country. I have liked the country so well that I have concluded to remain here for the balance of my days, notwithstanding the fact that I have been in every state and territory west of the Missouri river and from Sitka, Alaska, to Valparaiso, Chili [sic], and through all of Old Mexico. The sun shines brighter in Montana and everything here looks better to me than any place I have ever been, and here old George remains until the end of the chapter.

"It was in April, 1868, that I, together with 25 other white men, had the fight of our lives at Fort Phil Sheridan, located at the mouth of the Musselshell river. Most of the men in the party had been engaged in trading with the Indians near the fort for about a year, and in fact, we were the only whites in that portion of the country. The Musselshell river was the neutral point between the Crows and the Sioux. Everything was going along swimmingly, when one morning we awoke to the fact that the fort was surrounded by a lot of Sioux Indians, who we thought were planning an attack on the fort. We hustled around and the 25 men were soon in fighting trim. Chief Hairy Bear was the big mogul of the Sioux and the reception that our crowd of brave men gave Hairy Bear and his followers was certainly a warm one. He and his braves were looking for the Crows and not being able to find them they tackled our party. The Sioux numbered about 500 and only a few of them at that time possessed rifles, while all of our party had rifles that were loaded with powder and ball. After the first attack the Indians fell back and we made a rush for them. It was during this fight that Liver Eating Johnson received the

nickname that stuck to him up to the time of his death some few years ago, more of which will be told further along.

"As we charged the Indians fell back and the white men took possession of a coulee from which they did effective work with their old time rifles. After several volleys had been fired it was discovered that the Indians were in full retreat and upon counting, 17 were found lying stiff and dead among the sage brush, while none of our party were injured at all.

"At one time during the fight a big buck Indian arose close to where Liver Eating Johnson was standing and started to bring a heavy war club down on his head. Johnson had a 16-pound Hawkins rifle in one hand and a Red River knife, or cleaver, in the other when he discovered the Indian standing over him in a threatening attitude. He dropped the rifle and quick as wink grabbed a revolver from his scabbard, shooting the brave through his heart before he could finish the blow intended for his death. The brave began to stagger and before he reached the ground Johnson slashed him across the breast with the cleaver, exposing the red man's liver. Quick as a flash he grabbed the exposed part and bracing himself firmly tore part of it from the chest of the dying savage. He then held the bleeding piece of liver high above his head and with blood dropping all around him he turned around and asked the rest of the party, who were near, 'How would you like to have some fresh liver for supper?'

"One of the party dubbed him 'Liver Eating' Johnson on the spot and the name remained with that gentleman to his dying day. This is the true story of the affair. After he had held the bloody, dripping piece of flesh above his head for a few moments he turned on his heel and with a spirit of disgust, threw the once active part of the savage far into the bushes. I know positively that Johnson did not eat the piece of liver, for I was an eye witness to the whole proceeding and the facts are as I have related. This is the true version of the story.

"Several days afterward the finest specimens of the dead savages were boiled in a large tank by Dr. Andrews, hospital steward of the Thirteenth United States cavalry, of the regular army, and their *bones were strung on broom wire. After the boiling process the bones were strung together and then hung up in some trees to dry out thoroughly and bleached. All of these skeletons were afterward shipped to a national museum in the east, where they no doubt can be found at this late day."*

In yet another account of how Johnson acquired his ubiquitous moniker, the man earned his soap in a slightly different way. A compatriot and fellow traveler among Johnson's world—by various accounts a friend, trapping partner, or general roustabout who never shied away from a good fight—X. Beidler, in his autobiographical notes assembled into the book *X. Beidler: Vigilante*, had a different tale to tell about how Johnson earned his nickname:

One of the most noted Indian fighters of the frontier is Liver-Eating Johnson. At present he is past the prime but of magnificent physique and yet able and willing to take a hand with anyone—white or red—who wishes to collide with him. A sailor by occupation, he came from the coast about thirty years ago, and being exceptionally expert with his gun he was known as a bad man to impose upon. He followed wolf hunting and trapping with a big sprinkling of Indian fighting for over twenty years and the adventures and hair-breadth escapes of this man would fill a large volume. No man of the frontier is much better known than "Liver-Eating." The manner in which he gained his name is as follows:

At the mouth of the Musselshell River, in the summer of 1866, Capt. Hawley kept a trading post and quite a number of wolfers stopped at his place, doing nothing in the summer time.

One day in July, Mrs. Jennie Hawley, accompanied by a friendly squaw, belonging to one of the wolfers, were about three hundred yards from the trading post, engaged in picking berries. While busy filling their baskets, they were fired upon by Sioux Indians concealed in the brush. Mrs. Hawley fell, shot through the neck, and the squaw through the fleshy portion of her anatomy, but she was able to skip for the post, yelling at every jump. The wolfers responded quickly, but before they could reach the scene of the shooting, the noble sons of the prairie had relieved Mrs. Hawley of her scalp. On examination of her wound, it was found she was only creased, the bullet striking the chords of her neck, merely stunning her. Water dashed in her face soon restored her and she was assisted to the house, while a party of wolfers consisting of Johnson, Geo. Grinell, Jim Dees, and seven others, whose names have slipped my memory, went after the Indians.

The savages kept on the outside of the timber for about half a mile and then dropped into a washout on the river bank, intending to ambush the boys. Johnson's quick eye detected the ruse and the wolfers came down through the willows, and appeared close to the willows, so close, in fact, that the Indians dared not look out and the boys dared not look in.

The washout was about thirty yards long, ten yards wide, and about ten feet deep. The Indians would raise up their cue [coup] sticks and the boys would amuse themselves by shooting them in two. Various plans were devised for ousting the Indians from their stronghold. About sundown two of the boys went around to the mouth of the washout which they found barricaded with shields made from the necks of buffalo bulls; blankets were also hung up to keep the whites from taking aim. The two men being armed with Spencer rifles (at that time being considered a splendid arm) opened fire and the shields and blankets offering no resistance, the balls went whistling through. The Indians immediately commenced to sing their death song and climb out over the walls of the washout. It offered a splendid chance for the boys to avenge the injury to Mrs. Hawley. Thirty-two of the savages passed in their checks in nearly as many seconds. One of the Indians was shot through both hips and was sitting up. Jimmy Dees approached him, and drawing his revolver (a cap and ball affair) held it close to the Indian's head and snapped the cap, which being wet the revolver could not be discharged. The Indian winked, but finding himself still alive, pleaded for his life. He was informed that he was too good to live in this wicked world and that his home was in Heaven. After snapping the remaining five caps, with the usual amount of dodging, winking, and pleading by the Indian, Johnson stepped up and claimed him as his Injun, and putting his rifle close to his head blew his brains out. The boys then quartered the dead Indians and piled them up in one large pile, reserving the heads, scalps, and trinkets. Johnson picked up the liver of an Indian and holding it up asked: "Who will take some liver rare?"

Several ran up and Johnson devoured about half a liver; the other boys backed down and from that he got the name of Liver-Eating Johnson.

The heads of the Indians were taken to the post and the flesh boiled off, then the skulls were placed on a platform and labeled. They proved a great curiosity to the people aboard the steamboats plying between St. Louis and Fort Benton.

Mrs. Hawley survived the shock and is yet living, but wears a wig. Johnson is still living near Billings and bids fair to outlive many a younger man.[1]

Regardless of which account is accurate (if either), it's easy to see from such testimonies that Liver-Eating Johnson had little more to do to create and grow his own legend than survive. As long as he lived, his prowess as a mountain man would continue to precede him, a self-fulfilling prophecy.

In yet another ancient tome, one of the editors of the *Dakota Farmers Leader* on November 11, 1910, recalled his interviews with both "Liver-Eater" and the same compadre and storyteller, X. Beidler, who for most of his adult life was widely alleged to have been a trapping and hunting partner of Johnson. The editor wrote that he was republishing the article from the *Philadelphia Saturday Evening Post*. It concluded:

"X." Beidler, whose name was John Xenophon Beidler . . . was out on the plains one day with Liver-eating Johnson, another well-known Montana character, when they were chased by a band of Indians. Johnson had a better horse than "X" and was soon ahead. He turned several times and urged Beidler to hurry up.

"Hurry up, "X," he yelled. "Get a move on!"

Johnson partner John X. Beidler poses with his rifle for a studio photograph.

"Dod-gast you, Johnson!" shouted Beidler as he spurred his horse; "do you think I'm trying to throw this race?"

The first time we met X Beidler was in Helena, Montana, while visiting that city in 1887, and our first meeting with Liver-eating Johnson was at the Standing Rock Indian Agency while we were visiting Major McLaughlin, the agent.

We spent many a pleasant hour with X Beidler at Helena and his stories about his experience with bad gun men and road agents would make a good sized book. X was all crippled up from wounds received in fierce fights with the lawless characters that roamed Montana, when Virginia City was a great mining camp. To the best of his knowledge he never hung an innocent man or put one away with his boots on that didn't deserve his medicine.

On a trip one day from Helena to Marysville . . . X said the hardest fight he ever had was with a gang of road agents which he drove out of Virginia City and then had to follow them up until everyone was killed, and the last stand they made was in the Deer Lodge Valley after being driven from the mountains near where Butte City stands today. "I lost two men in that fight and got a bullet through my thigh," said X, "and I have been lame ever since. We got our men, five of them, and it was the last desperate fight we had with robbers in the territory."

X was about 5 feet 9 inches high and solidly built, and in appearance seemingly as harmless as any tenderfoot that ever washed gold out of Last Chance gulch, one of the richest ever found in Montana, and over the bed of that gulch Helena was built. . . . X and the writer met several times by appointment in order that we might get a detailed account of his services as a vigilante but we never got down to business more than five or ten minutes before someone would find us, seeking X on some business or other, and I left Helena without getting what I wanted.

Liver-eating Johnson was an Indian fighter pure and simple, and said he never met an Indian he didn't want to scalp, and the Indians made many a bold effort to get Johnson's hair. Liver-eating

Johnson was a great friend of Yellowstone Kelley, and they often hunted Indians together.

It was while General W. B. Hazen was in command at Fort Burford [sic] that Johnson got his blood thirsty name. "Liver-eating" had no reference to animal liver, it was good Indian liver that Johnson ate which gave him the name, and it was the liver of an Indian that Johnson followed for one hundred miles north of the mouth of the Yellowstone river.

A Ree Indian came into Fort Buford one afternoon and hunted up Johnson, who was a government scout and a mail carrier at times between the upriver forts. The Ree told Johnson that his chum and long-time partner Bill Jones was killed by a renegade outcast Mandan Indian while returning from Fort Stevenson to Buford with the mail. Jones had been ambushed by a Mandan named Black Feather, and was found dead and scalped beside his dead pony.

Johnson knew this bad Indian and he made a vow that he would follow him up and kill him and eat his liver, and Johnson kept his word, and when we last saw Johnson at Winona, opposite Standing Rock, he had that Indian's hair.

Johnson before starting out on his Indian hunt, visited the Ree and Mandan Indian villages and sought information of Black Feather's location and probable route towards the Canadian border. He learned that Black Feather intended to join the Canadian Tetons and make his home with them. Johnson returned to Buford and got the best horse among the scouts and a note from Gen. Hazen to the Canadian Mounted Police and started on a direct course for the Teton country, making no effort to follow the murderer, knowing where he would cross the line if he intended to go into Canada. Johnson made the boundary trail in two days and then concealed his horse to await events. On the third day a lone Indian was seen on the trail headed north and Johnson was sure it was the Indian he was after. Johnson was concealed near the trail and when he recognized Black Feather he determined to kill his pony and then kill the Indian. Johnson's first shot killed the horse and the Indian jumped to his feet with a war whoop knowing his time had come. The Indian started to run, not being able to locate Johnson, and then Johnson fired a second shot from his Winchester which caught Black Feather in the left shoulder and he fell, and Johnson soon discovered that the Indian could not use his gun. Johnson approached him cautiously, ready to shoot if the Indian raised his gun, but he was past fighting. Johnson, who could talk the Indian language fluently, told Black Feather why he followed and shot him.

"White dog coward," hissed Black Feather as he tried to reach his hunting knife.

"I told him to drop the knife or I would shoot his hand off," said Johnson as he sat on a bench in front of Ed. Westcott's saloon at Winona, gazing across the river at the teepees above Standing Rock. "The Indian threw his knife at me with all the power of bitter desperation and gave a war whoop, reaching for his rifle, which he was unable to handle.

"I told him he was too big a coward to go to the happy hunting grounds where warriors go, and that I was going to cut his liver out and eat it," said Johnson, as he pulled Black Feather's scalp from a pocket in his hunting shirt.

Neither spoke for a minute or more when Johnson resumed his story.

"The face of Bill Jones seemed to rise up before me as he lay wounded unto death behind his small pony, and I felt the time had come to make good my vow. I couldn't wait for the Indian to die as I was in hostile territory and liable to see a war party any moment. I took out my knife and ripped off the buckskin shirt from the body and raised the knife to drive it into the black heart of the murderer, but that was too easy a death for one who had murdered my best friend. I hesitated for a moment then I cut off his scalp, and the memory of Jones gave my arm strength as I ripped the body open and cut out his liver, but the Indian was about dead as I bit a mouthful of that warm bloody liver and ate it. Now you know why they call me Liver-eating Johnson and I am proud of the name.

"I returned to Fort Buford and reported to General Hazen and was given a furlough for 30 days. Yellowstone Kelley [sic] and Vic

Smith congratulated me for my good work, and there has been no more mail carriers ambushed on the Fort Stevenson route since."

We asked [Johnson] to have a cigar but he declined by saying he never smoked: "I chaw tobacco and drink red liquor but never smoke," and Ed. Wescott set 'em up for Liver-eating Johnson . . . a bad man to run against in a scrap, although very peaceable when let alone. It was after my interview with him that he went to Montana and joined X Beidler.

Fortunately for posterity's sake, Beidler had developed a habit of keeping a series of journals of his experiences—where he went, what he did, whom he met along the way, what experiences he encountered, and when. Johnson, on the other hand, wasn't nearly as meticulous, although he had a sharp and consistent memory. Thus, much of the material passed down from the two men, along with a handful of others, is most likely relatively accurate.

Where the falling out from reality enters the story above is with the reporter's "recollections" of the interviews he took. Newspapermen of the time had a propensity for writing the truth (or what they assumed might have been *passable* for the truth) while peppering it with spice for added reader appeal. It's in these hardscrabble cases in particular that the cautious observer must read between the lines to determine what is factual and what is fictional and weigh one man's account against that of another if he is to come up with an unvarnished picture of history.

"Less Is More"

In *real* life—in the world in which we mere mortals are forced to live—a commonsense dictum infiltrates our daily lives: The more absurd it sounds, the less likely it is to have happened. Unfortunately, in the building of legends, just the opposite is true: The less rational it sounds, the *more* likely it is to have occurred. After all, we're not talking about everyday mortals here. We're talking about supernovas, about men and women who are gods and goddesses, about people who can do no wrong, doing what is right regardless of the personal cost or sacrifice.

So it came to pass that one of the least likely and most absurd legends about Liver-Eating Johnson rose up from the grave, almost literally, to persevere into perpetuity.

According to many Wikipedia and other Internet accounts—as well as some recent print articles, television shows, and videographies—Johnson was the target of a Blackfoot Indian raid in which the braves captured the mountain man as he made his way on a journey to see his Flathead kin following his wife's murder. The Blackfeet took him prisoner, planning on selling him to the Crow, Johnson's mortal enemy, "for a handsome price." Stripped to the waist, he was tied with leather thongs and put in a tepee, leaving one young, inexperienced brave to stand guard outside.

Naturally, Johnson chewed through the straps, knocked out his young guard with a single kick, and scalped him before quickly using the brave's own knife to cut off one of the red man's legs Natty Bumppo style. Johnson escaped into the woods, relying upon the frozen limb as both a blunt weapon and a source of food until he reached the cabin of Del Gue—a fellow traveler and occasional trapping partner—a journey of two hundred miles.

The only problem with this remarkable tale is *not* that it *couldn't* have happened but, rather, that it *hadn't*. Certainly, if it had, some newspaper *somewhere* would have learned of the feat, picked the story up, and run with it. Instead, it wasn't until the distant passage of time that this one popped up, undoubtedly the result of tall tales told around a series of glowing campfires in the small hours of the night.

As is often the case with legends, the larger-than-life heroes who trigger them grow ever larger and more heroic with the passage of time. So it was only apropos that Liver-Eating Johnson fit the mold. Even in the twilight hours of his long and frantic life, he managed to generate news and interest among the American public, perpetuating a portrait of a superior human being already dozens of years in the making.

This story, published on November 11, 1910, a decade after Johnson's death, quickly burned up the wires from one end of the nation to the other. It involved the so-called petrified man, who had been discovered a decade earlier, in 1899, in the Missouri River near Fort Benton, where the body had remained in a perfect state of "petrification," preserved as if an embalmer had claimed it moments after the Grim Reaper had left the room. No one knew who the man was, how he got into the river, or how the petrification had come about, but everyone knew the mysterious man represented a gold mine to a curiosity-seeking public.

The man who discovered the corpse was quick to sell it for $2,500 to Arthur W. Miles, a prominent Livingston, Montana, businessman and former mayor of that town who happened to be the nephew of lauded general Nelson Miles. Miles placed the corpse in a pine box and carted it around the countryside "carnie-style" for viewing at 25 cents a head, paid by hundreds of curious gawkers from Washington State and Montana to Minnesota and several large cities in the East.

Miles's newfound "gold mine," like any other, was irreplaceable, so he took assurances that nothing would happen to his prized possession as it made its rounds. According to an article in the September 7, 1899, issue of the *Bozeman Chronicle*, "One of the most remarkable insurance policies ever issued has been taken out on the petrified man of Livingston. . . . The policy covers loss by accident in shipment and stipulates the payment of $5,000 should the strange freak come to harm while traveling from place to place."

On December 20, 1899, a new source for the "stone man's" identification stepped forward in the boot prints of none other than "the grizzled frontiersman, 'Liver Eating' Johnson," who by then was living in Billings. When the petrified man's remains finally filtered their way to Helena before being shipped off for exhibition to Paris, France, Johnson happened to be in town and—curious as to just what a petrified man looked like—coughed up a quarter to view the corpse.

Immediately, Johnson noticed a marked resemblance to his old partner Antelope Charlie, who had been killed by Indians two decades earlier.

Years after his disappearance, an article in the *Buffalo (NY) Evening News* dated December 26, 1899, recounted the reunion of Liver-Eating Johnson with his "old pard" in a mesmerizing story initially run a decade earlier in Montana's *Helena Independent*.

[The petrified man] has found a long lost friend who gives him a character and establishes his identity. This friend, who comes to the

aid of the silica man in his hour of doubt and trouble, is no other than "Liver Eating" Johnson, a famous Indian fighter and Scout of Eastern Montana, who declares that [the petrified man] is no less than all that is left of "Antelope Charlie," a character known at Fort Benton in the days when it could be truly said that the only good Indians were the dead ones, says the Helena (Mont.) Independent.

If "Liver Eating" Johnson tells the truth, the whole truth and nothing but the truth, the petrified man is liable for prosecution for selling whisky to Indians. At any rate, from what the old scout [Johnson] says of him it is evident that the petrified man was a hard case, or is one, in whatever tense he may be considered.

"Liver Eating" Johnson passed through Helena last week in company with James Nelson of Red Lodge, who is taking him to the Soldiers' Home at Santa Monica, Cal., where the old scout [Johnson] will probably spend his last days. The old man has been in poor health for some time, and as he expressed a desire to go to the Soldiers' Home, several of his friends among the leading residents, assisted by United States Senator W. A. Clark, secured him admission to that institution and the authorities of Carbon County paid his expenses there and provided him with an attendant.

There are a score or more of pioneers in Helena who know "Liver Eating" Johnson. They tell how, many years ago, he cut a piece of the liver from an Indian whom he had already leaded with the aid of his trusty shootin' iron, and eaten the gory morsel. From that time to the present day he has been known far and wide as "Liver Eating" Johnson. At the same time, his friends recognize the fact that he was one of the greatest romancers of his time, but that fact for the sake of the petrified man should be overlooked just now. "Liver Eating" Johnson, while at Billings on his way to California, called on the petrified man.

"Hully gee!" exclaimed "Liver Eating" Johnson, or in words to that effect, the moment he stepped behind the curtain and gazed at the stony features of the phenom. "I knew that fellow 25 years ago. That's 'Antelope Charlie' as sure as I'm a foot high. He went out to trade with

Indians one day and never came back. I looked for him a long time, and dum my skin, if I haven't found him at last."

"Liver Eating" Johnson gazed long and earnestly at the features of his old-time friend, and continued:

"You see it was this way: The Hudson Bay Fur Company did a land office business with the Indians and prairie men up there at that time, and 'Antelope Charlie' was a typical prairie man. Hundreds of white men made Benton their headquarters. They would organize themselves into expeditions and some of them go off into the Indian country on fur collecting tours, while others spent their time in trading with the red devils. 'Antelope Charlie' was one of the latter class. We all drank whisky in those days. The gang that he and I ran with had no other use for our money, and I helped to buy him 10 gallons of whisky, fitted him up a conveyance and sent him out to trade with the wild Indians down the Missouri river below Benton, but told him not to go to the mouth of Eagle creek, 25 miles down the stream, because the Gros Ventres and Piegans were camped in that neighborhood, and I knew that they would kill him.

"The crowd of bums waited around Benton two or three weeks for his return, but he failed to show up and we organized an expedition and scoured the country in search of him, but were unable to find any trace of his whereabouts. We did find, however, at the mouth of Eagle creek the irons of a wagon, which had been burned, but that is all that we could ever discover of the missing Charlie. But today the mystery of his disappearance is unraveled, and it all comes back to my mind as vividly and life-like as though I were passing through the events of 25 years ago at this time, because there lays the missing body in a state of petrifaction [sic], with the hands tied across his breast with a rawhide, which tells me all too plainly that he met his death at the hands of the Piegan Indians, and was thrown into the Missouri river.

"Charley came to Montana from Arkansas, but what his real name was I never knew, as everybody went by nicknames in those days, and a good share of the floating population were bad men from other States. Nobody in those days ever cared what a man's name was before he left home."

Johnson went on to explain that he had supplied Antelope Charlie, who at the time was some thirty-five years of age, with liquor and gear before seeing him off down the river to trade with the Piegan Indians. When Charlie failed to return after several months, Johnson assumed the Indians had killed him at the mouth of Eagle Creek, twenty-five miles below Fort Benton, before throwing his body into the river. And they had. That's where the corpse remained until late summer of 1899 when it was discovered by accident, still in a state of perfect petrification and looking as natural as it ever had in life.

In lending his firsthand testimony to the story, Johnson quashed two rumors together. The first was that Antelope Charlie had disappeared into thin air, never to be seen again. The second and even more important was that Liver-Eating Johnson was too old and feeble to remember with any great detail events from his own past. To the contrary, he could recount a story from decades earlier with little more than a hiccup in accuracy.

Well, *usually*.

THE TRUTH MAY SET YOU FREE

To a great extent, the recounting of a story ad nauseum, with appropriately progressive embellishments along the way, depended primarily on whether or not the story was worth recounting. What's important to realize when winnowing through the fields of time is that legends get perpetuated because their very perpetuation serves a purpose. Whether or not all of the stories are true, untrue, or *somewhat-basically-just-a-little-bit-in-between-true-and-untrue*—that's the historian's quagmire when writing about historical figures. What is fantasy and what is reality?

After determining the difference, the historian must identify the *source* of the story (who originated it?); the approximate age of the story (to what year was it first traced?); and the story's birthplace (where did the story first appear?). Only then, after weighing the answers and developing the irrefutable facts versus legendary suppositions, can we begin to place into perspective the veracity of the tales we read about or hear.

But even after all that, we need to remember that veracity is a bit like drawing a royal flush in poker: It's impossible to do until you do it. Some things we believe we "know" about our legendary heroes of the American West are impossible to verify until we verify them.

The only difference between poker and history is that drawing a royal flush is mathematically possible, while deciphering reality from legend often is not. And that is where the values of deductive reasoning and intuitive psychoanalysis come into play.

Liver-Eating Johnson was no god: He was a man. But he grew up to be a man only because he *portrayed* himself as a god—indomitable, indefatigable, unbreakable. Otherwise, he never would have survived childhood. The omnipresent spiritual aura standing guard over the person who would one day rise to become the legend of Liver-Eating Johnson helped rescue a young boy from the hands of a brutal father and a feck-less mother. As the aura around him grew and strengthened, so grew Johnson's self-image. Like a self-fulfilling prophecy, Johnson melded the man to the image. If he hadn't, we wouldn't be talking about him today. Sprung from the agony of subsistence throughout his teenage years, he developed the fortitude required to pack up, sail away from his family shackles for good, and set off to visit foreign ports of call in exciting new worlds.

And it all began on his very natal day in, of all places for a future mountain man, Little York, New Jersey.

Which is the very best place for us to pick up his trail.

CHAPTER TWO

The Birth of John Garrison

LIVER-EATING JOHNSON WAS BORN JOHN GARRISON IN 1824 NEAR Hickory Tavern between Pattenburg and Little York in Hunterdon County, New Jersey. He was likely one of two boys and five girls whom Isaac and Eliza-Metlar Garrison brought into the world.[1] Of his siblings, his brother died in Virginia during the Civil War, and his sister Matilda Tillman was the last of the surviving family to pass away in Rochester, New York, in 1923.

According to researcher Dorman Nelson, young Garrison's brother might have been named John while John's true birth name may have been William, a moniker he might have kept until forced to change his name to avoid prosecution years later.

One thing that's sure is that little is known of early family life for this most unlikely easterner turned mountain man. History has pieced together a vapid tableau of a tough childhood. Of Scotch-Irish or Scotch-German descent, Garrison was born into a home under duress. History has of necessity recorded less of his family's maternal lineage than that of his father, whose lifelong struggle with alcoholism was matched only by his violent temper.

As with most people who drain their courage from a bottle, Isaac Garrison rarely threw down against strapping, healthy, fully grown adult males but instead dumped most of his aggressive harshness and bottom-less brutality upon his wife and his sons, with John receiving the bulk of the father's fury. Nearly as soon as the boy could walk, Isaac showered him with abuse. When the lad was old enough, his father put him to work running errands and doing light jobs for the neighbors to pay off the father's own personal debts. As John grew into a strapping, sturdy young teenager, Isaac leased him out for even more demanding work—from building and hauling to plowing and planting. One account from a neighbor who knew the family states that the youngster was worked "nearly to the bone."

Sadly, the hardships he faced at home created in the boy a hardened, cynical outlook on life and a shell tough enough to harbor him from the pain of reality. Still, in time, the atrocities he faced became too much even for him. Young John, like his father, showed increasingly frequent outbursts of anger fueled by desperation. As time passed, Isaac's drinking grew progressively worse, and the family's financial woes deepened. That, too, was yet one more shortcoming heaped upon the boy's back until, at last, John could take no more.

Sometime around 1838, when John Garrison had reached the age of fourteen, he decided to run away from home to start a new life. Years of hard work and long days of intensive labor had honed the young man's physique into a toughened cog of chiseled steel. That was just what every employer of the day was looking for—and more than the captain of a whaling schooner setting out from port along the Atlantic coast could have hoped to find. When the boy showed up at the pier looking for a job one day, the captain hired him on the spot. And John Garrison, seaman, was born.

Young Garrison couldn't have picked a better time. American whalers had cornered the industry. An estimated seven hundred out of nine hundred ships plying the seas by the late 1840s—some 70 percent of them—flew the American flag. One of whaling's biggest years was 1845, at which time 525,000 barrels of whale and sperm oil were produced by American whalers alone. According to the US census, whaling had grown to become Massachusetts's third-largest industry by 1840. Direct employment on whaling vessels during the decade between 1840 and 1850 was estimated at ten thousand to twenty thousand men. Each vessel employed between twenty and thirty crew members.

The reason was simple: Whale products were invaluable to a growing nation. The main largess derived from the whaling industry included sperm oil, whale oil, spermaceti, and baleen, or whalebone. Sperm oil was waxy and could be burned in lamps or used as a lubricant. Whale oil was digestible and could be consumed just as any other type of animal fat. Spermaceti, or wax taken from the head of the sperm whale, was also called "head matter" and was a major component of luxury candles. Whalebone was used in place of plastic, which was still in its infancy and relatively unavailable to American industry. The whalebone was used to make things such as corsets, umbrella ribs, hooks, whips, walking canes, and just about anything else one could conceive. The bristle element of the baleen was used to make brushes and brooms.

But the whaling industry wasn't an entity unto itself. It helped create an offshoot economy through numerous other industries, including shipbuilding. In 1858 nearly $2 million was spent in New Bedford alone, fitting out the sixty-five vessels that sailed that year. The whaling industry also provided employment for the tens of thousands of men who made up the whaling crews, one of whom was named John Garrison.

Although we know Garrison hired on as a crew member on a whaler, piecing together a time line of young John's years at sea is difficult, as few records were kept. It appears as if he remained part of the crew for four to six years, after which wanderlust overtook him—a recurrent theme in his life.

With the possibility of war looming with Mexico, John saw an opportunity for excitement. When the schooner he was on set into port for supplies, he jumped ship and, lying about his age, joined the US Navy. There he served on a fighting ship in preparation for the Mexican incursion, which seemed all but imminent. Although numerous accounts claim he served during the tenure of the short-lived war, which ended in 1848, other records show him firmly ensconced on dry land, working his way west toward the Rocky Mountain wilderness long before then.

In all likelihood, Garrison served on one or more different naval and merchant marine vessels until around 1843. But even his short life as a naval enlistee proved fraught with perils. When a lieutenant in charge of Garrison's vessel struck one of his comrades with the butt of a sword, Garrison lost control and smashed the officer in the neck with a rock-hard fist, laying him out on the deck. Upon regaining consciousness and learning that Garrison had been the one who struck him, the officer placed him under arrest. For the next thirty days, Garrison was denied shore leave in what most researchers believe was San Francisco Harbor.

When Garrison's time in the brig was finally up, he took advantage of permission to go ashore, which he did—and then some. Setting off on foot, he followed the wharf toward the city and never looked back nor returned to the ship.

And John Garrison, naval deserter, was born.

CHAPTER THREE

John Hatcher's Cabin

By THE TIME HE REACHED NEARLY TWENTY YEARS OF AGE, JOHN GAR-rison had reinvented himself as John Johnston (he would later drop the *t* in his last name once he gained the moniker of "Liver-Eater") as he made his way west. There, he reasoned, he could match his new name to a new persona and avoid being caught and hanged for desertion. He likely worked his way westward in exchange for passage on the wood-burning paddle wheelers that plied the Missouri River from Kansas City to Fort Benton, Montana. Certainly, his knowledge of sailing would have served him in that capacity. Once he reached his destination, he planned on setting ashore and going to work as a woodcutter, providing steamboat fuel for boats traveling to and from Wyoming Territory.

Johnson arrived on the scene in St. Joseph, Missouri, sometime after 1844 and quickly went to work cutting wood. After a short period of that, he grew tired of the monotony, so he picked up and headed north and west to the Yellowstone region of Wyoming Territory, where he acquired a small plot of land and began raising cabbages for a growing westbound population.

When he discovered the remuneration for a full summer's worth of back-breaking labor tallied a scant 3 cents a pound, he made the fateful decision to give it all up and turn his back on society. He would venture even *farther* north, deeper up into Big Yellowstone Country, to where the mountains and the wilderness melted into one, a region so vast and sprawling that only God could find his way back. To survive, he would hunt and fish and trap and trade, never again to worry about where his next meal would come from—or how much money he could make toiling away in a field for someone else's benefit.

Outfitting himself with the necessities a mountain man required—a .30-caliber Hawken rifle, a bowie knife, several traps, and a sturdy horse—he headed higher up into the Rockies, stopping to take odd jobs along the way. In 1863, after several years of rousting about, he learned of a "fantastic gold strike" in the Alder Gulch area of Montana Territory. The news grabbed him by the throat. Rushing off to find fame and fortune, he arrived several weeks later only to discover that panning for gold was even less profitable than grubbing for cabbages. When he failed to make the killing he'd expected, he moved on once again, this time south through Wyoming into northern Colorado, picking up several more odd jobs along the way, including work as a woodhawk (supplying cord wood to passing steamboats), while dreaming of the day when he could turn to trapping and hunting full-time.

In a sense, Johnson was fortunate. Blessed with incredible good timing, he entered the Western Rockies' trapping trade at the peak of the industry. Still inexperienced and untrained in the ways of backwoods survival, he nevertheless managed to remain a trapper well past the industry's demise, somehow surviving the experience. In his initial interactions with the trappers he met along the way, he projected himself as a seasoned mountain man brimming with confidence and bravado. In fact, no one seemed to know where he came from, anything of his life's history, or any anecdotal memories that might eventually serve as the seeds of a legend. His physical size was helpful in selling the image, tipping in around 220 pounds by some estimates. Others claimed him as having a bulk closer to 280, with no fat and a "pair of paws as big as a bushel of Montana wheat."[1] He certainly appeared to be a mountain man, no doubt, underscored by the fact that he spoke in a perfectly developed "campfire vernacular."[2]

As difficult as his previous life at sea had been, his experiences served him well on land. He had learned at a young age the importance of self-reliance, not to mention developing his skills while using his brain to escape the trouble that already dogged his every move. Living and working in the mountains required a vastly different skill set than anything he had ever known before. It included self-defense and survival. The wilderness environment was, at best, "dangerous, arduous, [and] miserable."[3] Many veteran trappers had their lives snuffed out prematurely by a single misstep. Exposure to the brutal elements, the omnipresent reality of starvation, predatory animals, and Indian attacks all posed a relentless threat. Even in the best of times, trapping required wading through waist-deep frozen streams before the heaviest snows began tumbling from the sky in winter—and repeating that routine again countless times the following spring as the ice began to thaw.

Given the diverse ethnic origins of the trappers running their lines, a rudimentary knowledge of other languages proved invaluable. That meant being conversant in Spanish or French, with occasional forays into German, Portuguese, and Dutch, not to mention some of the dozens of local native languages and dialects.

Survival skills included total proficiency with a rifle, pistol, and knife along with the ability to swim, climb, and fight hand-to-hand whoever or whatever when called upon—and *win!* As a bonus, a well-trained mountain man had to be proficient in setting traps, skinning prey, and cooking, along with the less sedentary skills of knife throwing, tomahawk fighting, and spear tossing, all while honing an acute awareness of the local indigenous tribal habits and attitudes toward white men in general and trappers in particular. Often, mountain men were required to analyze and react to any potentially perilous situation instantaneously. Responding to danger both quickly and appropriately also required an expertise in sign reading, tracking, and horseback riding.

All these traits, though, amounted to nothing if a trapper was inexperienced in reading the weather patterns that played out all around him, any one of which could prove deadly. Add to his skill set a basic understanding of plants—planting, harvesting, and cooking vegetables, roots, seeds, and berries for those times when meat was scarce—and you begin to understand the mental and physical requirements of a successful mountain man.

Then, too, the rigorous lifestyle of a mountain man along with the emergencies he faced from one day to the next provided little forgiveness when it came to sheer physical endurance. Neither injury nor old age could depend upon mercy at the expense of a man's growing infirmities. Never was any explorer or adventurer in history more segregated from the rest of society. If a mountain man died far from his partner, he would simply disappear, never to be heard from again. If he were injured, he became prey for any predator, human or animal, to come along, so he had to mend himself quickly. In the event of illness, he had only whatever the land offered him as medicine.

In effect, a mountain man had to be a combination of farmer, fighter, prognosticator, trapper, hunter, linguist, physician, and survivor. It's no wonder that this unique breed inspired such near-mythical awe and admiration among the more genteel of the local Western populace.

Of course, Johnson, with all his skills and experiences—not to mention mental fortitude—would never have survived the first winter in the wilds on his own. With new, unique, and potentially deadly situations popping up daily, the skills of a mountain man required months if not years to hone. Fortunately, Johnson stumbled across the path of a skilled and experienced teacher in the form of a veteran mountain man who took a shine to him from the start. His name was Old Jack Hatcher.

Somewhat older than Johnson, Hatcher was a Virginian and an associate of the Bent & St. Vrain Company at Bent's Fort along the Santa Fe Trail. He and Johnson crossed paths in northern Colorado, and Hatcher was immediately impressed with the young man. He took Johnson under his wing, teaching the newcomer to be proficient with his bowie knife and a .56-caliber Hawken rifle he had gifted him (the .30-caliber was woefully underpowered for its purpose). Before long, Johnson learned the skills of trapping, tracking, hunting, and surviving as the pair settled into Hatcher's cabin on the Little Snake River to prepare for the onset of spring and the coming of a new trapping season.

The two men remained trapping partners until 1846, when Hatcher decided to return to Bent & St. Vrain to open up a series of trading posts in New Mexico. He released from service two Cheyenne women he had hired to cook and do chores for them, sending them back to their tribe. As a parting gift, he willed his cabin to Johnson, who was overwhelmed by the offer. Hatcher rode off and, when the war with Mexico erupted, signed on as an army scout, which he continued doing until the hostilities ended two years later.

Meanwhile, Johnson continued to put his newly honed skills to the test. Fortunately, he wasn't alone long. Another trapper by the name of Del Gue happened along, and he and Johnson agreed to a pact to hunt and trap together, splitting their spoils fifty-fifty.

Early in their relationship, Johnson saw a fortuitous jump in the hides they were bringing home. Still, life without Ol' Jack Hatcher—and particularly without the Indian cooks whom Johnson had so come to appreciate—wasn't the same. So, in the summer of 1847, he and Gue parted company, and Johnson set out for the Flathead (Salish) camps in the Bitterroot Valley of Montana, south of present-day Missoula. The year before, a sub-chief had offered his daughter, The Swan, to Johnson in a trade. But when the two met once again to discuss the details of the deal, Johnson surprised everyone by foregoing the routine of bartering, asking instead for the girl's hand in marriage—the quickest and easiest way he knew to replace the loss of Hatcher's Cheyenne housekeepers.

So, the customary exchanges were made, and Johnson and The Swan left on the trip back to the Little Snake. During their time on the trail, he gave his wife a rifle and some powder and balls and taught her to shoot so she would have meat during the fast-approaching winter. It wouldn't do to return from four long months of trapping only to find his new wife frozen and starved to death. In return, he learned to speak Salish, his wife's native tongue, so he could communicate with her and her Flathead friends and family.

By the time they reached Old Hatcher's cabin, fall had draped itself over the valley. Johnson had just enough time to settle into the notion of being a family man. He jumped into the task as easily as any before in his life. As trapping season drew close, Johnson spent the rest of the season putting together an ample supply of dry goods for his wife's winter stay.

Finally, the day came when he bundled up, packed his horse and mule, and kissed his wife good-bye before heading out for the deep snows and frigid streams and the promise of a rich winter season of trapping. Life at last, it seemed to him, had taken a turn for the best. Everything was working out better than he could have hoped. For John Johnson, the reality of finally being a family man filled his hardened heart with joy and gave him a real reason for living.

Or so at first it *seemed*.

CHAPTER FOUR

Liver-Eater

THE SUN LAY LOW ON THE HORIZON OVER BATTLE MOUNTAIN IN northwestern Colorado. The big man on the imposing black stallion veered off the trail and onto the shale and gravel scattered along the hillside and dismounted.

He stood for a moment, sniffing the air. Satisfied that there were no enemies nearby, he unfastened his pack, lifted the load from his horse, and threw it like a pillow full of feathers off to one side. It was no problem for the most powerful man who ever strode the Rocky Mountains. Or, at least, so legend said.

The man who had come to be called Liver-Eating Johnson, or *Dapiek Absaroka* by the Indians and "Crow Killer" by the whites, uncinched and removed the saddle from his horse. The setting sun silhouetted his six-foot-three-inch frame and 240 pounds of muscle below the thick red beard that had become his calling card.

Staking his pack animals in a small patch of greenery among the stones, he whispered to them that all was well and they'd be safe that night. Mountain men often talked to their animals when no one else was around. Johnson hadn't seen another soul for weeks.

Near the belongings he had thrown to the ground lay an oblong pile of stones in the shape of a grave. He removed the two top layers, reached down into a hole, and removed a hinged copper kettle. He loosened its latch and opened it up. Reaching in, he lifted out the skull of a woman followed by a second, smaller one. After that, he removed an eagle's feather and several mementos, including a necklace and armbands. He checked the items carefully before putting them back in the kettle and returning it to its hiding place. He mortised in the stones and, as darkness settled over the mountainside, he sat back against a boulder and pulled on his pipe while he watched Battle Mountain shimmer against the twilight.

He thought back four years to the day he had made that monument of rocks. He had returned from a winter's trapping in the Uintah Range to find his world uprooted. When he neared his cabin on the banks of the Little Snake, he noticed no one there to welcome him home. The previous fall, when he had bid his Flathead wife good-bye, they had exchanged tender words to one another. Now, only stillness greeted his return. The greatest tracker in the mountains knew the danger of silence in the wilderness, so he tethered his animals and sneaked up toward the cabin on foot. Peering from a hiding place, he felt a dead emptiness until, suddenly, the fluttering wings of a huge vulture lifting off startled him. The emptiness turned in an instant into anger.

Cursing, he stepped forward with his Hawken fully cocked and hoping to find an enemy to send to the happy hunting ground. But when he barged through the door, only emptiness greeted him. Emptiness except for two skulls and other bones near the doorway. He shouted as two more vultures lit out. He picked up the small skull and shook his head. He'd had no idea his wife had been carrying his child when he'd last said good-bye. He knew instinctively what had happened. And if the killers could have seen his eyes at that moment, they would have shuddered in fear.

Stepping back outside, he discovered the spot in the shrubs where the braves had hidden. When he picked up the eagle's feather, he knew the killers were Crow.

Returning to the cabin, he located a heavy wooden box that the Indians hadn't taken, although they had spirited off most everything else of value, including two packhorses from the corral near the house. The red-bearded giant removed from the box a hinged copper kettle, gathered together what remained of his family, and placed their bones in the vessel along with the feather.

It was 1851 when Johnson found himself again on a layover along the trail to Fort Laramie. His pipe glowed in the darkness as he pondered a plan for revenge. He knocked out the last remaining ashes, climbed to his feet, and sniffed the clean, pungent air. Reassured that he was alone (he could smell an Indian a mile away, he insisted), he finally rolled up in his blanket and fell off to sleep face up on his back.

The wives and daughters of soldiers stationed at the old fort had heard of his coming. So, when he rode in, they closed their shutters and peeked through the cracks at the mighty man of the mountains as he dismounted and strode by, bloody scalps dangling from his belt. They shuddered at the sight of his red beard, thinking of the bloody vendetta and bloodier livers for which he had a reputation of devouring raw, and they pushed their children back behind their skirts. Some of them—the bravest boys of the bunch—wanted to get a closer look at the Crow Killer, but their mothers had caught the cold gray glint in the killer's eyes. One later recounted that she felt the chill of Death in his passing.

Men who had met him before spoke to him in the byways but were repelled by his eyes, which seemed fixed on something afar. He said nothing to anyone—not even to "Bear Claw" Chris Lapp and Del Gue, his staunchest allies. According to Raymond Thorp, writing of the incident in *The West* in September 1964, Lapp raised his hand and began to speak when Gue suddenly quieted him. "Leave the Liver-Eater alone, he's on a trail."

The mountain man turned into a store, where he bought some salt, sugar, and flour, trading several scalps he had taken. Some of the gawkers wondered if he had eaten the livers of those braves, but no one dared to ask. From the man's belt dangled a bowie knife with twelve-inch blade sheathed beside a Colt Walker revolver, each with rosewood handles.

The man went about his business as silently as the wind as he made up his pack and strode off toward the corral where his horse was quartered. Several men had gathered there and watched him saddle the powerful black before tying on his supplies. The owner had talked before about how the animal stood watch over Liver-Eater while he slept, neighing a warning whenever an Indian got within earshot.

Liver-Eater heard the crowd mumbling as he prepared to mount but thought nothing of it, for it was nothing unusual. Finally, he climbed aboard the saddle, placed his Hawken behind the horn, and pointed the beast's flaring nostrils west.

"Wonder whar he goes?" someone asked.

"Wherever ther's Crow Injuns," another answered. "Thet ol' coon is on a death trail."

The stallion threw back, whinnied, and broke into a trot.

FERRETING OUT HIS PREY

Fifty Crow Indians from the tribe of the fabled chief Big Robert, whose young men had created Johnson's vendetta, were riding toward the Bitterroots. They were warriors chosen for their fighting skills, for the Crow had made as many Indian enemies as they had white. In addition to their own mounts, they had thirty horses loaded with bulging packs to trade with the neighboring Flatheads for horses. They were the best tanners in the West and carried buffalo robes (the softest), beaded leatherwork (the fanciest), and grizzly bear-claw necklaces (the largest). Trading was something the Crow did each spring, and on this particular day, they rode military style, two abreast, with scouts leading and trailing and sentinels off to either side.

The warriors were unaware they were being followed. Johnson kept a wary eye out for a trap as he lagged a safe distance behind. No one could say how he knew of their presence or their destination, but he did. And before long, he would have his revenge—not against all fifty warriors at once, of course, for that would have been impossible. The Crow were fierce warriors and renowned fighters. So, he set out to beat them to the Flathead encampment and convince his kinsmen to set an ambush.

Stumbling across the hot ashes of several Crow campfires at the forks of the Beaverhead, he rode on, proceeding just fast enough to pass the tribe without growing careless. Coaxing his horse off the trail, Johnson dismounted and, taking four horsehide covers from his saddlebags, wrapped them around the animal's hooves before continuing. After several minutes, he watched a Crow scout ride by, never once spotting a track. Johnson forced himself to suppress the urge to kill the solitary Crow, which would have alerted the rest of the tribe. Instead, he waited for nightfall and, when he saw the flickering of their campfires against a canyon wall ahead, he climbed the rimrock and looked down upon their encampment. Returning to where he had left his horse, he unsaddled the animal, placed it on a long lead, and went to sleep with the horse standing watch.

Waking two hours before daybreak, Johnson once again looked down upon the Indian camp. Two Indians stood sentry—one tending the fires and the other, a huge man for a redskin, walking back and forth between the camp and their baled goods. Their horses were scattered about, some dragging the picket pins that had worked themselves loose in the hard, rocky ground.

When the sentry turned away, Johnson slipped down to a vantage point near the stacked robes and packs. The moon was just right for him to stand in the shadow of the trade goods while he planned his next move. He would kill the sentry, scatter the horses, and put half a hundred Crow braves afoot.

But how? He couldn't use his pistol; it would wake the entire tribe. His bowie was silent, but his victim likely wouldn't die before crying out as the instrument penetrated his side. Johnson looked down at several good-size rocks that had washed down from the creek bed in a flash flood. He picked up one the size of a grapefruit, hefted it, and waited. The warrior sidled up, stared for several seconds out over the camp, and turned to go back. Liver-Eater hurled the stone against the back of the man's head, striking the Crow's skull as if it had been shot from a cannon.

For a moment, Johnson froze, listening, but the rebounding stone had failed to attract any attention. He grabbed the brave and dragged him into the shrubs at the edge of the ravine. A few seconds later, he was back among the horses, humming softly to reassure them as he pulled the remaining picket pins. When all were free, he scraped up a handful of pebbles and pelted the animals while whooping out loud.

Within seconds, the Indians began pouring out of their tents, yelling above the shrill neighing of the herd but quickly drowned out by the sound of hundreds of thundering hooves on a dead run to the north. Johnson threw the body of the huge sentry upon his shoulders as if it were a feather pillow and disappeared with his trophy among the trees. A short while later, with the big black saddled and ready, Johnson seized the greased scalp lock of the unconscious Indian, cut around it with his bowie, and snapped it free. A tremor ran through the brave's body as Johnson deftly cut his throat.

Liver-Eater pulled a bull-hide belt from around the waist of the dead Indian, noticing a long-dried scalp dangling from it. In an instant, he knew that the scalp wasn't that of a white person. The tresses were too coarse, dark, and long, barely finer than a horse's mane. Looking closer, he felt his heart shudder. Holding it up to the early morning sky, he knew in an instant: It was the scalp of The Swan. Through some quirk of luck or justice, he had met and killed the murderer of his squaw and unborn child.

But there was more to do and little time in which to act. He quickly braided the topknots of his squaw and her killer together and looped them through the headstall of his bridle. Taking his bowie, he made a deep incision below the ribs of the dead warrior. He inserted his hand and wrenched the liver free. Wiping the blood from his knife blade with his thumb and forefinger, he mounted his horse and rode off toward the northwest.

When Liver-Eater came within sight of the foothills of the Bitter-roots, he knew he was a day's ride ahead of the Crows, who would have run down their scattered horses by then and resumed their journey to the Flathead encampment. In his hurry to arrive there first, Johnson had pushed his stallion hard—too hard. Within five miles of his goal, the horse stumbled and fell, and Johnson was forced to put the animal down with his Walker Colt, carrying his saddle, blanket, and bedroll on foot the rest of the way.

When he finally arrived, the Flatheads greeted him as their brother and took him to the tent of Bear's Head, the tribe's chief and Johnson's father-in-law. They sat on the tepee floor made up of soft, smooth sand as Johnson held out the two scalps. The chief took them, dropped one, and held the other to the light, which danced off the stilled mane. The chief's hand trembled. "It is The Swan," he said finally, and Johnson nodded.

"She had a papoose," he added. "It was killed within her. I have the bones buried in a kettle."

The old chief's eyes roiled with hate. He picked up the second scalp. "They belong together?" he asked.

Johnson nodded again. "There were fifty Crows," he said. "Forty-nine come to trade tomorrow."

The voice of Bear's Head quaked like the threat of thunder. "We will trade death," he said. *"You are Dah-pih-ehk Absaroka.* Everyone knows of your trail of death. Now, The Swan's kinsmen will do their part. They have waited a long time."

An hour later, mounted on a new long-limbed, coal-black three-year-old, the Crow Killer rode out of the valley of the Flatheads. He turned south as soon as he passed the sentry. He was going to visit an old friend in the Snake River Plains, Wahni (The Fox), chief of part of the Northern Shoshoni tribe. The Crow Killer walked his new mount slowly: He was in no hurry.

Johnson spent two days in his campsite, getting his horse to know him. He had a lot of training to do now that his stallion was dead. Ever since old Joe Robidoux had given Johnson his first fine black pony when he had arrived in the west, he vowed never to ride another color. The pony was eventually shot out from under him, but he killed the three Cheyenne braves in that fight and secured their horses and scalps in retribution.

At Red Rock Creek above Fort Hall, Johnson came upon two Shoshoni warriors whom he'd never seen before. They didn't recognize him either, and he didn't tell them who he was. They were carrying two Flathead scalps and wouldn't take kindly to hosting one of their enemies. He knew that Shoshoni had joined the Absaroka in battle, and he had something special planned for them. He watched them hawk-like so that they didn't get the jump on him that night.

When the three arrived at the Shoshoni camp on the Lost River the following day, Johnson went directly to the chief's tepee. Several older warriors recognized him, acknowledging the "great white chief who kills the Crows and eats their livers." He was no sooner presented to The Fox than he told the old warrior of the two braves who had accompanied him, saying that they had killed two Flatheads and scalped them, adding that the two slain Flatheads were his kin. He said he brought the two braves along with him so the Shoshoni could "take care of the matter."

The Fox clapped his hands and called in his son, a young warrior with a long scar on one side of his face. "Many moons ago," the chief said, "my son was but a child and went out to hunt rabbits. A big cat sprang upon him and would have killed him but for your old partner. A rifle ball went through the heart of the beast, saving my son's life. The shot was fired by Hatcher."

"*Jehosophat!*" Johnson blurted out. "Is this the one? Well, Ol' John Hatcher never missed a target." He said Hatcher had told him that tale long ago.

"Tomorrow, when you leave," said The Fox, "you will carry the scalps of my two braves who fought beside the Crows. I am sorry for their families, but they went against tribal law."[1]

A short ride later, Johnson was back in the Flathead camp, where he laid out four scalps on the floor for Bear's Head. Two Flatheads, two Shoshoni. He didn't have to say anything, for the tale was plain to see: two victims and two atonements. But Bear's Head had something for him, too. Thirty-six Crow scalps, nearly enough to buy out Jim Bridger's trading post. Thirteen Crows had escaped to tell the tale of the Flatheads' prowess. In the process, sixty-two Flatheads had also fallen. Ambushed and attacked by a force of four to one, the Crows had upheld their reputation for giving their enemies a fierce fight.

A hundred Flathead warriors escorted the suddenly affluent Liver-Eater out of the valley. Two packhorses laden with Crow finery, for which the Flatheads had traded death, accompanied the black horse adorned in regalia that included a rare white buffalo robe as a saddle blanket on which was placed a richly beaded Crow saddle. And in that saddle sat *Dapiek Absaroka*, looking like King Arthur at a jousting tournament. The bridle was a braided work of art, and Johnson himself was dressed in white doeskin as soft as silk, beaded and fringed—topped with a luxurious beaver cap and new buckskin moccasins and leggings. From his wide belt of buffalo calfskin hung, in bright scabbards, the rosewood-handled Colt and bowie knife.

When he arrived back at the cabin, Liver-Eater was greeted by his partner, Del Gue, who grinned at the spectacle. "Yer looks just like a Crow chief," he said.

Once safely back home, he went to his sepulcher. The Swan and her baby would sleep better, he knew. With the kettle before him, he took out the skulls and the lone eagle feather which had first told him the identity of his enemies. Now, from the doeskin bag he had brought from his spoils in the Bitterroots, he pulled the scalps, twined together, along with the killer's eagle feather and the body ornaments of the brave.

While he sat there fingering his keepsakes, his nose began to quiver, and he knew live Indians were present. Black eyes glistened from behind the rocks somewhere, but a mountain man was a fatalist with no fear of sudden death. Very slowly and carefully he returned his property to the kettle, closed the lid, and placed it in his family tomb. He took the time to mortise it in, knowing that his observer would have killed him from ambush long ago, had he so chosen. Then, still as carefree as a bird, he got to his feet and ambled back down to the cabin.

The word would go forth from Johnson's Indian stalker that the Crow Killer had a reason for his madness. He had seen Liver-Eater's two skulls—one tiny and one from a grown woman—two feathers, two scalps, and several ornaments from a successful skirmish. What Indian wouldn't make the connection? As for the watcher, was he Arapaho, Sioux, Gros Ventre, Blackfoot, Cheyenne, Piegan?

It was impossible to know. Regardless, news traveled ahead to the forts and settlements, the trading posts and encampments—wherever men gathered throughout the wilderness. Why had a man with no sentiment started such a bloody vendetta? He was incapable of love, according to those who knew him, and most certainly he was incapable of loving a *squaw*.

But those who knew him had forgotten that the Crow had destroyed not only his squaw and his young child but also his *property*. The squaw and baby had belonged to him.

Suddenly, as news of the reason behind the vendetta spread, the lonely white women of the frontier found themselves empathizing with him instead of standing against him. Liver-Eating Johnson had become practically overnight their knight in shining armor, their patron saint of retribution.

He had proven his single-handed, single-minded determination to right the wrongs done to him and his family. It was more than a personal vendetta; it was the Code of the West. Little could anyone have known, but Johnson was far from finished. In fact, he was determined to carry on the feud with his archenemies for the rest of his life—or until every last one of them had paid the price. Which meant he would continue waging war against the mighty Crow Nation for close to a quarter century. By then, his victims would total more Crow warriors than there are days in the year.

CHAPTER FIVE

Captured!

WORD OF JOHNSON'S VENDETTA SPREAD AS QUICKLY AMONG THE INDIans as it had swirled around his own people. The Crow appeared helpless to respond—not that they hadn't tried. But with every attempt came yet another failure until the Crow had been completely humiliated. The entire tribal nation had fallen victim to a single man! According to an article in the Ada, Oklahoma, *Weekly News*, the Crow couldn't visit the local trading post without a Blackfoot or a Sioux brave running his index finger across his torso, as if to say, "Whose liver is next?"

If the Crow Nation was to survive, Johnson had to be stopped. But the Crow couldn't send their entire tribe out after a single foe. The ridicule would be worse than their failures. So, Crow chief Big Robert decided to gather together twenty of his best warriors with the goal of sending them out to end Johnson's "mortal, solitary battle"[1] against them forever. One at a time, they found Johnson's trail; one at a time, they closed in on him before attacking; one at a time, they perished. And every single one of the twenty braves was discovered with that wicked gash across his chest and his liver missing.

The Crow warriors were doing their best. They had their orders; they made their plans; they set up their ambushes and stalked their prey into Johnson's camps and along his trap lines. And to a one, Johnson had smelled them coming and killed them.

The Crow most assuredly realized the severity of their dilemma: To them, Johnson was an evil spirit, someone to avoid at all costs. Yet, if they were to survive as a tribe, they could no longer choose avoidance as an option. The vendetta went on for nearly twenty years when Johnson killed the final member of the twenty-brave party—all to satisfy a deep-seated gnawing within him to avenge the murder of his wife and child.

But author Alan Bellows believes that The Swan's murder was not the only impetus for Johnson's onslaught, suggesting that the "uneducated, unprincipled, insensitive" mountain man was "contemptuous of Indian culture" as a whole.[2] Bellows notes that Johnson waged other wars against other tribes with equal laser-focused ferocity, suggesting that the mountain man once poisoned a band of twenty-nine Blackfoot Indians who had stumbled upon his camp, giving them strychnine-laced biscuits for no other reason than he felt he could.

In reality, the poisoning—like everything Johnson did relating to his Indian nemeses—has a strong dose of logic behind it. The act was in response to the Indians who had invaded his cabin and stolen his property while he'd been away hunting and trapping. The only way to get them out, considering their superior numbers, was to kill them quickly and efficiently—all at once, if possible. It worked. Furthermore, the poisoning served as an apt warning for other Blackfeet who might be tempted to choose Johnson as an easy mark. The message was clear: So great was his "Big Medicine" and ferocious nature, he was to be avoided at all costs. By making an example of the braves, Johnson had issued an unmistakable warning to the Indians of the mountains and the plains: *Stay away!*

The Blackfoot and Sioux got the point. Still, from the tribes' points of view, the more the spirit guiding the white "interloper" succeeded, the harder the tribes had to fight to stop him.

Once, according to legend, Johnson was ambushed and captured by a band of Blackfeet as he returned from a second visit to his Flathead kin. The Blackfeet saw in him a valuable bargaining chip for obtaining horses from the Crow, whom they knew to be Johnson's sworn enemy. But Johnson turned out to be anything but a manageable "prisoner,"[3] chewing through his leather straps and slipping out without creating an alarm. The Blackfeet had underestimated Johnson's backcountry skills by posting a solitary warrior outside the tent. Despite the Indian's size, Johnson killed him with a single blow to the nose, allegedly sawing one of the man's legs off with the Indian's own knife and using the stump as a weapon to fight his way out of camp.

Once deep inside the woods, he used the leg as food on his two-hundred-mile journey home. Weeks later, he reached the cabin of his old partner, Del Gue. After recovering from the ordeal, the ritualistic deaths among the Crow—which had inexplicably halted while Johnson was recuperating—resumed in that same "symbolic completion of revenge slaying[s]."[4]

That's according to legend. Gue, who is said to have relayed much of the information he'd gathered about Johnson to White Eye Anderson, who later recalled the incidents in his memoir, *I Buried Hickok,* swore it was true, even admitting how shocked Gue had been when Johnson showed up at the cabin weeks after he had disappeared—presumably for good. Most likely, the basis for the story was true while the facts were somewhat exaggerated—hardly a startling state of events for the day and times. Such were the vagaries of the press.

While Johnson undoubtedly benefitted from the tall tales building around him, he often set about correcting some of the greatest exaggerations, including the one legendary feat synonymous with his nickname. In recounting his life's story to a newspaperman from Montana's *Anaconda Standard,* Johnson debunked the notion that he had ever killed an Indian and eaten his liver, claiming he got his moniker from someone who *thought* he had.

He also confirmed to the reporter that his real name was John Johnston (with a *t*), and he was born in 1824 near Little York, New Jersey. He acknowledged arriving in Montana in 1867 after guiding a train of a hundred wagons from the East, although that year is open to debate. He claimed he'd had seven Indian fights during their journey, never losing a single member to the frays. He confessed to having scouted along with Yellowstone Kelly for General Miles in 1877, and he nearly single-handedly saved the general's life.

But strangely enough, he never mentioned gnawing his way to freedom from a band of blood-thirsty Blackfeet preparing to turn him over to the Crow.

Was that proof that the incident never happened? Perhaps. Perhaps not. Johnson may have had a skirmish with some Blackfoot braves and escaped unscathed. He may have been greatly outnumbered and fought his way out, leaving a swath of blood in his wake. He may have told a "tall one" to Del Gue—who later amplified it—simply because the story sounded more exciting than admitting he'd run across an Indian maid and, getting liquored up, lost track of the time. Or perhaps Gue himself exaggerated the story to make his association with the legendary Liver-Eater all the more impressive.

What is undeniably true is that the severed-leg tale is no taller than every other story about Johnson that wound its way out of the backwoods of the Rocky Mountain West to resurface repeatedly among civilization. What's critical to remember when examining the tallest of tall tales is not whether or not they are true but why they came to be in the first place. In the case of Liver-Eating Johnson, the man was larger than the legend, so anything written about or by him *could* have been true. It is only when the man is *smaller* than the legend that the veracity of the tales hangs upon the ridiculous.

Of course, even if Johnson's entrapment by the Blackfeet wasn't true, he had plenty of other tight scrapes with many of the tribes of the area, including the Sioux, that were. This account from the January 24, 1889, edition of the *Billings Weekly Gazette* documents one such event:

> *Some of the adventures and hairbreadth escapes of this strange individual [Johnson] are, without doubt, among the most wonderful that have ever occurred in the west, and yet, singular to note, they have never yet appeared in print, chiefly, perhaps, for the reason that Johnson, though he cannot read, has a superstition that if his name were to appear in the newspapers it might, perchance, bring him into disrepute among his old acquaintances.*
>
> *The old-timers have a peculiar reverence for Johnson, and whenever his name is mentioned they shrug their shoulders and give up that his record of perilous deeds and thrilling encounters excel those of any other settler in the upper Missouri region. Johnson was one of the very few white men who followed the occupation of hunting*

*and trapping from away back in the '60s, and right in the midst of
the Sioux reservation grounds, and while they were the most deadly
enemies of his race, but he always managed to elude their most crafty
efforts at capture. In his fights with the red skins, he always came off
victorious, and one or more of the copper-skinned race was sure to bite
the dust through the unerring aim of his rifle.*

*Of course, he was eagerly sought after by the Sioux, and every
hour of his existence in those days his life was in jeopardy because of
their determined hostility. But, like the famed Hannibal, he had the
simon-pure grit, and made an oath to be the mortal enemy of the
tribe, an oath which he invariably kept; nor did he ever lay down
his arms and smoke the pipe of peace until the last Sioux was driven
beyond the hunting-ground of that vicinity. The chief cause of his
indignation toward that tribe was because the warriors of Sitting
Bull and other chiefs molested his beaver traps, stealing his beavers
and interfering with his chances of securing pelts and other trophies
of a hunter's prosperity. In those days, to use Johnson's expression, he
slept with both eyes "chock open" and ready at all times to meet any
emergency that might arise. Brush and swamps were his principal
places of concealment, and the highest hilltops he used for points of
observation. Raw meat, or "meat straight," was his principal food,
and when he was tenanted to build a fire it was done with great
caution.*

*He kept a strict account of every Indian that he killed, but the
numbers grew so large that his acquaintances, although they did
not doubt his claims, yet laughed so heartily at the idea of one man
slaughtering so many Indians of one tribe that he never forgave many
of them for their apparent unbelief of his statements; and now he
invariably avoids going into numerical details, but is fond of relating
stories of how he played many tricks on the crafty savage. At one time
he occupied a small log hut, or block house, full of port holes and in a
commanding position from whence he kept numerous war parties at
bay, slaying so many of them that the balance were quite willing to
leave him alone and decamp without his scalp. Once however they
surrounded this little fortress of Johnson's in such overwhelming*

numbers and sent such showers of lead and arrows that defense was useless, hot arrows setting fire to his block house in many places.

The red devils, on observing progress of the flames, howled with the most keen and fiendish delight, supposing that their paleface enemy would now perish sure. But Johnson was prepared for just such an emergency. He had secretly constructed an underground passageway, and into this he crawled and remained until darkness came on when he escaped unharmed. The Indians never forgave Johnson for this trick, but called him the "Fire Devil," and a great many ponies and numerous wives were offered by the chief to the warrior who would slay him.

Another trick which he played on them they'd not soon forget. One day he constructed a good sized tepee, and after arranging things as if he had made a hasty departure, left some poisoned pieces of meat inside of the tent, which some of the Indians discovered and ate, and in consequence died immediately. They were some of the bravest warriors of the Sioux, and the tribe went into mourning. For months Johnson was practically besieged, and the only way in which he could obtain any food in his little fortress was by slipping out at night, and if he failed to kill any game, gather a quantity of berries and herbs.

On returning from one of these excursions late at night, he was greatly surprised to discover signs which indicated that his home was occupied by the enemy. How many of the Indians were inside he could not ascertain, but he determined to investigate. As usual he had provided a secret passageway to his abode, of which no one else knew or would be likely to discover. Into this passageway he crept slyly to make explorations. Through a crevice he soon ascertained that there were three Indians, all well armed and watching for his return. Johnson could not depart from his usual custom of shooting a Sioux whenever such a good opportunity offered. So he drew a bead through the crack on the largest Indian and fired. The latter jumped plump to the ceiling and fell dead, shot through the heart. The other two Indians were so astonished at the noise and sudden death of their comrade that they snatched up the latter's body and fled in the wildest consternation. But Johnson threw the secret door open and sprang after them, causing them to relinquish their hold on the dead comrade and flee for safety. He then caught up to the dead Indian and carried the corpse to his fortress, where, 'tis said, he mutilated it with his teeth in the most shocking manner, and drank the blood as it flowed trickling from his victim. For a long time after this incident, Johnson was left almost undisputed master of this portion of the Yellowstone valley, the Indians regarding him with that fear inspired by an evil spirit, and he hunted and trapped at his own leisure without any danger of being molested.

But the last, and probably the most terrible, adventure of Johnson's happened about 1870, near the Musselshell river, in this territory. He and another companion were out hunting and killed quite an amount of game, and had just made preparations for camping when all at once they were set upon by a dozen or more Sioux, who raised a tremendous war-whoops *with the expectation of frightening the trappers away from their prize. The latter, however, were all experienced in Indian cunning and warfare, and stood their ground bravely. Fortunately the Indians were not so well armed as the whites, or the encounter might have proven more disastrous for the latter. At the moment when the affray began, Johnson was returning from the brush with a load of wood, intending to build a fire. Six of the Indians sprang in front of him, hoping to cut him off from his companions and kill or scalp him at their leisure. Several of them fired their guns at him at close range, but by reason of excitement, missed.*

Seeing that the Indians had the advantage in number, Johnson threw down his wood, and, snatching his large navy revolver from his belt, where he kept it for just such emergencies, he darted into the brush. The Indians followed, but Johnson being fleet of foot, gained on his pursuers and was soon secreted beneath a bunch of dense underbrush.

Three of the Indians turned their attention toward the two trappers, but the other three rushed on after Johnson. He was now ready for them, and no sooner had they shown themselves around the edge of the brush that he fired twice, killing one and disabling another.

The leader of the party, who was a very powerful Indian, snapped his gun at Johnson but it failed to go off. Instantly he threw it down, and drawing a long hunting knife with a yell, dashed at his antagonist. By a quick stroke of his revolver Johnson, in warding off the blow of the knife, belabored the arm of his enemy so severely that he let fall the knife to the ground. Both now grappled, and an intense struggle took place to get possession of the weapons, the revolver also having fallen beyond Johnson's reach.

Down a steep bank rolled the two combatants neither having any dangerous weapons, but each endeavoring to prevent the other from breaking away and thus securing one of the weapons first. The advantage in strength was with Johnson, and he held his enemy firmly, determined that he should not get away. At last the sound of guns in the direction of the encampment died away, and in a few minutes more Johnson's two companions came to his rescue having with their rifles driven away all the Sioux who attacked them. Johnson begged them not to shoot his enemy but to give him a knife. On getting hold of it he plunged it into the Indian several times, until the latter was unable to rise, and then, his companions state, he cut out the red man's liver while the latter was still alive, and ate it, the hot blood dripping down over his whiskers in a stream. Johnson's companions were so astonished at the sight that they on their return thrillingly described the scene to their friends, who at once applied to Johnson the name of "liver eating," an epithet by which he has ever since been known and to which he seems to have no objection, and he also admits that the account is about correct.

The reference to Johnson's admitting that the newspaper's account was "about correct" is typical of newspaper articles of the day wherein what actually happened was never as important to the writer as what *might* have happened. The account is riddled with inaccuracies. But the goal of yellow journalism—then every bit as much so as it is today—was not to disseminate fact but to snare readers into reading the account and talking about it later. The more breathtaking and extraordinary the tale, the more likely the paper (and, by inference, the reporter) would be to live to see another day . . . and to prosper handsomely! Taking all these early accounts with a grain of salt is the key to understanding the real man, Liver-Eating Johnson, and the real-life experiences he lived.

Oh, yes, and for the record: Johnson could read and write just fine.

Chapter Six

Peace in the Bitterroots

At some point following the Musselshell Valley attack in which the woodhawks had turned back the Sioux, Johnson decided to reconcile with the Crow, ending his war of vengeful attrition. He never said why. Perhaps by that time, he was tired of the constant attacks and killings (with three hundred Indians dead by some accounts, although probably closer to half that number). Or perhaps he had come to recognize that the Crow, while cantankerous in nature and disciplined in fighting, weren't the *real* enemy to western civilization that the Sioux were. He certainly would have recognized that an alliance with the Flatheads would not save him from the antagonists among the members of the other tribes in the area—the Sioux, Assiniboine, Blackfoot, Crow, and Piegan.

So, according to legend, Johnson signaled his intentions to enter into a peace agreement with the Crow by riding into the camp of Chief Gray Bear and brazenly requesting a truce. The chief, relieved at last to see an honorable end to the years of failed mutual antagonism, readily agreed.

Finally, after nearly two decades, the vendetta was over, and no more deaths were reported among the Crow, whom Johnson soon came to look upon as his "brothers."[1] And after that, Liver-Eating Johnson—regardless of whether or not he had actually done so—never touched another human liver to his lips.

Some historians question why the Crow would have accepted such a powwow for a truce, considering that Johnson could have been captured or killed easily had the Crow chosen to rush him in a group.

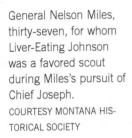

General Nelson Miles, thirty-seven, for whom Liver-Eating Johnson was a favored scout during Miles's pursuit of Chief Joseph.
COURTESY MONTANA HISTORICAL SOCIETY

It may be that the various honor codes of the region had dictated the wisdom of entering into an agreement after such a marked show of bravery by a solitary mountain man. Most Indian societies projected an image of strength among their men and honor for those who fell in battle, and they appreciated the same valued machismo displayed by their enemies. On the other hand, it may have turned out that the legendary revenge killings were not as important as reports claimed them to be and that the Crow may well have looked at them as more of a nuisance than a threat to their existence. In that case, entering into a peace agreement would not have been that significant an arrangement.

A counterargument persists, as Johnson's chronology and his relations with the Crow Nation continue to elude confirmation. In addition to disagreements as to when Johnson had arrived in the West following his naval service, multiple researchers insist he openly admired the Crow. If he had made war against *any* Indian tribes, they suggest, his true enemies would have been the Sioux and the Blackfoot nations.

Regardless, the legend of the long-lived Crow vendetta persists, and Johnson himself never denied it in person. In an article in Montana's *Anaconda Standard* on February 11, 1900, appearing only one month after his demise, Johnson had supposedly relayed to a reporter his true story. The omissions and misinformation, though, could not have come from Johnson. More likely, the reporter may have spoken with Johnson briefly or pieced together that and all other Johnsonia available to him at the time, claiming it all came from the very lips of the late, great Liver-Eating Johnson. Nevertheless, the main thrust of the piece shows an attempt by the reporter to chronicle the life and passing of one of America's true heroic pioneers:

> *Death has called another old-timer to the long last journey over the great divide, and the rapidly thinning ranks of Montana's frontiersmen are mourning the loss of one of the most typical of civilization's trail-blazers—Liver-Eating Johnson, the name by which he was universally known.*
>
> *Few men in the world to-day have passed through so many years of daring and adventure; few there are who have hobnobbed so intimately with danger and peril and been boon companions with death upon so many occasions. Johnson came to the territory when a man's life was a lottery with daily drawings, and that he drew the prize so long shows the splendid stuff in his manhood.*
>
> *Liver-Eating Johnson was an Englishman by birth, and little or nothing is known of his early life. Soon after the gold excitement broke out in California he came to the United States and joined the rush to the gold fields. It was his initiation into the ways of frontier life, and he learned it well. From California he wandered all over the West, joining many of the stampedes, but never at any time striking the yellow fortune in which he was in search. It was this life of adventure that made him a frontiersman with few equals. Woodcraft was an*

open book to him and necessity bred in him the cunning to match the savage of the plains and the wild animals of the vast forests, against both of which he was at perpetual war in a keen struggle for life and existence, and in which the least failure meant death of frightful torture.

At the breaking out of the civil war Johnson enlisted and fought through the whole war. His experience as a scout permitted him to make a most enviable record. At the close of the war he returned to the West, again to take up a life of peril and adventure, an existence which had now become second nature to him. During the many years of his life on the Montana frontier he served in nearly all the Indian wars and was chief of scouts at various times for General Miles. There is no phase of frontier life in which he did not play a part. When not with the army he was hunting buffalo, bears and big game; now prospecting, then spending a winter wolfing; again at his war with Indians; smuggling whiskey across the [Canadian] line; or cutting cord wood on the Missouri for the steamboats.

Liver-Eating Johnson was a magnificent specimen of physical manhood. He stood over six feet high and weighed 220 pounds of solid brawn and muscle which his arduous life had hardened to the strength of steel. Fatigue was almost unknown to him and he had greater endurance than an Indian. His personal appearance was startling and striking from the fact of a shaggy growth of jet black whiskers and an enormous head of long hair, which hung over his forehead and down his back in unkempt profusion. He seldom wore a hat or if indeed started away on an expedition with one, he always returned bareheaded. So shaggy and hairy was he that the Crows, with whom he was always on friendly terms and with whom he lived a great deal of the time, called him Black Bear, a most appropriate soubriquet. Cold, shrewd, steel-gray eyes were truthful indices of character. Johnson did not affect the fancy dress of some of the frontier dandies. He was usually clothed in buckskin, but it was simple and unornate in the extreme.

Johnson was known and feared by the Indians of the Northwest, particularly the Sioux and Blackfoot, while the Crows were his friends and allies. He never got the worst of any encounter and the superstitious fear of him was enhanced by the tremendous carrying power of his big buffalo gun, in which he used 120 grains of powder to propel a bullet which looked like a great spike. When Johnson killed an Indian the redskin looked as if he had been coquetting with a buzz saw. It was in this way that he won the respect of the Sioux and Blackfoot, and it was, in fact, about the only possible way do it.

The newspaperman, obviously confused about numerous points in Johnson's life, had him being born in the wrong country, possessing the wrong color beard, allying with the wrong Indian tribe (although he did make peace with the Crow later in life), ascribing the wrong length of military service, according to him a lifelong pursuit of gold, and saddling him with the wrong rank (he worked as a scout for General Miles). The reporter *did* manage to get the nom de guerre correct: "Liver-Eating Johnson." And, in fairness, he recorded relatively accurately some of Johnson's latter-day exploits—the period in his life after he had decided enough was enough and set out to make peace with the Crow.

The reporter's take on how Johnson got his nickname rivals several similar theories, lending at least partial credence to them all. It came about in an encounter with the Sioux upon the Musselshell near its junction with the Missouri. According to the same *Anaconda Standard* piece:

There were two parties of white men, 15 in all, camped there cutting bull pine and cottonwood for the steamboats. At that time the blood- thirsty Sioux under the chieftainship of Sitting Bull were undisputed masters of the vast, trackless plains which stretched far beyond the horizon on both sides of the Missouri. Between the whites and Sioux eternal war had been declared and the bloody campaigns and raids which ended several years later in Sitting Bull's defeat had just begun.

The Sioux were masters of the plains and it took courage of more than the ordinary sort for a small party of whites to tempt fate by throwing themselves in the way of certain death. But the steamboats were obliged to have wood, Indians or no Indians, and were ready to pay good prices for it. It was another case of mixed motives—avarice

Liver-Eating Johnson posing in buckskin coat and pants with a telescopic rifle that helped earn him the reputation as one of the most deadly shots in the Rocky Mountain wilderness.

and the love of adventure. Every party which left the forts for the river bottom to cut wood knew for a certainty that a large proportion of its members would never return—that their bones would whiten and crumble on the prairie and that their scalps would dry and stiffen in the smoky lodge of some Sioux brave. Yet the steamboats never lacked for wood.

The year previous several wood cutting parties had been massacred, but the next season found Johnson's party at the mouth of the Musselshell in spite of the warning given by the Sioux that the land was theirs and that they would allow no white dogs to trespass upon it.

But Johnson and his party went prepared for trouble and determined to teach the hereditary foe a lesson which would not be soon forgotten. Breech-loading rifles had been just introduced and were in the hands of the choppers, who were ready to give the Sioux a surprise party when they made their expected and inevitable appearance, and they did not have to wait long. One morning, Crow Davis and [his] squaw happened to be the first up in one of the camps. They were a short distance from the camp getting wood for the breakfast fire, when suddenly the squaw told Davis in a low, frightened voice as she continued to pick up wood, that the camp was surrounded by Indians. Davis was shrewd enough to show no signs of his knowing of the danger, and after picking up a few more sticks of wood walked slowly and unconcernedly back to the camp as if nothing had happened out of the ordinary. The squaw kept on gathering wood to keep up the bluff, all the time her cunning black eyes searching the surrounding woods for signs of Indians as she slowly worked herself back towards the camp. But the strain was too much for even her stoical nature and finally, a moment after Crow Davis reached the camp, she gave a frightened scream, dropped her armful of wood and ran for the cabin. She never reached it. When about half way to it a bullet from an Indian's gun found her and stretched her on the ground, a victim of too much courage or too little fear. The wound was not fatal, however, and she lived for many years afterwards.

In the meantime the camp had been alarmed by Davis and the shot brought them all to their feet ready for business. It did not take long to get the sleep out of a man's eyes in those days. Like a flash they dropped behind nearby trees and stumps, ready for the attack. But it did not come. The plan of the Sioux had been spoiled by premature discovery and they were never anxious to attack a foe that was prepared to receive them. Unless in overwhelming numbers they would never take any chances in their conflict with the whites.

So slowly the Sioux who had completely surrounded the cabin crept away out of the timber up on to the bluff out of range to hold a council of war.

In the meantime Liver-Eating Johnson, who with seven other men were encamped on the other side of the river, had heard the shot and had hurried across just in time to see the Indians leave the timber for the plains. The white men then held a council of war. Quite a number of them thought it better to let the Indians depart in peace instead of taking any chances in following them, but Johnson and a majority of the party thought the present an elegant opportunity to treat the Sioux a lesson altogether too good to be neglected. To let an Indian escape, particularly a Sioux, went against the grain. Finally it was decided to fight, and Johnson was given the command.

And it was full time for decision, for as the men drew out near the edge of the timber they found that the Indians had decided upon an attack and were moving towards the camp in a wide circle with the evident intention of surrounding it and finishing their work of slaughter, even if it cost them a few braves as the expense of their audacity. They were evidently relying upon their superiority of numbers. But as the white men appeared at the edge of the timber a new plan was evolved and a cunning trap laid. The Indians started off in mad gallop towards the distant hills. A moment more and they were lost to sight in a rolling depression of the prairie, but they were soon seen climbing the rise on the other side in the far distance.

It was a clever trick, but it did not for a moment fool an old Indian fighter like Johnson. While a small party of Sioux had ridden towards the hills, trusting to the distance to confuse their movements, the larger part of the Sioux had made a detour and returned to a deep coulee which opened into the Musselshell bottom. Pomp Dennis offered to reconnoiter while the rest of the whites kept up their bluff of not knowing that the Sioux were near. Dennis had with him in camp two Newfoundland pups. They were untrained and followed him as he craftily crawled to the top of a small hill which commanded a view of the coulee. Dennis had hardly had a chance to size up the contents of the coulee, which he found full of redskins, before one of the pups ran up to the edge and looked over. In a second there was a whir and the dog fell to the ground pierced with a dozen arrows which quivered in his body and a dozen others fell around him. The other dog ran up to its mate and in an instant met a similar fate. The arrows had been falling too close to Pomp Dennis for comfort—it was a miracle he was not hit—and so, having got all the information he was after, he crawled back the way he had come and reported the result of his investigation.

Johnson then developed his plan of campaign. Three men with Winchesters were sent across the river to take up a protected position which commanded the coulee, while Johnson divided the rest up so that no avenue of escape from the coulee was left open. After the men were all placed the music began, and it was very lively. It was a complete surprise to the Sioux, who were picked off like rats in a trap by the men across the river, and when a redskin would stick his warlock above the bank of the coulee he at once became good and virtuous.

The men across the river did not waste a shot . . . [and] they began to dig holes in the bank as protection against the murderous fire. But it availed them but little. The men on the river bank would change positions a little and find them out.

Seeing the hopelessness of the struggle, the Indians demanded a pow-wow. Johnson answered them. They told him that they had got all the fighting they had any stomach for; that they wanted to quit and call the affair a draw. But Johnson would make no terms . . .

"If you want to go," he said, "you know the road and there is nothing to hinder you from hitting it."

As he said this, an Indian who had crept and crawled beyond the lines sprang up and made a dash for life. An instant later he sprang into the air and fell with a bullet through him.

There was no more pow-wowing after that and the Indians understood that their own merciless cruelty was being meted out to them to the order of "No quarter."

For some time afterwards the whites kept potting the Sioux in the coulee, while the Indians were unable to do any damage at all with their arrows and the few guns they possessed. Finally they concluded to take the desperate chance of a rush in a bunch from their trap. They crept up to the edge of the bank and then, yelling like demons and running like antelope, made a break for the open prairie and life. But they had simply got into another trap. Their maneuver in the coulee had been observed, and Johnson, guessing what they were planning to do, had posted most of his men in a little hollow towards which the Indians, their ranks frightfully thinned, were heading. The men across the river kept raking the running Indians with a deadly enfilading fire of which every shot rendered a good account of itself. And then, when in close range and not a hundred feet from the hollow, they ran into such a merciless hail of lead that they were mowed down like grass. One volley and the fight was over and 60 dead Sioux were stretched lifeless on the plains, a good day's work for a little band of 15 pioneers.

But the affair was not yet completed. Quite a number of the wounded had crawled off to hide in the bottoms along the river. It was decided to let not a single one escape, as it would mean certain death for some one of the white party. Several Indians were found. Some begged piteously for life and others received the finishing stroke with the traditional stoicism of their race.

Johnson found one buck as he was crawling away towards the prairie, seriously but not fatally wounded. He trailed him for some distance by the blood splashes on the ground and grass and as the Sioux warrior heard Johnson approach he turned to make a last desperate fight for life. Crawling behind the sage brush, he waited until Johnson was close upon him and then let fly his last arrow on its errand of death. But the Indian was well nigh exhausted by the loss of blood and the shaft was poorly aimed. It whizzed dangerously, but harmlessly, by Johnson's head.

Johnson was upon him in an instant, but found the Indian was now unarmed and defenseless. Johnson dropped his rifle and pulled out his hunting knife and felt its edge on his nail.

"I am going to kill you," said Johnson to the Indian, for he spoke Sioux like a native. "I am going to scalp you first and then cut your throat like a dog's."

The Indian listened to him with cynical indifference and met his fate like a stoic. Grabbing the scalp lock, Johnson pulled it tight with his knee against the Indian. With the other hand he gave a quick slash of his knife around the roots and then a sharp pull and the trophy of Indian valor came off with a report like a small pistol. Frightful agony as it must have been, yet not a moan or a word escaped the Indian's lips, but two great tears rolled down the doomed Indian's face.

Seizing the Sioux by the big brass ring which he wore in his ears, with a quick movement Johnson threw the Indian over his bended knee, and, twisting the head around until every cord and muscle of the neck was tense and taut, gave it one quick, ugly sweep of the knife and the painted head came off in his hand, dripping a crimson flood, while the blood spurted in gushes from the headless trunk, which slipped to the ground.

He walked quickly back to his comrades, his rifle in one hand and his bloody knife in the other. When he reached the group, one of them, a pilgrim, noticed a little strip of flesh hanging to the knife blade, and inquired what it was.

"That," said Johnson, glancing at the knife, "is a piece of Indian's liver. I just had a feast off of one and thought maybe some of you would like a taste. Try it."

And he passed the knife with its little piece of flesh around the circle, but none of the men appeared to be hungry for that particular cut. With apparent offense at having his tid-bit slighted, he said:

"You don't know how good it is. I eat nothing else when I am out on the plains if I can get Indian livers. They taste best raw."

With that he lifted the knife to his mouth and made a motion as if he was eating the stuff. In reality he had dropped it to the ground by a twist of his hand, but the broad red splatch across his black beard *gave the spectators a contrary opinion. From that day he was known far and wide as Liver-Eating Johnson.*

The reporter went on to write that the Sioux gave the woodcutters no more trouble the rest of that year, but the following spring, seven squaws walked down to the river, where they gathered up the bleached bones of their slain tribe members in blankets and chanted their mournful dirges. They sat down in front of Clen Denning's trading post and continued their ceremonies, "mutilating themselves horribly, as was the custom of their tribe, and working themselves up into a frenzy of passion." Soon afterward, a war party of 160 Sioux came dashing down the bin intent on stirring up trouble, but Johnson's group was ready for them and fought them off, holding their post for several days until the Indians gave up and went away, carrying with them the bones of the warriors who had fallen in the previous year's fight.

Johnson, who had recently developed an unusually close relationship with the Crow considering the antagonistic history between the two, often called upon them for counsel. He, in turn, warned them of news of warring tribes or raids planned against the Crow village. The Crow came to admire Johnson so much that they called him Black Bear and made him one of their own tribe. It was not an impulsive or arbitrary thing to do. The Crow and the Blackfoot were traditional enemies. From time immemorial, they had been at war, showing one another little quarter in times of battle.

The hostilities exploded in a series of annual raids. Every year like clockwork, a band of fifteen or twenty Blackfeet set out on a horse-stealing expedition against the Crows. Coming from the north, they crossed the Missouri River below Fort Benton and traveled south through the Judith and Musselshell valleys, across the Yellowstone, and into the very heart of Crow country.

From there, they hung around, concealed near some Crow village while awaiting their opportunity to strike on some dark, moonless night. When the time was right, the Blackfeet crept in between the horses and the village, killed the solitary sentinel, and slowly worked the herd up toward the open prairie. When at last out of earshot, several more Blackfeet joined them and urged the horses to run as fast as possible. By the following morning, the Indians were far away to the north.

By that time, of course, the Crows had discovered what had happened and set out to right the wrong and retrieve their animals. Johnson often joined in the fray.

Occasionally, the Crows failed to catch up with the Blackfeet and gave up the chase the worse for wear. Most often, though, they overtook them and bloody battles spilled out in the Musselshell Valley—victory sometimes falling to the Crows and sometimes to the Blackfeet.

Along the wide valley, the war houses of the northern marauders provided a place for the Blackfeet to make a desperate stand if the battle went badly for them. Spiraling, heavily timbered buttes of solid rock rose from each side of the draw, and behind the rocks the Blackfeet arranged a nearly impregnable fortress from which they could launch a deadly volley into the pursuing Crows, thus delaying them while the main body of the Blackfeet made their escape across the Missouri River to safety.

It was on account of Johnson's participation in these revenge raids that the various tribes of Blackfeet had targeted him for the better part of a decade. They stalked him, watched his every move, and waited for him with their usual vigilance—but with no success. Once, on the banks of the Missouri, they came close to succeeding when three Piegans jumped him from the thicket and rushed in to kill him. Leaping to his feet, he swung his rifle wildly, knocking two of them down with a single blow before turning and running "like a whirlwind" for the safety of the post.

Even the bravest of fighters has to learn that discretion is, indeed, the better part of valor. And Johnson was a quick learner.

CHAPTER SEVEN

A Good Scout

NEWS OF THE AMERICAN CIVIL WAR IN 1860 TRAVELED SLOWLY UNTIL Johnson finally learned of the fighting sometime in 1861. A strong opponent of the enslavement of any group of people, he thought that if he were to enter the war, he would do so on the side of the Union against the Confederacy. And that's exactly what he did.

In the winter of 1863, Johnson entered the war, which had been raging for more than three years. Whether for reasons of guilt over having once deserted, or of conviction to the Union cause, or—and this is far more likely—of a desire to escape the hardships and the constant struggle of the wilderness at least for a while, he made his way to St. Louis to enlist. He appears to have been assigned to Company A of the Third Colorado Infantry until it was absorbed into the Second Colorado Cavalry, Fourth Brigade, H Company, where he served as a "veteran recruit," according to the Record and Pension Office reports of the War Department. He apparently lied about his age to enlist, claiming to be thirty-three when he was actually closer to thirty-nine and above the maximum acceptable limit allowed by law.

True to his past military history, Johnson still believed that he could walk away from an organization such as the army whenever he chose. And, barely five days after enlisting, he did just that, disappearing from his unit without any clear explanation (or even fuzzy conjecture!) as to why. Perhaps he had acquired a substantial sum of money selling whiskey to an increasingly large clientele and found the shock of a scout's meager pay too paltry to bear. Or maybe he simply needed some time to conclude other dealings going on in his life. Or possibly he had a change of heart and decided that five days of wearing the Union blue was enough.

Whatever the reason, he had chosen precisely the right time to abandon his post, for shortly after that, he rejoined his company. In the interim, the Second Colorado had accomplished exactly nothing and had gone precisely nowhere, its daily regimen consisting of hurrying up to await further orders as the troops lived a totally stagnant life.

By all historical accounts, few officers or colleagues had even noticed Johnson missing. Of those who had, fewer still cared. Whether out of a punitive gesture or simply as a reassignment due to some bureaucratic need, Johnson was sent to the Second Regiment without any apparent penalty for his actions, even though the Descriptive List of Deserters included his name and the notation that he had returned to his unit "without being apprehended." As strange as that may sound today, soldiers going AWOL were not uncommon during the Civil War.

In her book *Desertion during the Civil War*, author Ella Lonn claims that "one hundred thousand Confederates had left the ranks while more than two hundred thousand Union soldiers had done the same." Those staggering numbers amounted to one out of every seven soldiers in the Union Army and one out of every nine serving the Confederacy.[1]

On April 23, 1864, Johnson was reassigned from Benton Barracks to Fort Leavenworth, Kansas, where he immediately fell back in line and was listed as "awaiting transportation to company."

Finally, in October 1864, Johnson—who had been enlisted as a "sharpshooter"—saw his first real action at the battles of Westport and Newtonia, Missouri. Under the leadership of General James Blunt, he was shot in the shoulder and again in the leg. He applied for and was granted a small pension (which he received for the rest of his life) due to a gradual "withering away" of muscle tissue in his shoulder.

Johnson was discharged from service on September 23, 1865. Not long after in November, the Army of the Border was disbanded "by directions of superior authority," and the men in Blunt's command were mustered out.

Back to Montana

Following the war, Johnson—with nothing in particular better to do—headed home to the wood camps of Montana. A December 1939 article in the *Flathead Courier* recalled the event:

> *Then he came to Montana and had a wood camp on the Missouri river, near the mouth of the Musselshell river. There was a small trading post there which was run, I think he said, by Clendenine, and at the time about 16 white men and a few Indian women were camped there. The hostile Indians were killing the woodchoppers wherever they could surprise them at work. The cottonwood trees were cut in suitable lengths and piled and dried and sold to the steamboats going up or down the river. These wood camps were not uncommon along the upper Missouri at the time of which I write.*[2]

But woodhawking, as it was known, was far from an easy way of earning a living. It was particularly dangerous where Johnson had established his wood camp. Only the most rugged of men were fit to handle both the physical and the mental rigors of that line of work in the very heart of the Sioux Nation.

A slightly different account of Johnson's activities following his mustering out and return to Montana was provided by author Will Carpenter:

> *He returned to Fort Benton and obtained a job as a teamster with the Diamond R. freighting company out of Fort Benton on the Helena run. He worked at this until the summer of 1867, when he went into a partnership with a man named Sims to cut cordwood for the Missouri River steamboats. The two men established a wood yard just below the mouth of the Musselshell River and spent the winter of 1867–1868 cutting wood.*[3]

This latter account may be more accurate, since Diamond R freighting was owned by E. G. MacKay and Company and would have provided quick and easy employment for men returning from the war. The company held the government contract giving them the right to haul freighting goods to army posts scattered across the frontier. The Diamond R was one of the largest freight haulers in Montana Territory.

Regardless, Johnson allegedly had a falling out with Sims about his partner's drinking habits and elected to get rid of him. In addition, Liver-Eater had heard that at least three different war parties were camped in the vicinity, and the last thing he wanted was trouble, so he closed up his business and hopped a steamboat back to Fort Benton, where he stayed until the following spring.

Fort Benton was a popular place, one of the earliest trading posts built at the head of the Missouri River. As such, it attracted both the best and the worst of river-going clientele—and, as always, *trouble.*

An April 22, 1902, article in the *Anaconda Standard* documented the death of a prominent local who once shared quite an experience with Johnson:

"Prof." James House, a pioneer prospector and one of the early-day settlers of this section of the country, died this morning at Parsons' hospital after a confinement there of almost six weeks. He had been suffering with heart trouble for a long time. He was 73 years of age and would have celebrated his next birthday in June. He was one of the familiar characters in this part of the state, being a friend of every one who needed one and did much to promote mining in Western Montana. He was sometimes called the father of the Wallace mining district.

James House came from St. Louis in 1864 and came up the Missouri river by boat, stopping at Fort Benton for the summer and winter. He prospected around that country during the summer and with a man known as "Liver Eating" Johnson had a thrilling experience with the Blackfeet Indians. House and Johnson were corralled by the Indians and had to remain within a prescribed circle for many days. They had a reasonable amount of food on hand at the time, but it soon was exhausted. They were three or four days without food, and becoming desperate, decided to leave the spot, either to kill their foe or to be killed. They started in to fight their enemy and every shot brought *down an Indian. The nearest one that fell to the spot where House and Johnson were was dragged into camp by Johnson and his liver torn out. It was in this manner that Johnson became possessed of the cognomen given him. From Benton, they proceeded to Oregon, where Professor House continued his prospecting. In Oregon he became the owner of a rich mine. He sold it for $6,000, and he considered himself well off. He took up with a woman [and] before the professor was aware of it his "baby," as he had always called her since, got all he possessed.*

BACK IN FORT BENTON

Back in Fort Benton, Montana, it didn't take Johnson long to lose on drink what little money he'd managed to scrape together. Broke again, he signed on once more with the Diamond R, this time to haul supplies to the gold miners at the Forks of the Musselshell.[4]

Whether or not Johnson had returned to woodhawking before running into his partner X. Beidler is a matter of speculation. What is clear is that, once the two hooked up in the late fall of 1868, they quickly settled again into an easy alliance.

Their partnership was immediately successful for several reasons. For one, the steamboats plying the river required an endless supply of wood to keep the boilers steaming and the paddle wheels turning—some twenty-five cords of hard wood or thirty cords of the softer, faster-burning cottonwood a day! For another, no two men anywhere worked harder at life than X. Beidler and Liver-Eating Johnson. Worlds apart in physical stature (with Beidler a good foot shorter than his compatriot), they shared the commonality of tremendous strength and pride in their work.

The duo's success was all the more remarkable considering the constant danger from attacks they faced by the Sioux. Perhaps it was Johnson's reputation as "bad medicine" that kept the two out of harm's way. Perhaps it was something even more metaphysical. Regardless, Liver-Eating Johnson never stopped to question the fact that he and Beidler were trespassing upon land designated as Sioux territory. By the very act of his ongoing presence there, he had made the statement to the Sioux that there was only one way he would ever leave his wood camp, and that was "potted" (killed).

Painting an illuminating portrait of Liver-Eating Johnson as a humanitarian and a caretaker (far from the reputation he toiled hard at creating), author Joe DeBarthe sat down for an interview with the man who, in the spring of 1869, served as chief of scouts for General George Crook. The purpose of the interview was to see if Frank Grouard could recall enough information from his illustrious career for DeBarthe to write Grouard's biography.

As it turned out, he could.

Grouard not only recalled every incident of his career, but also did so without notes or input from anyone else. And he did so, apparently, with the same sort of honesty and integrity that marked his career as an army scout.

"In my relations with [Grouard]," DeBarthe wrote in the book's preface, "he has never given me occasion to doubt a single statement he has ever made, and I can thoroughly appreciate the confidence reposed in him by Gen. Crook, who, in 1876, referring to Grouard in his official correspondence with the War Department, said: 'I would sooner lose a third of my command than Frank Grouard!'"[5] Grouard's written recollection of Liver-Eating Johnson is particularly enlightening:

In the spring of '69 I came down to Seven Mile creek, seven miles from Helena, and went to breaking horses for the Holliday Stage Company. I broke horses there all that fall, or close to fall, and it was during this time that the Blackfeet Indians commenced to get ugly. The people had to do something to protect the outside settlers. It was at this time that the Montana militia was organized. I came down with them into the camp about forty miles from Diamond City. Huntley had got the contract to run the pony express from Diamond City to Fort Hall on the Missouri river, and I hired out as carrier. The militia went into camp about forty miles from Diamond City on our right, on the head of the Mussellshell river. I came down while they were getting things ready, and they were to overtake us. I was there at the time the militia were in camp, and camped right there with them. I was waiting for C. C. Huntley to come down. He and his party were to come on into camp, and we were to start out from there, and some of the militia were to go there with us as an escort. I was there about a month with this militia before the Huntley party did come down. There was an escort of twenty men ordered to go with us.

There was one of these militiamen who afterwards became quite a notorious character, and is so at the present day, being known by the cognomen of "Liver Eating Johnson." At present he is marshal of Red Lodge, Montana. One day it was pretty hot, and an antelope came close to us. Johnson says:

"Wait a minute; I will kill that antelope."

He shot at it four or five times and missed it, and the antelope still stood there. That made him kind of hot, for he was a pretty good shot, and he says:

"I will eat your liver out if I do kill you," and he kept his word.

After he killed it he ate its liver. He was blood from one end to the other. That is how he got his name. Everybody called him "Liver Eating Johnson" after that. Huntley, I think it was, gave him the name.

We went on then to Fort Hall on that trip and fixed everything up, and turned around and came back over the same road. When we got back the militia had disbanded, and we went through to Diamond City. It was about a week afterwards that I took the first mail through, leading one horse packed and riding another. The distance was about two hundred and eleven miles from Diamond City to Fort Hall. It took me four days and nights to make the trip. I made one trip down one week and the other week made the trip back.

Diamond City was a mining camp—not much of a place. I think it was in November the Blackfeet captured me. I had not made many trips. I was going from Diamond City to Fort Hall when the redskins got me.[6]

DeBarthe wrote that, as Grouard neared Judith Springs, he passed along a ridge spiked with "little points of rocks standing here and there."[7] His attention was attracted by an immense herd of buffalo grazing off to his left, and being intent on watching the animals, he paid no attention

to the trail before him. Suddenly, he looked up at twenty Blackfoot Indians in full war dress. One of the Blackfeet yelled out to him in perfect
English, "Hold up!" DeBarthe continued Grouard's story:

*Grouard was incapable just then of doing anything else. It was his
first experience with Indians, and he was frightened nearly to death.
In a scabbard on his horse he carried an eighty-dollar Henry rifle, and
had two revolvers stuck in a belt about his waist; but the possession of
the weapons never crossed his mind, he had imagined he was armed
well enough to kill all the Indians in the country; but matters assumed
a different light when he sat on his horse in the midst of twenty of
the worst looking cut-throats he had ever heard of or read about. The
redskins seemed to enjoy poor Grouard's fright and discomfiture, but
did not keep him long in doubt as to their intentions toward him.*

*They partly pushed and partly pulled him off his horse, and
stripped him of every vestige of clothing.*

*Then they pointed in the direction he had come and told him to
go. Emboldened by the fact that they were not going to take his life,
Grouard asked them to give him one of the blankets they had taken
from him. For an answer they mounted their horses, drew their quirts
and lashed their defenseless victim until his body was filled with gap-
ing gashes, from which the blood flowed in streams. Realizing that his
only chance of escape lay in flight, Grouard struck out across the sandy
plain, the Indians following for over two hundred yards, raining
blow after blow upon his bleeding head and body.*

*Darkness was settling over the earth. The sun had sunk behind
the western hills about the time the Indians [had originally] captured
Grouard. The night was warm, and scarcely a breath of air was stirring. It was nearly seventy miles by the nearest known route from
Judith Springs to Fort Hall.*

*The country was covered with patches of cactus and prickly pears.
Into these the fleeing man rushed, lost to all sense of pain in the
haunting fear of death. His imagination peopled the semi-darkness
with pursuing savages on horseback. He had no hope but the present
chance of escape.*

On he sped and on, covering mile after mile of the distance he must travel to find safety at the fort. He realized nothing but fear of pursuit, and that fear lent wings to his feet.

If, during that awful flight, he stopped for breath, he does not remember it. He had tasted no food since the previous morning, yet he knew not a pang of hunger.

No liquid had passed his lips since the preceding noon, but he would not have slackened his pace to slake his thirst if the purest of springs had invited him.

Onward into the cruel cacti, over the prickly pear vines, fled Grouard, the phantom horsemen lashing their steeds into a foam in a vain endeavor to overtake him.

Suddenly he stops.

Like a flash through the heavens the black veil of night had been lifted.

He could not tell at first whether he were waking from a horrid dream or had lost his reason.

One hundred yards ahead of him stood Fort Hall, and as he gazed the heavy gates swung open and a man appeared.

"In that single moment," says Grouard, "I realized all."

At his side flowed the river; behind him were the familiar cotton-woods and willow groves.

A trembling sensation seized upon the muscles of his body.

His brain was in a whirl; it was getting dark again. He raised his arms high above his head and tried to shout.

He knew no more.

Four days later Grouard opened his eyes. The first face he recognized was that of "Liver Eating Johnson." His condition was pitiful. His body was covered with festering sores, and his feet were swollen twice their natural size. His limbs were so stiff and heavy that he could not raise them, and he had not the power to utter an audible sound.

For three long months he lay upon his bed of furs, suffering the tortures of hell itself. "Liver Eating Johnson" nursed him with all the care and solicitude of a mother. The needles from the cacti which had *entered his flesh as he had rushed through them in his efforts to escape the Blackfeet, worked their way out of his limbs through the festering sores, some of them appearing at the surface of the flesh as high up as the knees.*[8]

Although the account is riveting in its recollection of the beating Grouard, a novice in the way of the woods, received, there are a few hiccups in the chronological alignment of his tale. For one, Grouard's recollection that Johnson was marshal of Red Lodge, Montana, in 1869 jumped the gun since Liver-Eater wouldn't hold that position for another two decades. Nevertheless, the notion that Big Bad Liver-Eater was a warm-hearted soul at heart is something few other accounts have managed to reveal.

True to his friends? Undoubtedly. Fair-minded and respectful of others? Absolutely. Brutally unforgiving to his foes? Wholeheartedly. But, as was the case with Calamity Jane, another western pioneer whom Liver-Eater wouldn't meet for years to come, deep down inside beat a warm heart and a kindred spirit—something he sought, as had Calam, to disguise from others for his own defense.

LEAVING THE WOOD CAMP

Despite their success as woodhawks along the Missouri, Beidler and Johnson felt instinctively it was time for all good things to end. Rationalizing that there was more profit in running illegal whiskey than there was in chopping legal wood, the duo packed up their horses sometime around 1870 and, according to various articles and oral histories, headed north into western Canada. Wherever they stopped along the way, Johnson joked about having eaten raw Indian livers, creating an atmosphere of growing intrigue, curiosity, and fear among those he met.

As they worked their way from one camp to another, the two men peddled the whiskey they'd made in their own stills. Of course, they also killed hostile Indians, trapped, and in general enjoyed some time away from the Montana wilderness to, as Johnson may have described it, "get the rust out of our pants."

Artist's rendering of Fort Whoop-Up on the Canadian frontier, where Johnson and Beidler peddled illegal whiskey for several months before returning to the States.
COURTESY INTERNATIONAL FEATURES SYNDICATE

Regardless of wherever it was that Johnson stopped to do time, he never slowed down or slowed up. Nor did he shy away from controversy or a good fight. At one town, a professional boxing promoter engaged him for a match, and Johnson "agreed to a little sport" behind a popular saloon.[9] The professional "champion" was taking on all comers, and Johnson never hesitated before accepting the challenge of going a few rounds of light sparring with the champ. Even though neither man wore gloves (a nod to John L. Sullivan's bare-fisted approach to pugilism), neither wanted the fight to get out of hand.

And it didn't.

Johnson's first swing caught the champ squarely on the jaw and, according to legend, sent the younger man crashing through a board fence with the blow. A second devastating punch convinced the man to call an end to the festivities.

With that out of his system, Johnson and Beidler worked their way through what is today Alberta, Canada, where they crossed paths with a former army scout who wrote of the encounter in Whoop-Up Country, an especially wild and dangerous wilderness area that ran from northern Montana east of present-day Glacier National Park up into Canada:

> *While scouting through the whoop-up country, we bumped into the old pioneer Liver-Eating Johnston, who jogged along with us for a while. He said he was just sort of pi-utin' around, and he certainly had room to do so, for there was not another soul in sight, and it was a notoriously bad region, where everybody got whooped up, both red men and white. One of our scouts told me that Johnston was safe anywhere, for the Indians were superstitious about him, and kept out of range of the big telescope rifle he carried. It was also said that he really did not eat the Indian's liver, but had merely drawn it across his mouth so that the other Sioux could see and think he had eaten it after shooting an Indian and jumping over the breastworks at Fort Pease and cutting the liver. Liver-Eating Johnston hated Indians and was given the nickname, because of his threat to eat the liver of any Indian who came near his place.*[10]

The Sioux land remained one of the most dangerous places in North America for a white to travel. Mountain men had named the region Whoop-Up appropriately enough, although Johnson was likely the only white man ever to escape death if caught there. The Sioux, in particular, regarded him as an evil spirit.

Writing of the memoirs of White Eye Anderson in the book *I Buried Hickok*, editor William B. Secrest relayed the story of just how volatile a run-in with the Sioux could be. According to Anderson's account:

> *On the south side of the Republican River, at the head of Drift Wood Creek, two hide hunters had made their camp. I did not know their real names, but one was called Blue Dick because he came from the Blue River area of Nebraska. The other fellow was called Fly Speck as his face was covered with small freckles. They had a light wagon and a span of mules. One afternoon they were in camp cooking and baking bread. They were making what we call frypan loaves; bread baked in*

a fry pan tipped up in front of the fire. They had baked quite a lot of them and put them in their grub box—a heavy, old tool chest. The box was overloaded and the lid did not fit down tight on account of the bread. Two Indians came to the camp and said they were hungry and wanted some of the bread to eat.

The hunters would not give them any, so one of the Indians slipped his hand into the box when he thought they were not looking. Blue Dick saw him and made a quick jump right on the lid of the old tool chest grub box and pinched the Indian's fingers and hand pretty bad. The Indian did not get anything to eat, but got his hand hurt and they went away very mad.

Fly Speck told Blue Dick that he had made a bad break in treating the Indians as he had done and they would have to look out for trouble. They picketed their mules that night and took turns watching them. Spreading their blankets on the ground close by the mules, Fly Speck lay on the top of the bed with his gun in his hand until midnight when Blue Dick took his turn. It was not long until he saw someone crawling through the grass toward the mules. He waited until he saw the Indian with a knife in his hand just about to cut the picket rope, then he took a dead aim, shot and killed him.

The Indian he killed proved to be Whistler, the chief of a Cut-off band of Sioux. Before this, these Indians had been peaceful. They lived in that country, hunting and trapping. The squaws tanned buffalo hides for robes, deer hides for buckskin and rawhide and jerked great stacks of meat. They had large herds of horses and if the white people had only treated them right and not tried to cheat and rob them on every turn of the box, there would not have been any trouble with them.

There were two or three other Indians along with Whistler when he got killed and it was not long until the whole tribe knew about it and all went on the warpath. They killed lots of the whites who were locating homesteads and settling on the frontier. All the hide hunters and trappers had to get out. We heard the news that Whistler was killed from some fellows who were getting out of there as fast as they could.[11]

85

Meanwhile, oblivious to the Sioux activity in the territory, Johnson and Beidler continued their foray through southern Canada. In between periods of hunting, trapping, and picking up odd jobs in the Whoop-Up Country, the partners peddled their homemade whiskey for the next two years, hiding their activities from Canadian authorities during the day and working by night. Only boredom finally forced them to give up that trade, and by the middle of the decade, Liver-Eater and X had agreed to go their separate ways in pursuit of more respectable forms of employment—*whatever* that might have proved to be.

So, in the spring of 1874, Johnson decided to sell his services as a pack guide and quickly found all the work he could handle, leading tenderfeet up into the mountainous regions of the south-central and southeastern parts of Montana Territory. With an intimate knowledge of that part of Montana—better, it was said, than any other man alive—Johnson was the perfect choice as a guide. But, with a growing number of settlers heading west through the recently discovered mountain passes and aboard the rapidly expanding railroad, the mountain man's wilderness was beginning to shrink.

Working as a pack guide proved to be harder than Johnson had at first realized, and the pay was low. For no extra effort, he came to realize, he could serve virtually the same purpose and make substantially more money *and* have more excitement. So, in 1876, he left the pack-guide business and signed on as a "contract scout" for General Nelson A. Miles, who had been at the forefront of virtually every major Indian action and event of the Plains War. More than a decade after Johnson's military service had ended, he found himself at war once again, although this time against a far more elusive and, some would say, savage enemy.

IN THE ARMY NOW

Johnson's return to service came some four months following General George Armstrong Custer's disastrous defeat at the Little Bighorn. Soon enough, Johnson found himself embroiled in the ongoing Plains Wars. After Custer's defeat, hundreds of Northern Cheyenne had joined the Sioux and Chief Crazy Horse in the Powder River country, set on completing one more major victory against the whites.

But it was not to be. They met and were soundly defeated, driven back by Colonel Wesley Merritt's Fifth Cavalry at War Bonnet Creek in July 1876. The Cheyenne subsequently retreated to the nearby Red Cloud Agency.

The next major skirmish in the Indian Wars brought Civil War veteran General George Crook up against Sioux chief American Horse and his braves at Slim Buttes. The leader was mortally wounded during the battle, and his warriors surrendered to Crook.

When Liver-Eater decided to sign on as a scout, he chose General Miles, who had put out a notice that he was searching for some of the best fighting men in the country. As one writer later noted: "Miles gathered around him a band of old-time frontiersmen as scouts that filled the bill to a nicety. There was Liver-Eating Johnson, George Johnson, Vic Smith, Tom Cushine, Bob and Billy Jackson, Bat Shane, George Fleury, and Milan Tripp."[12]

In the fall and early winter of 1876–77, Miles and his command marched up the Tongue River to the Wolf Mountains, where they encountered Crazy Horse and his warriors. In the short skirmish that followed, the scouts, headed by Johnson, "captured a buck and a squaw." Several soldiers were killed while the Indians lost one man, Big Crow, their medicine man.

Aware of the daunting task he faced from the entire hostile force of the five Indian tribes he would have to confront in battle, Miles decided to hunker down for the cruelest part of the Montana winter and set about building a cantonment to survive the next few months. But never far from his mind were thoughts of the Hunkpapas (Sitting Bull), the Oglalas (Crazy Horse), the Northern Cheyenne (Two Moons), and the Minneconjous and Sans Arcs whom he knew would be planning a strong attack at the first break of spring.

In a move that ranged from desperation to genius, Miles went to General Alfred Terry to request authority to launch an attack on the five tribes over winter, catching them off-guard. Reluctantly, Terry granted his permission.

The *desperation* came in realizing that, if he waited until spring to launch an attack, he would be forced to face an enemy that was well fortified, well armed, and well prepared for battle, with numbers far superior to anything Miles could throw up against them. The *genius* came in knowing that, by forcing the Indians into a tough winter battle where the cavalry had the advantage of mounted militia, he would either force the Sioux into surrendering or squeeze them out of their stronghold and into a retreat far north to Canada.

In his autobiography, frontiersman Yellowstone Kelly, who was Miles's chief of scouts during the campaign, summed up the Indians' dilemma: "Your wild Indian in order to live comfortably must camp where there is game and [food] for his pony herds and where the women can dress hides to barter for flour, cloth, powder and shell ammunition, salt, and sugar."[13]

Miles knew that when placed under duress, the Sioux would be forced to retreat to their hunting grounds to replenish their supplies and rest up for the next skirmish. Johnson knew that those hunting grounds were in the vicinity where he had worked his wood yard for years and understood the terrain inside and out.

But as the troops moved in on the Sioux, the soldiers met with fierce fighting. After several hours, the general finally ordered a three-inch howitzer brought up to dislodge the enemy from their position. He followed that up with two companies of men who drove the Indians back down the ridge from where they had come. The Sioux and Cheyenne ultimately retreated up the Tongue River and the protection that Wolf Mountain offered them. The government had won the skirmish, but the war was far from over.

Later that year, on a chilly spring morning in 1877, Johnson set out on a routine scouting patrol and stumbled across a band of fifty Sioux and Cheyenne warriors on the Rosebud River. The duty to track them fell to him and fellow scouts George Johnson, Vic Smith, and Bob Jackson. After a brief parlay, the four men decided to ride their mounts into the center of the Indian camp between the tepees and a sprawling herd of horses grazing placidly beneath the clear open skies. Rounding up the herd, the scouts spirited them off into the nearby valley. The warriors, cut off from their animals, raced for cover in the surrounding hills.

By the time Miles's troops arrived, scout Bob Jackson allegedly had killed and scalped the two chiefs, Lame Deer and Iron Star, as the battle raged. Before long, fourteen Indians and four of Miles's men lay dead. The army confiscated nearly a thousand Sioux horses, which the Indians reportedly stole back a short while later.

Following that campaign, Johnson moved on to Fort Vancouver to scout for generals Miles, Otis Howard, and Samuel Sturgis and the Second Colorado Volunteers attached to the army. With the Sioux and Cheyenne campaigns slowly winding down, the Nez Perce were only beginning to exert their influence.

The origins of the Nez Perce War are similar to those of nearly all Indian wars. Whites encroached upon lands claimed by the Indians, who eventually struck back. The result: inevitable defeat.

In the 1870s, the Nez Perce inhabited sections of a wide area that included parts of present-day Oregon, Washington, and Idaho, although their hunting area extended as far east as Montana. Since the days of Lewis and Clark, they had been at peace with the white man, and in 1855 a formal treaty with the United States established a "generous reservation area" for them.

But as a growing number of white people entered the region—flooding the area after the discovery of gold—increased antagonism developed between the Indians and the whites. It was capped in 1803 when the federal government, at the demand of the whites, reduced the size of the reservation substantially. Although many of the Nez Perce chiefs rejected the new boundaries, principal chief Lawyer accepted them, and the government took that to mean the new treaty was binding on the entire tribe. Those who did not accept the treaty of 1803 and remained off the reservation were designated as "nontreaty Nez Perces."

One strong, large band of nontreaty Nez Perces was led by Joseph, who claimed as tribal domain the entire Wallowa Valley in northeast Oregon. There, during summer, the Nez Perce came to hunt, fish, and graze their stock. A clash of cultures was imminent.

In the summer of 1876, almost two years after Howard had taken command of the department, two settlers killed an Indian in the Wallowa

Valley. The situation was becoming tense, and there was a strong possibility of war breaking out between the whites and the nontreaty Nez Perces.

The Indian Bureau attached to the Department of the Interior was at the time following a mandate of placing *all* Indians on reservations and attempting to teach them the ways of the white man. The report of Commissioner J. Q. Smith in 1876 stated: "The civilization or the utter destruction of the Indians is inevitable. The next twenty-five years are to determine the fate of a race. If they cannot be taught, and taught very soon, to accept the necessities of their situation and begin in earnest to provide for their own wants by labor in civilized pursuits, they are destined to speedy extinction."

Needless to say, Chief Joseph and his tribe disagreed.

Joseph, a renegade known to many as "the Red Napoleon," had recently orchestrated an astonishing retreat from the US Army, coming within forty miles of reaching safe harbor in Canada. Liver-Eating Johnson's regiment had pursued the Nez Perce through the Big Hole Valley at Yellowstone and the Bears Paw Mountains in northern Montana. The Nez Perce had killed several miners along the Clark's Fork, stealing their horses in the process. They also raided the ranch of JMV Cochran, killing two trapper guests of his. Afterward, several warriors rode into the town of Coulson and burned down the saloon!

In order to help stamp out the carnage, Lieutenant George Houston named Cochran and Johnson to an elite cadre of guides known as the Yellowstone Scouts. Author Mark H. Brown wrote, "Howard engaged a prospector named George Houston for a guide and enlisted about twenty others as scouts in a body called the 'Yellowstone Scouts.'"

Chief Joseph and his brother Ollokot were away from the camp during the Indian raids of June 14–15. When they returned the next day, most of the Nez Perce had departed for a site on White Bird Creek to await General Howard's response. Joseph considered issuing an appeal for peace to the whites but realized it would be useless in light of the recent killings. Meanwhile, Howard mobilized his military force and sent out 130 men, including 13 scouts who were friendly to the Nez Perce, under the command of Captain David Perry. Their goal: to punish the Nez Perce by forcing them onto the reservation. Howard anticipated that

An 1886 photo of General O. O. Howard, for whom Liver-Eating Johnson scouted during the Indian Wars.
COURTESY MONTANA HISTORICAL SOCIETY

his soldiers "will make short work of it."[14] Instead, the Nez Perce defeated Perry at the Battle of White Bird Canyon and began their long flight eastward to escape from their pursuers.

Looking Glass and his band joined Joseph at White Bird and, after several battles and skirmishes in Idaho during the following month,[15] approximately 250 Nez Perce warriors and 500 women and children along with more than 2,000 head of horses and other livestock began a remarkable retreat. They crossed from Idaho over Lolo Pass into Montana Territory, traveling southeast, dipping into Yellowstone National Park and then moving back north into Montana, roughly 1,170 miles. They attempted to seek refuge with the Crow Nation, but, rebuffed by the Crow, they ultimately decided to try to reach safety in British-held Canada.[16]

According to Charles Erskine Wood, an eyewitness on the scene, "The battle in White Bird Canyon was the first armed conflict of the Nez

Perce War. I helped bury the dead in that canyon. The next clash was the two-day battle on the north fork of the Clearwater, July 11 and 12, 1877. Then Chief Joseph's retreat through the Lolo Pass began, only to end at Bear Paw Mountain, Montana, within about thirty miles of the British line and safety. (Joseph could easily have made his escape by pushing his march a little farther, but, as General Howard anticipated, he kept his eye on our rate of progress and when we slowed down, he did the same.)"[17]

Following the retreat, a small number of Nez Perce fighters, probably fewer than two hundred, defeated or stood off larger forces of the US Army in several skirmishes. The most notable was the two-day Battle of the Big Hole in southwestern Montana Territory, a brutal conflict with heavy casualties on both sides, including numerous Nez Perce women and children. Until the Big Hole, the Nez Perce had held the naive view that they could end the war with the United States with terms favorable, or at least acceptable, to themselves. Afterward, the war "increased in ferocity and tempo. From then on all white men were bound to be their enemies and yet their own fighting power had been severely reduced."[18]

According to Wood:

After the battle of the Clearwater, came skirmishes at the beginning of Lolo Trail, then the battle at Big Hole, where Gibbon was wounded; then the early morning attack at Camas Meadows, where Joseph ran off with our pack train and we, recovering only about half, had to stop at Henry Lake and send into Virginia City, Montana, for pack horses and wagons. Then we built the bridge across the Yellowstone River and brought over it the first wagons that had ever gone through the National Park. Joseph's trail had let us so far through some of the most terrific fastnesses of the Rocky Mountains.

Howard had wired Sturgis to have his six or seven troops of the Seventh Cavalry watching for Joseph's debouchment from the mountains somewhere in the neighborhood of Hart Mountain, for we judged by his line of trail and the trend of the water-courses and passes that he would have to descend from the mountains at that point. We tried to send messengers ahead of the Nez Perce to give Sturgis definite information of our coming, but not one of our couriers got through, all being killed by the Indians. Nevertheless it did not seem possible for Joseph to make the maneuver in this country which he had done at the eastern end of the Lolo Trail—that is, go over the hills and around the waiting enemy. I shall never forget the actual pass through which he made his exit into Clark Basin near Hart Mountain. It was the spout of a funnel—the dry bed of a mountain torrent, with such precipitous walls on either side that it was like going through a gigantic rough railroad tunnel. Had Sturgis remained at Hart Mountain in accordance with instructions, ready and watching, Joseph's escape would certainly have been blocked. But in the night Joseph had sent a few of his young men quietly around Sturgis' force toward Hart Mountain. There, at daybreak, they stirred up a great dust by tying sagebrush to their lariats and riding around furiously, dragging the bundles of brush along the ground. Sturgis thought Joseph's whole body had got past him, and started in pursuit of the long dust trail, abandoning the mouth of the pass. When he saw it clear Joseph went through safely. The young men who had acted as decoys made a long circuit and joined Joseph out on the easy plains of the Yellowstone and Missouri Rivers.[19]

Howard, wanting to put an end to the stalemate, sent a written order down the Yellowstone by boat to Miles at Fort Keogh advising him that Joseph and his band had eluded Sturgis and continued their retreat toward British Columbia. The reason: to unite with Sitting Bull's forces in Canada. He advised Miles that Joseph was traveling at a rate of about "twenty-five miles a day; but he regulates his gait by ours."[20] He advised that he would lessen their speed to around twelve miles, thereby enticing Joseph to slow down, delaying his escape into Canada and allowing Miles to intercept him. The purpose of the communiqué to Miles was to alert him of Joseph's location and the direction and rate of his flight and to allow Howard to meet with Miles as they overtook the Indians south of the Canadian border.

The messenger returned and said that Miles had immediately issued orders to his command to prepare to intersect the Indian line of march. Besides rations, Miles prepared ammunition, feed for the horses, and two howitzers and set out on a diagonal line the following morning.

General Samuel Davis Sturgis, 1822–1889, for whom Johnson scouted during the final days of the Great Indian Wars.

Wood picked up the narrative from there:

In the afternoon we saw a man at a distance across the prairie, evidently puzzled by our appearance. General Howard sent a couple of our scouts to bring him in. He turned out to be a bearer of mail and dispatches for Miles from Miles' post at Fort Keogh, and was trying to find him. He was a frontiersman called Slippery Dick or "Liver-Eating Johnson"—because, by his own story and popular report, he was supposed to have eaten a piece of the liver of an Indian whom he had killed and scalped, thereby following the tradition of the Indians, that if one ate a part of the heart or liver of an enemy, he would acquire all the bravery of the dead man.[21]

As the two armies converged upon the retreating Indians, light snow covered the ground. The Nez Perce stopped to make camp and rest on the prairie adjacent to Snake Creek in the foothills of the north slope of the Bears Paw Mountains in northern Montana Territory, only forty miles from the Canadian border.

They believed that they had shaken off Howard and their pursuers, but they were wrong. Unaware that the recently promoted Brigadier General Nelson A. Miles had been given command of the newly created District of the Yellowstone, they had no way of knowing that Miles had been dispatched from the Tongue River Cantonment to find and intercept them. The general led a combined force composed of units of the Fifth Infantry and the Second and Seventh Cavalries. Several Lakota and Cheyenne Indian scouts accompanied the troops, many of whom had fought against the army only the year before during the Sioux War.

Finally, on the morning of September 30, Miles and his men launched a surprise attack on the Nez Perce camp. After a three-day standoff, Howard arrived with his command, and the stalemate was broken. Chief Joseph surrendered on October 5 and declared in his famous surrender speech that he would "fight no more forever."[22]

In total, the Nez Perce had engaged two thousand American soldiers of different military units, along with their Indian auxiliaries. They fought "eighteen engagements, including four major battles and at least four fiercely contested skirmishes."[23] Many people praised the Nez Perce for their exemplary conduct and skilled fighting ability. The Montana newspaper *New North-West* stated, "Their warfare since they entered Montana has been almost universally marked so far by the highest characteristics recognized by civilized nations."[24]

By the time Chief Joseph formally surrendered, European Americans described him as the principal chief of the Nez Perce and the strategist behind the Nez Perce's skilled fighting retreat. The American press referred to him as "the Red Napoleon" for the strategic military prowess attributed to him, but the Nez Perce bands involved in the war did not consider him a war chief. Joseph's younger brother, Ollokot, along with Poker Joe and Looking Glass of the Alpowai band, was among the chiefs who had formulated the fighting strategy and tactics and led the warriors in battle, while Joseph was responsible for guarding the camp.

Nevertheless, Chief Joseph became immortalized by his famous speech:

> *I am tired of fighting. Our chiefs are killed. Looking Glass is dead. Toohoolhoolzoote is dead. The old men are all dead. It is the young men who say, "Yes" or "No." He who led the young men [Joseph's brother, Ollokot] is dead. It is cold, and we have no blankets. The little children are freezing to death. My people, some of them, have run away to the hills and have no blankets, no food. No one knows where they are— perhaps freezing to death. I want to have time to look for my children and see how many of them I can find. Maybe I shall find them among the dead. Hear me, my chiefs! I am tired. My heart is sick and sad. From where the sun now stands I will fight no more forever.[25]*

It had taken some of the most grueling battles in US military history, but in the end, Johnson and the other scouts had helped to write the history of Chief Joseph's people in blood. Johnson was present when Joseph formally surrendered to General Miles on October 5, 1877, at 2:20 p.m.

Throughout the glory years, Johnson received more respect and notoriety than he had at any other time of his life. Famed fellow scout Yellowstone Kelly, who served with him under Miles, referred to his colleague as "the celebrated huntsman and frontiersman on whom rested the sobriquet of 'Liver-Eating Johnson.'"[26]

In an interview with a reporter from the *St. Louis Globe*, General Sturgis, for whom Johnson served throughout the Chief Joseph campaign, paid tribute to one of the army's most famous and appreciated—if

Chief Joseph, a leader of the Nez Perce, who led his people on an epic flight across the Rocky Mountains before surrendering to the US Army, ending the Great Indian Wars.
COURTESY MONTANA HISTORICAL SOCIETY

not sartorial—scouts. The interview was republished in the *Bismarck Tri-Weekly Tribune* on February 7, 1878. It announced the death of "Liver-Eating" Johnson on the Yellowstone—somewhat prematurely, as soon became evident.

The reporter asked Sturgis for some background on his relationship with the "recently departed" Liver-Eater:

> "*I met him when we were at the mouth of the Stillwater, and there engaged him as a scout on account of his knowledge of the country which we were to go over last summer.*"
>
> "*What do you know of his Indian fighting, General?*"
>
> "*Personally, I know nothing; though, from all I heard, he had killed quite a number of Indians, by whom he was greatly feared.*"
>
> "*That's a rather peculiar nom de guerre he travels under, General.*"
>
> "*Well, yes,*" laughing, "*That's the name he was known by, though, universally—'Liver-eating Johnson'—and I have no doubt earned it honestly. He was as you may suppose, quite a character. I never heard the full particulars of his liver-eating exploit; but I have the best reasons in the world for believing its truth—he told the story himself.*"
>
> "*He possessed the accomplishment of truth, then, among others?*"
>
> "*He was a perfectly truthful man. In all my dealings with him I never knew him to deviate a line from the truth. He never professed knowledge which he did not possess. When it became necessary for us to go into a part of the country with which he was unacquainted, he at once acknowledged his ignorance; and when he was leading us through territory which he professed to know, everything he indicated concerning localities which we were to enter—where there was water, where there was none, where a hill would be found, where a shortcut could be made—turned out exactly as he had stated.*"
>
> "*What sort of a looking man was he, General?*"
>
> "*'Looked like a quiet going farmer. He was a man of about fifty-one years of age, stoutly and powerfully built, with a sober, resolute face, dark hair and eyes, and heavy beard.*"

"*Quite picturesque, then?*"

"*No he wasn't at all picturesque. He might have been if he chose, but these guides as a rule make no attempt at personal adornment, and Johnson in particular was utterly regardless of his clothes. He was very carelessly dressed at all times; consequently it was impossible to guess at his merits from his personal appearance. Well, well, I'm sorry he's dead, but (looking at the slip again) it doesn't say how he came to be killed. Have you heard any further particulars?*"

"*Nothing further than what you see there. Maybe he has been killed in a fight probably.*"

"*I hardly think so. Very few people in the country would care to engage him, and he never sought trouble. On the other hand, he always avoided personal encounters, though when he was to run into one he could take care of himself admirably. No, I do not think he has fallen in a fight.*"

"*I suppose there were occasions when he was invaluable to you?*"

"*Yes, indeed, and never more so than when I crossed the river in order to go Miles' relief, fearing that Sitting Bull might come to the rescue of the captured Indians. I heard that he had intercepted the Nez Perces, so I crossed the river with the whole command to the scene of the fight. Johnson was my guide on that occasion. Everything depended on him—no one else in the command knew anything about the country we had to traverse—and he led us straight to our destination.*"

"*What sort of a man was he socially?*"

"*These men are pretty much alike. They live from hand to mouth; make a little money and spend it as soon as made; live principally by the chase and seem to have no care for the future.*"

"*Married or single?*"

"*Oh, I've no doubt he was, or had been married. The marriage relation is not very seriously regarded in that country. Such men marry squaws generally according to the Indian custom, but the relation is not considered very binding, and Johnson may have been married more than once.*"[27]

Another report of Johnson's premature death—and the manner in which he was thought to have garnered his Liver-Eating moniker—appeared in the book *Frontier Folk* by George Booth, published in 1880. Beyond shedding light on Johnson, the book in only a few short paragraphs paints an intriguing and insightful picture of scouts, scouting, integrity, and the relationships between white scouts and Indian women in general:

> *On occasion of any military expedition, scouts are hired to discover the position and circumstances of the "hostiles," as Indians are called, for attacking whom orders have been issued. Their rewards are usually regulated by the importance of the information they bring and the risks they have run. Many of these men will do excellent service, and sometimes in a modest way. Many more, on the other hand, will lie perdu until their rations are consumed, and then come back with some startling but highly untrue information. They have proved themselves to be not too good to burn the grass, to efface the trail of the enormous body of Indians they pretended to have seen. These men usually don a costume like that of the hero of a dime novel. They wear long hair, occasionally neatly bound up into a queue with a snake-skin. Sometimes they cut out the roof of their sombrero, to permit their flowing topknots to wave forth like feathers. They use much of the Indian's ornament, often adorning themselves by sewing elk-teeth on their garments; they also imitate some of the least excusable customs of the savage. All of them endeavor to adopt some prefix to their name. A Mr. Johnson, who was drowned in the Yellowstone, acquired the soubriquet of Liver-eating Johnson, by eating and pretending to prefer his portion of liver in an uncooked condition; and he was as well satisfied with this name and the notoriety it implied as are Indians with their zoological titles.*
>
> *"Squaw-man" is the name given to a white man who has married one or more Indian wives, and been regularly adopted by their tribe with whom he lives. With the exception of being of occasional use as an interpreter, he is an utterly worthless person. He has completely left his own race and taken to the ways of the savage, and is*

equally despised by the whites and by his adopted brethren. Many of the woodcutters who supply fuel to steamboats on the upper Missouri marry, or rather buy, Indian wives; but they do not form part of the tribal family, as does the "squaw-man." Often it is policy for them to take wives from tribes which are dangerous to their safety. A wife insures protection from the depredations of her tribe; and when her lord and master is tired of her, or wishes to form other business relations, he simply tells her and her progeny to go home.[28]

Despite Johnson's success as a military scout—or perhaps *because* of it—his days battling the Nez Perce tribe didn't always receive unanimous praise. On December 24, 1884, the *Pioneer Press* of St. Paul, Minnesota, published a letter written by an "unnamed officer" of the Seventh Cavalry under whom Johnson allegedly served during the Nez Perce War. The author heaped some uncomplimentary charges onto Johnson's back regarding the time he had served as a scout for General Miles. The anonymous writer was identified only as an "officer of the Seventh horse" (Seventh Cavalry):

The first time I ever met Liver-Eating Johnston . . . was in '77, when we were out after the Nez Perce. It was a pretty lively campaign that summer, and what with Howard, Miles and Sturgis in the field, all trying to capture Chief Joseph, good scouts were in demand; for every small party detached from either of the three columns operating against the Indians must have a guide; and he must be one who knew his business, able to detect the faintest signs of Indians, and quick and sure on the trail.

Johnston came to us from the Crow Agency at Stillwater, where he spent most of his time. He was what is called a "squaw man," that is, one who has one or more squaws to wife, and who practically lives with the Indians. A tall, burly fellow, standing over six feet in his moccasins and weighing over two hundred pounds, his strong, well-knit muscular form and his face, framed in an amplitude of flowing beard and curly locks, would have made him conspicuous in a crowd anywhere. He was a first-rate scout, bold and quick to scent danger.

But with all his keenness while scouting, I noticed Johnston took mighty few chances himself, and ran no risks that could be avoided. Coming across some very fresh signs of bear while hunting, I asked him to go in the brake with me and see if we could find the game. With a perfectly sober face, he said, "Well, lieutenant, you and your man go in and stir him up, and I'll shoot him when he comes out the other side."

One day while scouting near the mouth of the Musselshell, he pointed to a belt of timber near at hand and remarked "there is where I got the name of Liver-Eating Johnston. You see, there was a party of twenty of us hunters and trappers camped here in 1868. The country was full of game and Indians, and beaver was almost as thick as buffalo. We was having splendid luck, and our camp was just piled with peltry. But one morning we was jumped by a band of about fifty Sioux, who circled towards us, whooping and yelling like devils, and firing under the necks of their ponies. We gave them a volley, and the Indians, thinking we were armed with the common rifle, rushed in. But most of us had repeating rifles (it was the first season we had them in the territory), and as they came on we gave them another round which fairly staggered them, but when we pulled on them again, a more surprised lot of bucks you never saw. They skinned out quick, but we gave it to them. I saw one buck tumble from his pony and crawl into the brush, so I went after him. Putting my knife into him I gave it a turn, and when I pulled it out there was a piece of his liver sticking to the knife. So I held it up and yelled to the fellow next to me, 'Say Jim, won't you have a bite?' That's all there is to the story. Some say I ate it, but it's a lie."

They do say that Johnson really ate a piece of the liver as Indians sometimes do, believing they acquire the brave qualities of the man they had killed.

I remember one day while scouting with a detachment we came upon Chief Joseph's trail. It was near the foot of the Heart Mountain, and miles away from the column of Sturgis. The trail was very fresh and at a little distance ahead of us could be seen the bodies of two white men. As soon as Liver-Eating, who was in the lead, struck the trail, and saw the bodies lying there, he came galloping back, and yelled out, "there will be more than a million Indians here inside ten minutes." Well sir, you could have knocked me down with a feather, for I was scared; and when I looked around, and saw the white faces of my men, more than half of who were green recruits, I was afraid of a stampede. But I instantly gave the word to dismount, leaving every fourth man to hold the horses of the others. This, of course, prevented the men from stampeding; and then I ordered the scout to ascend the hill in front and look for Indians. He refused at first, but I told him he was a dead man if he disobeyed. Having seen I meant business (and I would have shot him sure), he rode on. Cautiously, he ascended the hill but found no Indians.

Johnson, clearly no admirer of the letter's author or its contents, was incensed. He rattled off a response to the *Post* of Billings, Montana, which had originally republished the *Pioneer Press* letter the day before. On Christmas day, 1884, the *Post* ran Johnson's rebuttal. Although Johnson could read and write, the style and vocabulary of his rebuttal lend credence to the supposition that he had dictated his thoughts to a ghostwriter, who put them down on paper.

In the Pioneer Press of the 21st instant [21st day of December], nearly a column is devoted to a sketch about myself and some of my adventures as detailed to the credulous reporter of that paper by a Jim Crow subaltern of the 7th Cavalry. The smart aleck who undertakes to tell the Pioneer Press about me has not the manhood to back up his statements by publishing his name. However, I suspect who he is and am inclined to think him as big a poltroon now as he showed himself to be when a petty lieutenant in the Nez Perce war. He says that when I was guiding the 7th through the mountain region, I showed the white feather when I struck the Nez Perces fresh trail.

Now, the less a good many of the officers of the 7th have to say about the Nez Perces war the better, for their reputation for valor. Some of these days I shall publish what I know about the march of the Nez Perces from Bald Ridge to Bears Paw, and I can promise my friend the fresh lieutenant who is so anxious to tell the Pioneer Press his adventures that I shall add some reminiscences of great interest to himself and some other of his brother officers who I know to be much braver in attacking a beefsteak than a hostile camp.

When the 7th was in the region of Clarke's Fork Canyon, I discovered the Nez Perces on Bald Ridge. I told the lieutenant in charge of the detachment that I had found the Indians we were looking for. He looked through his field glasses but said he could not see them. He didn't want to. He hadn't lost any hostile Indians, I guess.

The Crow scouts present at this time also saw the Nez Perces and told this brave officer so, but he wasn't open to conviction. None so blind as those who won't see. When the Nez Perces were discovered at Clarke's Fork Canyon, General Sturgis asked my opinion as to the best route to overtake them. I advised him strongly to remain just where we were, as from the lay of the country the Nez Perces must pass close to our encampment that they could then be attacked to advantage, and the campaign ended. General Sturgis saw the truth of my reasoning and agreed with me, as did Captain French and Colonel Benteen. All the other officers of the command demurred and overruled these three officers. They did so because they were afraid to fight, and I told them so at the time in the presence of the command.

This bluntness on my part offended some of these sucking warriors, and one of them, the Pioneer Press's informant, has undoubtedly never forgiven me. The result of the council was that we moved on towards Stinking Water, and the Nez Perces passed by our rear and went on their march to Bear Paw, thanks to the blundering and cowardice of these carpet knights.

During the balance of the campaign, I was leading scout [head scout] and guide for Sturgis's command, and part of the time for Howard's and at times for both together. Both these officers during the campaign and after its close gave me the highest praise for my knowledge of the country, skill in guiding troops and intrepidity in a hostile country. I deny that I am or ever was a squaw man or ever kept a squaw as a wife or otherwise. Any statement to the contrary is a malicious falsehood.

As far as "sand" goes, I don't need to go to any second-class lieu-tenant for it. I have been in forty different Indian fights, and have fought them from California to the Gulf of Mexico. I have killed more Indians than all the officers of the 7th Cavalry put together, throwing the regiment in. If the dirty, cowardly officer of the 7th Cavalry who has tried to stab my reputation, through the Pioneer Press, will pub-lish his name, the first time I strike his trail I'll make him think that a section of the Day of Judgment has struck him.

My adventures and my conduct are pretty well known through-out the west, and I don't need to go away from home to get a certificate of good character, but it does rile me when a whelp of an officer that was nearly scared to death in one little campaign, comes barking and snarling at my heels, who can count twice as many coups as he can toes and fingers.

If the anonymous author of the letter appearing in the *Pioneer Press* ever read Johnson's response, he never acknowledged it. Not another word on the allegations was exchanged between the two men, anony-mously or otherwise! And, in the end, few men's reputations built upon the backs of the Nez Perce War and the natives' eventual defeat could match that of Liver-Eating Johnson's—or come even close.

CHAPTER EIGHT

The Yellowstone Years

LIVER-EATING JOHNSON SERVED THE US ARMY AS A SCOUT, A WELL-documented fact. But just how valuable he proved to be during the Indian Wars might never be known without the meticulous notes provided by Luther "Yellowstone" Kelly. Working as a scout for General Miles, Kelly, Johnson, and three other men shouldered the burden of running down and bringing to bay three powerful Sioux tribes led by chiefs Pretty Bear, Gall, and a man named Sitting Bull. The three other scouts were Club-foot Boyd, Charley Bass, and Billy LeBeau.

Kelly's full Christian name was Luther Sage Kelly. To the Sioux, he was known as "Lone Wolf," "Little Man with the Strong Heart," or "Man Who Never Lays Down His Gun." To the white men who knew the northern plains country of the American West throughout the 1870s and 1880s, he was Yellowstone Kelly, a man whose accomplishments transcended the region that spawned his sobriquet.

If any single scout projected the image of a handsome, buckskin-clad, straight-shootin', poetry-spoutin', damsel-rescuin', Indian-fightin' frontiersman, it was Kelly. A man who in an earlier generation might have served as the inspiration for a James Fennimore Cooper novel, Kelly was dashing, lithe, and muscular—Cooper's venerable Natty Bumppo transported to the West. He wore a full mustache below coal-black, shoulder-length hair. His garb most often consisted of animal skins and beaded moccasins, and his .44-caliber Henry repeating rifle, which he affectionately called "Old Sweetness," was encased from muzzle to butt in the skin of a giant bull snake.

Liver-Eating Johnson, scout, 1876–77, with General Miles, commissioned hunter and trapper in Yellowstone Company.
COURTESY INTERNATIONAL FEATURES SYNDICATE

In an era that boasted many noted frontiersmen, Kelly was among the most respected of all. General Miles is reported to have considered Kelly's ability as a scout equal to that of Kit Carson and Daniel Boone combined and found his knowledge of the Missouri and Yellowstone river valleys "exceedingly" valuable. Buffalo Bill reportedly called him a "good man to tie to."

Further setting himself apart from most of his frontier contemporaries, Kelly was an educated man. He enjoyed reading, delighting in the works of Edgar Allen Poe, Sir Walter Scott, and William Shakespeare. Pioneer Montana photographer L. A. Huffman, who operated a studio in Miles City during the 1870s, recalled that Kelly liked to relax in the back of his studio where, stretched out on a pile of buffalo robes, he'd consume a book.

Although fond of intellectual conversation, he preferred reticence. Soldiers at Fort Keogh in southeastern Montana called him "Kelly the Silent" and "Kelly the Sphinx." Grant Marsh called Kelly "extremely taciturn." Marsh was best known for his epic piloting of the *Far West* riverboat from the mouth of the Little Bighorn River down the Bighorn to the Yellowstone and Missouri rivers and Bismarck to deliver to the medics fifty wounded troopers who had survived the "Custer Massacre."

Kelly's natural shyness may have been nurtured by years of solitary wanderings in the out-of-doors, a habit that he had cultivated since his days as a boy in upstate New York.

Born July 27, 1849, near Geneva in the Finger Lakes region of central New York State, Kelly was a direct descendant of Hannah Dustin, a heroine of colonial New England. Dustin was reputed not only to have survived a seventeenth-century Indian raid and abduction but also to have killed and scalped ten of her captors in the process of escaping. In later years, Kelly suggested that his affinity for the outdoor life may have been a trait inherited from his illustrious ancestor.

"Along Seneca lake and the deep woods that bordered it," Kelly wrote, "I passed many a happy day of my boyhood, encroaching, no doubt, upon many hours that should have been devoted to school. The inclination I had for forest life and scenes, and later for the free life of

The erudite Luther Sage "Yellowstone" Kelly, 1849–1928, came to the West to find adventure and was not disappointed. He served along with Johnson and several others as a military scout during the Great Indian Wars.

the plains and mountains of the Far West, may have been derived from ancestry."[1]

Like Liver-Eater and other young men of his era, Kelly saw the American Civil War as a grand adventure too exciting to pass up. But with the war drawing quickly to a close, he feared the fighting would be over by the time he had an opportunity to contribute. In early 1865, at the age of sixteen, he talked his mother into allowing him to join the military. He left Geneva Wesleyan Seminary in Lima, New York, and headed for Rochester to sign up in the Army of the Potomac. But the minimum age for enlistment was eighteen, so Kelly was rejected. Persistent, he tried again at a different location, and on March 28, 1865, he was accepted into Company G, Tenth US Infantry. Naive about military matters, Kelly had unwittingly signed up for a tour of duty with the regular army rather than with the volunteers. The mistake committed him to serve three years of his life regardless of the war's duration.

As in the case of Johnson, Kelly barely had time to don his uniform before the conflict was over. The closest he came to the action was serving as a guard during the great victory parade down Washington's Pennsylvania Avenue. As he recalled in his autobiography: "All day long that column passed, and our arms became numb with saluting and holding our rifles at a carry. Some regiments were arrayed in white collars, and many had new uniforms: other regiments, perhaps direct from the field, had no time to make requisition on the quartermaster for new clothing. So they passed, horse, foot, and artillery, followed by camp followers and 'bummers' in strange and quaint attire gathered in foraging forays on the flanks of armies."[2]

Shortly after the parade, Kelly's unit departed for duty at Fort Ripley, Minnesota, on the upper stretch of the Mississippi River near present-day Brainerd. Kelly remained there for a year before being transferred to Fort Wadsworth and then to Fort Ransom in Dakota Territory, where he eventually received his discharge.

While stationed in Dakota, Kelly fell under the spell of the sprawling vistas of the trans-Mississippi West. In his free hours, he often hunted, providing fresh meat for the garrison and honing the skills he would need later as a mountain man. He saw buffalo for the first time, as well as Sioux Indians, who were to play an important role in his life in the years to come.

When his enlistment expired in the spring of 1868, Kelly wanted to see more of what lay beyond the Missouri River. Returning to St. Paul, he cashed in his pay vouchers and embarked in pursuit of a long-enduring dream. He made his way to the Canadian settlement of Fort Gary (now Winnipeg), from where he laid plans to travel west to wherever the "spirit of adventure might lead me until I had reached the wild country at the headwaters of the Missouri River."[3]

At Fort Gary, Kelly joined a party of Montana miners who had chosen to winter on the Red River instead of in the less-affordable gold camps. From these miners, Kelly added to his growing store of knowledge about the northern plains tribes, including the Sioux. The miners tried to convince him not to continue on alone, but Kelly was determined. He struck out from the Red River camp, crossed the Assiniboine River, and joined a party of mixed-blood Indians headed for the Souris, or Mouse, River. The river wandered from the Yellow Grass Marshes north of Weyburn, Saskatchewan, south through North Dakota past Minot to its most southern point at the city of Velva, North Dakota, and then north again back into Manitoba.

It was during this phase of his westward journey that Kelly met Sitting Bull, a Hunkpapa Sioux who had not yet attained the reputation of his later years. Kelly recalled that Sitting Bull had a "round, pleasant face, and wore a head scarf of dirty white cloth, while most of his followers affected black head-gear."[4]

Leaving the Indians, Kelly forged a trail toward the Missouri River country, which he found sprawling and inspiring—if less than awesome. In later years he retraced the journey in his memoirs:

I rode leisurely along until I had topped the low divide of grassland, with here and there scrub timber in the hollows and ravines, and from this viewpoint I saw, not the valley of the Missouri, but the country beyond, with rough hills and ridges covered with dark timber like cedar. It seemed a forbidding-looking country, under the shadow of low-lying clouds far on the western horizon. It was, indeed, a land of broils and feuds, where dwelt many tribes of men of different tongues, whose pastime was war until the white man came, who warred against none, but fought all, because all opposed.

I rode at a good pace and suddenly arrived on the bank of the great Missouri, which rolled along between narrow bluffs with no valley or timber on either side. Perhaps not in hundreds of miles could the river have presented to the stranger a more unattractive aspect than at the bend where I touched it. Yet its potential power, mighty in its confinement between gray bluffs of sandstone, was apparent at once.

Man and horse took a refreshing drink of mighty Minnishushu, then I marked the places where Lewis and Clark's boatmen must have trod while cordelling their clumsy boats up the river, for there was no shifting of the channel in that rockbound bend.[5]

During the winter of 1868–69, Kelly spent some time at Fort Buford at the confluence of the Missouri and Yellowstone rivers in Dakota Territory, presently North Dakota. The commanding officer asked for a volunteer to carry dispatches to Fort Stevenson some fifty miles down the Missouri. The two regular riders had not shown up on schedule and were feared lost to a Sioux war party. No one stepped forward until Kelly raised his hand. He was quickly passed over because of his youth, but his persistence paid off, as it had when he'd joined the Union army, and he was assigned to the mission, if reluctantly.

But Kelly allayed all doubts when he reached Fort Stevenson without incident, although on the return trip, he stumbled upon a pair of Sioux warriors. In a quick, gruesome attack, Kelly lost a finger and suffered a wound in the leg by an arrow from one of his attackers before he managed to kill them both. When he reported the incident back at the fort, news of Kelly's exploits spread quickly. Before long, he was heralded as one of the most skilled scouts and best marksmen in the entire Missouri River valley.

By the spring of 1873, Kelly was itching for more action. His commanding officer recommended him as a guide to Colonel George A. Forsyth, who had made a name for himself in the Battle of Beecher

Island, Colorado. During that skirmish in September 1868, Forsyth led a command of civilian scouts in a fight against a large contingent of Cheyenne. He'd been preparing for a military reconnaissance of the Yellowstone River from Fort Buford to the mouth of the Powder River, a point farther upstream than any steamboat had dared travel before. If he found it could be done, the army could begin hauling supplies upriver to a military base camp established at the mouth of the Powder, where soldiers were needed to protect Northern Pacific Railroad surveyors from Indian attacks.

The Yellowstone Valley at that time was still unmapped and mostly unexplored. To rectify that, Forsyth needed a reliable guide with previous experience in the area. Captain Marsh, upon hearing it, immediately thought of Kelly. Anchoring the *Key West* near Kelly's cabin along the banks of the Missouri near present-day Williston, North Dakota, Marsh disembarked and paid a visit to the scout. Kelly had spent the previous five years hunting and trapping in the region and knew the area better than any other white man alive. He confessed he was less familiar with the upper reaches of the Yellowstone but could barely restrain his excitement at the thought of being among the first Americans to explore it. Kelly accepted on one condition: Marsh had to agree to transport Kelly's supply of pelts to Fort Buford and safety.

So, the expedition went forward. Kelly set off to scout the river as far as the headwaters, eventually reporting back that the water was indeed deep enough to be navigable by boat to the point where the army hoped to establish a fort. Forsyth later related his thoughts regarding Kelly's service: "Our guide, known as 'Yellowstone Kelly,' was another capable character, who gave us much information of the country on each side of the river through which we were passing, and he has since won a lasting reputation on the old Western frontier as an able scout and a reliable guide."[6]

Of Forsyth, Kelly recalled that the colonel was a "very pleasant gentleman, quiet and reserved, not much given to recounting past deeds and events, never a word of Beecher Island [in which Forsyth and fifty scouts stood off several hundred Northern Cheyenne, Arapaho, and Oglala Sioux] or the stiff fight and defense made there."[7]

Kelly spent the next several years working part-time as a guide and filling out his days hunting and wolfing in central Montana's Bears Paw Mountains and the Judith Basin. Meanwhile, relations between the US government and the Indians of the northern plains were strained to the point of breaking. The Horse Creek Treaty that was enacted to offer specific lands for each of the different tribes failed to produce lasting peace. The problem was exacerbated with reports of gold discovered in the Black Hills of Dakota Territory, an area long considered sacred by the Sioux. As white settlers from all parts of the country poured into the Indian lands, increasingly frequent clashes broke out. Things were not about to get better.

The Sioux, who considered the Black Hills the center of the earth and a place to communicate with the Great Spirit, had controlled the area consisting of most of modern-day western South Dakota for decades. The United States finally ceded the land to the Indians following Red Cloud's War and the Treaty of Fort Laramie in 1868. But even though whites were forbidden from entering the Black Hills, the allure of gold proved too great a temptation to resist.

As the inevitable clashes between the two cultures increased in ferocity, so too did whites' demands for protection. Finally, General Phil Sheridan petitioned President Ulysses S. Grant to build a fort at the southwest edge of the reservation to deter future raids on white settlers and their encampments. Grant approved the request, and Sheridan assigned his favorite commander to the task of siting the fort—the fair-haired wunderkind of the Seventh Cavalry, Lieutenant Colonel George Armstrong Custer.

Beyond locating a suitable site for the fort, Custer was charged with clandestinely looking for something even more valuable than a military fortification: gold!

So, ten companies of the Seventh Cavalry set out from Fort Abraham Lincoln on July 2, 1874. Along with them were several scientists, geologists, and reporters. If the companies found gold, the geologists were to examine it, and the press would report upon it, providing Custer with some welcomed positive publicity back East. If they didn't, they still had their main mission of locating a suitable site for the new fort to fall back on.

But when the reporters began sending their earliest dispatches back to their papers, they all focused on the same mission: "Looking for Gold—Custer's Exploring Expedition," the July 25 headline of the *Baltimore Sun* rang out. Some three weeks later, the headlines grew even bolder as the reporters learned of a find. The August 27 headline of Chicago's *Inter Ocean* screamed, "GOLD!"

Even though Custer's expedition had found only a small sprinkling of the precious ore, the reports in the papers made it sound as if he'd made the largest strike since the mother lode in California.

Within days, prospectors began pouring in, desperate to strike it rich. And some did at Deadwood Gulch in November 1875—enough, anyway, to keep the rush of prospectors funneling through the area. By the following year, some five thousand fortune-seekers had flooded the Black Hills, and the town of Deadwood sprang from the mountain grasses and prairie-dog holes. All thoughts of restrictions against trespassing on the Sioux-owned Black Hills evaporated into the sun-drenched skies.

Rather than acting to remove the interlopers, the US government sought a rationale for grabbing the land back from the Indians. That would certainly have gone far toward pacifying the voters back East who were clamoring for "manifest destiny"—an America that stretched from sea to shining sea. When a delegation of Sioux representatives traveled to the nation's capital in May 1875 to petition the federal government to enforce the 1868 treaty, US officials offered to purchase the land from the Sioux for $25,000 and a guarantee of safe relocation to Indian Territory in present-day Oklahoma. The Sioux refused.

The following March, the Great Sioux War erupted as Plains Indians across the territories lashed out. Custer, already familiar with the area, was assigned to defeat the Indians and force their return to the reservation. Bravely (or foolishly), he marched his troops into battle at the Little Bighorn, an encounter known by the Lakota and other Plains Indians as the Battle of the Greasy Grass or "Custer's Last Stand." On June 25, 1876, some 263 soldiers including Custer engaged the combined forces of the Lakota, Northern Cheyenne, and Arapaho in the largest battle of the Great Sioux War. It took place along the Little Bighorn River in the Crow Indian Reservation in southeastern Montana Territory. By the end of the second day, every member of Custer's Seventh Cavalry lay dead or wounded.

The following day, two Union army scouts—Liver-Eating Johnson and Yellowstone Kelly—rode out ahead of the rest of the scouts who accompanied General Miles and his troops, following close behind. Miles's command was charged with the Herculean task of bringing to justice the "savages" who had annihilated an entire US cavalry division. Writing in the book *Yellowstone Kelly*, author Clay Fisher recounts the episode:

It was 2 p.m., June 26, 1876.

Twenty-four hours earlier on the barren treeless slopes above the Minniconjou [sic] Ford of the Little Big Horn River, the last of Lieutenant Colonel George Armstrong Custer's gallant Seventh Cavalry had been martyred to the dashing "boy general's" incredible military ignorance and political ambition.

The next two months were the hardest, most dangerous in Luther Kelly's life, calling for the expenditure of every last ounce of physical endurance, tracking skill, hunting prowess and Indian scouting ability at his command. Yet in the end he had to admit the wily Sioux had dealt him a defeat as crushing and total, if not as fatal, as Custer's.

For sixty-one days he followed Gall and the Hunkpapa of Sitting Bull. In a classic of plains scouting not surpassed by Bridger, Carson, Meeker, Smith or any of the earlier mountain immortals, he hung on the trail of the moving Sioux from the first mile of their flight from the [site of] the Seventh Cavalry's tragic demise toward the Big Horn Mountains to the last somber days of that 1876 summer when Sitting Bull knew beyond final doubt that the hour of his people grew short.

For nearly the whole of that time Gall knew he was being followed and strove constantly to ambush his white shadow. Yet so wary was Kelly and so determined that this time he would not be denied Crow Girl [Kelly's mate, who was being held captive by the Indians] short of death, that in the entire eight weeks of his herculean hunt not one hostile Sioux came within rifle shot of him. More than that, he went the whole time without seeing or speaking to a fellow white man, making all his few contacts for food and information with the chance bands of friendlies who were in part trying to emulate his own course—avoiding the post-Custer hostiles with which the tributary valleys of the Yellowstone were literally acrawl through these desperate days of July and August.

Thus it was that the most the Irish scout received for his perilous sixty days in the Sioux wilderness was a detailed addition to his former knowledge of the unexplored lands north of the Yellowstone. These were the same lands which history even at that moment was leading George Crook's erudite adjutant, John Bourke, to label terra incognita. *And they were the same lands whose blankness on the existing military maps was at that identical August hour causing Colonel Nelson A. Miles to dispatch up and down the river his historic summons for Luther Kelly to join him in his camp on the banks of the Yellowstone at the mouth of Tongue River.*

Thus it was, also, that on the murky hot morning of August 25 the latter, coming back down the Big Dry Creek Range from below Fort Peck on the Missouri, having lost the village trail of Sitting Bull's and Gall's band twenty-four hours before in the charred ash and clotting smoke of an Indian-lit prairie backfire, rode his little appaloosa stud up out of a blind draw to collide, dead on, with a disreputable old friend from his Fort Buford days.

"Liver-eating" Johnson was in that era and place as celebrated a sobriquet as "Yellowstone" Kelly. And it was so largely for the same reasons of its owner having successfully kept his long hair from being shortened while poaching the sacred game preserves of the Hunkpapa and Oglala Sioux. Thereafter, however, all resemblance between the two delighted white scouts ceased. While they "howdied and shook" and slapped one another thunderously on the back, a hidden observer would have found it difficult to believe they followed the same profession.

To match the Irish scout's clean-shaven chin, carefully trimmed mustache and respectable buckskins (albeit they were torn, faded and

*alkali-stained now) Johnson presented a picture from another day
and time.*

*Ragged leather shirt and leggins unbeaded and black with the
grease and soot of a thousand cookfires, wild hair frizzled and sun-
faded, unkempt beard dirtied by chaw spittle, tobacco-ruined teeth
rotted to the gumline, illiterate, unwashed, profane, roving-eyed,
raucous; he was the remaining classic chromo of the last of the Big
Horn beaver trappers.*

*But it was not the way his friend looked, nor his raw language
nor even his gamy odor downwind, which unhinged Kelly's jaw. It
was what he had to say. And what he had to say brought to Kelly a
suddenly leaping new hope to replace the waning one which had just
died out in the ashes of the Hunkpapa grassfire.*

*But Liver-eating made him wait. First off, knowing the hunger
of a lone white man long weeks away from the river for news of his
fellows, he brought him up to date on the general situation.*

*The Army had just sent Crook a new commander from clean
down to Fort Leavenworth in Kansas, Johnson began. This latter
was only a full colonel but he had hell's own reputation as an Indian
fighter. Kelly would likely recall having heard of him. Fellow named
Miles. Nelson A. Miles. Same Miles that had knocked the liver and
lights out of the Comanches down south in '74.*

*Well, anyways, Liver-eating went on, this Miles's orders were
to "set on" the hostiles that had "done for" idiot-child Custer over on
the Greasy Grass. He had been campaigning with Crook and Terry
the past weeks getting the "feel of things," mostly down around the
Rosebud, Tongue and Powder. Then Crook had been sent on southeast into the Black Hills, virtually out of the Sioux campaign, and a
couple of important things had happened. Just before old "Three Stars"
pulled out, General Wesley Merritt had broken up a big Cheyenne
column moving out from Camp Robinson to hook up with Sitting
Bull, weakening the Hunkpapa plans aplenty. Then that young feller
Anson Mills had caught poor old American Horse trying to join his
Oglala up with Crazy Horse's and had completely routed them, killing*

American Horse and cutting the Oglala strength in half before the big fight ever got started.

Miles and Terry had then marched north to the Big Dry and right back south to Glendive Creek on the Yellowstone. Here Terry had loaded his boys on the Far West and four other steamers and "gone south for good," leaving Miles's Fifth Infantry with orders to "build a cantonment on the Yellowstone and occupy the country during the coming winter."

But it looked as though "Bear Coat," as the Sioux called Miles, had other ideas than just "occupying" the country.

He wanted to go after the Indians and reckoned he had a ring-tailed good chance to catch up with them and give them a little northern dose of Palo Duro and Adobe Walls. There was just the one little hitch. None of his scout staff knew the Yellowstone country well enough to shag hostiles through it with the snow up to a tall horse's belly and the mercury stuck in the bulb at sixty below.

At that point, Liver-eating claimed proudly, he himself had thought of "Old Yellowstone."

It was what came then that dropped Kelly's jaw.

Miles wanted him to come in and talk about taking over his scouts and guiding the command after Custer's killers in a full-dress winter campaign the likes of which had never before been planned or put on by white troops in Montana or Dakota Territories.

It developed, via Liver-eating's excited insistence, that this was not a mere suggestion. It was a concrete offer. With no strings whatever tied onto it.

All Kelly had to do, apparently, was go see Miles.

After that it would be squarely up to him whether he kept on chasing the Hunkpapa all by his lonesome, or gave in and let the U.S. Army back him up with somewhere around six hundred Comanche-trained troops of the Fifth and the Twenty-second Infantry.

Having delivered himself of the Colonel's "gelded edge" invitation, Johnson eased back in his saddle to await his companion's reaction. He did not get eased very far back. The Irish scout took less than ten seconds to reach his decision. After that, they both "got down

*and sat a spell," risking a fire to boil up a fresh can of coffee and bake
a hasty batch of frying-pan bread, the first of either civilized delicacy
Kelly had tasted since leaving Tern's column two months before. They
then shook hands again and went their careful, separate ways.*

*It was well within the hour of his chance meeting with Liv-
er-eating Johnson on the Big Dry Creek Fork of the Missouri that
Yellowstone Kelly started south to keep his date with destiny and
Colonel Nelson A. Miles on the south bank of the Yellowstone at the
mouth of Tongue River in Montana Territory.*[8]

After "narrowly escaping a spirited dance with an overzealous
grizzly," Kelly returned to report to General Miles of some Indian
sightings, but the general was off on an errand. Kelly left word with
the quartermaster to tell the general he had important news. Although
Miles was still a colonel who wouldn't make the rank of brigadier until
1880, his officers and men invariably deferred to his Civil War brevet
rank in addressing him as "general." The same was true of his civilian
employees—the packers, stock handlers, scouts, and others. The only
person who refused to call him "general," according to Kelly, "was old
Liver-eating Johnson, who would not knowingly defer to the Devil or
'grant one inch of undue credit to Jesus Christ himself,'" as the scout
had put it.[9]

Not long after, Miles's scouts set out once more, leading a column
headed by Miles in pursuit of the Sioux, and Kelly stumbled upon the
very spot where the three tribes had smoked their last peace pipe together
and parted ways one last time. Tremendous billowing clouds filled with
snow and wind threatened from the northwest. Kelly read the signs and
quickly sized up the situation as he turned to his fellow scout, half-breed
Billy LeBeau.

> *"You had better," said Kelly softly to his companion, "get the General
> up here right away. I'll sit on this sign till you get back. Best hop to it,
> Billy. This lull won't hold long."*
>
> *The other nodded quickly. "Wagh! no waste," he grunted uneasily.
> "Pretty quick him snow blow every which way same damn time."*

It was a good enough description of a Montana blizzard. Kelly did not argue it. "Tell the General to hump his tail," he said. "Tell him," he added, with a peculiar intensity of emphasis, "that I've found Sitting Bull for him."

The dark-faced scout bobbed his head again. He took a last peering look along the fading trackline of his Indian brothers, shook his head slowly. "Him poor damn devil," murmured [the half-breed] and sent his shaggy pony on the gallop to bring up Colonel Nelson A. Miles for the keeping of his forgotten bargain with Luther S. Kelly.

Miles came forward in a matter of minutes. He had been but a mile behind Kelly, two ahead of the column, riding with Liver-eating Johnson, Clubfoot Boyd and Charley Bass. Now he studied the three diverging lines of Sioux ponytracks, turned on Kelly and demanded bluntly, "Well, what do you make of it?" As bluntly, Kelly told him.

"They left here within the hour. The main bunch, about two hundred or so, went straight ahead, down the Red Water. The second bunch, less than one hundred, went east across the Fork. Third bunch, no more than thirty or forty, split off northwest, back toward the Big Dry. It's their last gamble; you've got them, General."

"We'll push on at once," said Miles, excitement beginning to light his pale eyes. "Baldwin's the best Indian fighter in the army; we'll give him the big band. I'll take the bunch that went east and Snyder can take the handful that headed northwest. What do you think they have in mind, Kelly?"

"It looks to me, General, as though the second bunch is pulling out and will quit. But the other two are heading north and will likely reunite. Now we know Sitting Bull has always said he would go to Canada before he would stay here and surrender. We also know that Gall is not the kind to quit." Kelly paused and Miles was at him instantly. "Well, well, man! go on, go on!"

"There's hardly a doubt, General. Your big due-north bunch is Sitting Bull's. Your east-turning quitters are Pretty Bear's. Your little band of northwesterners is Gall's."

"Good, good," cried Miles, in a rare show of feeling. "Now as for scouts, Johnson and Bass can go with Baldwin, Boyd and LeBeau with Snyder, and you can stay with me. That way, we can—"

"That way," broke in Kelly, low-voiced, "we can forget."

"What the devil do you mean?" snapped Miles, scarcely accustomed to being countermanded in midstride.

"I mean," said his chief of scouts levelly, "that we made a deal. With all due respects, General, I intend to hold you to it."

"Well!" huffed the latter, staring down his high-bridged nose at his wolfskinned guide. "I must say your Celtic insubordination is exceeded only by your Irish optimism. However, a deal's a deal. What was it I promised you, sir?"

Kelly pointed north along the trail of the main Sioux band. "You said if I would find you Sitting Bull, you would give me Gall. Yonder goes Tatanka's track. Baldwin will be up to him before this blizzard blows itself out."

Miles's searching look picked the pockets of his mind with a single deft glance. His familiar decisive head-bob cemented the brief inspection.

"All right, Kelly, you go with Snyder. Who do you want along?"

"Only LeBeau, sir. And thanks, General. I'll never forget it."

"Don't thank me, man!" snorted Miles. "I only hope you know what you're doing—that you've picked the right bunch of redskins to go after."

Kelly's dark eyes narrowed as they flicked again to the faint track-line veering northwest. And narrowed yet further as they singled out the peculiarly twisted left forefoot print of a certain blue roan gelding a hundred and forty-four days familiar to him since the great silence along the Little Big Horn. "Don't worry, General," was all he said to Miles. "I have."[10]

With the end of the months-old campaign to find and overtake the three Sioux tribes drawing close, Miles split his troopers into thirds, with Johnson and Kelly traveling in the opposite direction. Within a matter of hours, Kelly and LeBeau had caught up with his quarry, Chief Gall, who had crossed paths with Kelly many times over the years. Putting the chief's mind to rest, Kelly explained that he had no intention of battling the Sioux warriors under Gall's direction.

"A life for a life," said Luther Kelly. "It is a law written in the old book of my people's god."

"I am waiting."

"Many moons ago it was within your power to take my life—or worse."

"You mean the hinmangas *my brother?" Gall shrugged self-dep-recatingly. "It was a moment of weakness. I could truly not help myself. You fought too well." The least trace of a grim smile lit the Hunkpapa's savage face. "My people were very unhappy with me, Lone Wolf." The smile was gone. "They said that I was no longer fit to lead them. That I was become an old fool. That because I fought for the love of a woman half my age and honored a white warrior for a great fight, I was no good anymore, that they could not trust me to lead them as before." He paused, his mind weary with remembering, then asked with the unaffected guile of a child hoping to find parental agreement or approval of some minor sin of omission. "Do you believe that, Lone Wolf?"*

Kelly grimaced, nodded slowly. "Yes, I believe it, my brother. Your people are right. This can happen to a man. Love and war do not sleep well in the same lodge."

"You walk in circles, as if you were going around a trap. What is it you are saying?"

"That my people, too, are the same. That if they were to know what is in my mind now, they would never trust me to lead them again. And they would be right."

"What is in your mind, Lone Wolf?"

"As you said yourself—many things."

Gall only nodded. Like all Indians he knew the golden rule of silence, and practiced it with a chief's pride.

"I have heard that Tatanka will go to the Land of the Grand-mother. Is that true?" said Kelly.

"Yes."

"And also that you will go with him?"

"We were to meet beyond the mouth of the Musselshell if we escaped Bear Coat [General Miles] and could come together again."

"Would you still do it?"

"With the last breath of life that is in my body."[11]

And so, the final chapter of the last major Indian resistance in the American West had been closed, exactly as two visionaries had predicted it would. Luther Yellowstone Kelly and John Liver-Eating Johnson were worlds apart and yet cut from the same cloth.

With Gall removing himself from the Plains, the hostiles' house of cards came tumbling down, never to be rebuilt again. Meanwhile, Johnson and General Frank Baldwin had caught and routed the main band of Sitting Bull's tribe. Miles, also successful, forced the surrender of Pretty Bear and his followers. And Ranald Mackenzie, moving up from the south in independent command, trapped and smashed the last of Dull Knife's Northern Cheyenne. Wesley Merritt had already broken up the Camp Robinson Cheyenne, and Anson Mills had blanketed American Horse and his Oglala Sioux. It remained only for Miles to track down and destroy Crazy Horse, which he did on January 8, 1877, only a few short days after his December 16 defeat of Sitting Bull's Hunkpapa.

Catching Tashunka, Witko's main Oglala band, on the headwaters of the Tongue in the snowbound wilderness of the Wolf Mountains less than eighty miles from his cantonment on the Yellowstone, Miles, backed by full artillery support, hammered the last of the major Sioux bands to shards. Completely routed, the remaining Oglala fled deeper into the mountains.

Miles did not go after them. Instead, at Kelly's plea, he sent Johnny Brughiere in with the surrender terms. Crazy Horse was beaten. He came trundling in. His simple reply to Miles was delivered by his friend Little Chief. Facing Miles, the proud Cheyenne dropped his buffalo robe to the ground, drew himself erect, and spoke without humbleness or arrogance: "We are weak, compared with you and your forces; we are out of ammunition; we cannot make a rifle, a round of ammunition, or a knife; in fact we are at the mercy of those who are taking possession of our country; your terms are harsh and cruel, but we are going to accept them and place ourselves at your mercy . . ."

It was the end. In the tumultuous weeks that followed, various ragged bands straggled in, their chiefs repeating to Miles Gall's prophetic promise of "fighting the white man no more from this day on." Little Hawk, White Bull, Two Moons, Hump, Little Big Man, He Dog, The Rock, Horse Road—the list read like a who's who of the Dakota Sioux and Northern Cheyenne high commands. And, with the stoic surrenders of their chiefs, came upward of another two thousand fighting Indians of the plains to add to the like number of Sitting Bull's brokenhearted followers already headed back to the reservations.

With the news of Crazy Horse's surrender, Gall and Sitting Bull, with what ragtag band of Hunkpapa followers remained, kept their word and fled to Canada. The Sioux and Cheyenne wars were over.

William B. Secrest, editor of the book *I Buried Hickok: The Memoirs of White Eye Anderson*, provides a lucid explanation as to why the Indian Wars ended so decisively. He wrote:

After the Custer battle of June 25, 1876, [at the Little Bighorn massacre] the Sioux scattered to be able to more effectively elude the military. They had neither the will nor the ammunition to fight any more than they had to, and with winter coming on, they would be able to hunt more easily and safely in small groups. All that summer and fall, however, the Sioux harassed the miners in the Black Hills. General Crook was on the move, and the Indians knew there was to be a reckoning for the Little Big Horn. Colonel Nelson A. Miles, his troops well-equipped for a winter campaign, chased Sitting Bull and his followers across the border into Canada in February of 1877. Crook's calvary [sic], under Colonel Ronald [sic] MacKenzie, had meanwhile attacked a Cheyenne camp the previous November and driven the Indians into the camp of Crazy Horse. The noted

Sioux chieftain quickly fled with his people, but the Indians were wearying fast. Colonel Miles and his troops caught up with them in January, but after several battles, the Sioux again escaped into the bitter cold mountains.

Out of ammunition, his people freezing and starving, Crazy Horse was at last forced to listen to the white man's promises and to the agency Indians' pleas to return in peace. The Deadwood newspaper reported Crazy Horse and some fifteen hundred warriors camped on Bear Butte, some twenty-five miles northeast of the city in April. On May 5, 1877, the great Sioux chieftain marched his people into the Red Cloud Agency and the Indian war was at an end.[12]

Kelly, at last freed of his responsibilities to the military, requested a leave of absence from his service to Miles. He left the country in redemption of the pledge he'd made following his failure to report his final grim meeting with Gall. He later returned to work, once again with Liver-Eater, to bring to bay Chief Joseph and his desperate Nez Perce after General Howard and nearly four thousand troops from three commands had been unable to achieve the same result in fifteen hundred miles of army-Indian "cat-and-mouse."

But for Kelly, the chase was not the same. Something had gone of his spirit after Gall's defeat. By his own admission, his latter days were never quite the same for the romantic scout as those earlier ones along the Yellowstone had been.

Still, Luther Yellowstone Kelly went on to more of a life filled with continuing adventure. He rose to be a major in the regular army, a confidante of two presidents, governor of a Philippine municipality, and an agent of a great Arizona Indian reservation, along with surveyor, cartographer, Indian Bureau troubleshooter, Alaskan adventurer, and California rancher.

True to his word, Gall never rose up against the white man again, while Sitting Bull clung to his retreat in a protected wilderness of southwestern Canada for upwards of a year before, on July 19, 1881, starving and sickly, he rode into Fort Buford with a small remaining band of Hunkpapa Sioux and surrendered. And that was the formal conclusion of three decades of confrontation between the government of the United States of America and the mighty Sioux Nation.

The Indian Wars were finally over. The trail for Yellowstone Kelly and Chief Gall had come to an end. And two scouts, Kelly and Johnson, went on to claim their roles in military scouting history.

For Yellowstone Kelly, the wars had been yet one more day in his life as usual, just another series of campaigns as a dedicated scout and military man. For Liver-Eating Johnson, they had been a diversionary lark, a side trip along his journey through life, a steady paycheck. For Liver-Eater, the wars helped cement his legend, setting him apart as more than mere mountain man for decades to come—as an intrepid US Army scout and Indian fighter unmatched in the annals of American history.

CHAPTER NINE

Partners in Crime

WHILE BIOGRAPHERS OFTEN QUESTION THE VERY EXISTENCE OF DEL Gue as one of Johnson's on-again/off-again trapping partners, there are enough instances of his mention throughout accounts of Johnson's various escapades to repel those historians who have come to doubt his existence. Like Johnson himself, the diminished version of Gue is probably more in keeping with the level of notoriety of most mountain men of his time. They rarely kept journals or gave interviews or—in some instances—even mingled with other people socially. It is the extraordinarily colorful, verbose, and outrageous characters who got most of the public's attention—Johnson and Hickok and Calamity Jane and Buffalo Bill. For whatever the reason, it seems obvious that Gue was more than a mere fictional character whom Johnson had poetically woven from the fabric of his mind.

No doubt, fueling the skepticism about Gue's actual existence is the powerfully fictionalized account of the man as Johnson's wily, enigmatic trapping partner in the film *Jeremiah Johnson*. In that depiction, Gue, fictional or not, summarizes the mountain man's environment by describing the Rockies as "the marrow of the world."[1]

With most scholarship on Johnson straddling the line between reality and fantasy by necessity, another popular source sheds doubt upon Gue's actual existence. Skyler Gabel, a student-writer looking to strip the doubtful romanticism surrounding history, took a hardened if simplistic view, which he published on the Internet. Along with that is a review of *Crow Killer* by author Dorman Nelson, who, despite several errors in his logical evaluations, managed to conclude that Gue was surrounded by the literary camouflage of the day and most likely never existed in reality. Nelson concluded his findings: "Del Gue was one fella I could never find any historical facts about."[2]

At first blush, that seems to confirm that Gue may simply *not* have existed at all, making the skeptics right. But in a deeper vein, the days of the mountain men yielded more "Del Gues" than "John Johnsons." Most men came into and departed from this world with little more than a casual nod in the newspapers, magazines, and memoirs of the time—if that. It is quite understandable that Gabel's search for historical facts about the man may have yielded little in the way of factual corroboration.

Unfortunately, the young man may have come up empty not so much for lack of a definable real-life person as for lack of diligent research. In his memoir, *I Buried Hickok*, White Eye Anderson had his biography committed to paper by author/researcher William B. Secrest, who quotes Anderson:

> *My brother Charlie and I left Fort Assiniboine in July of 1871, when we were well enough to travel. We bought two good saddle horses and used our old horses for pack animals. Each of us also got a good rifle, six-shooters and plenty of ammunition, then traveled south down the Red River for several days. We struck across the country southwesterly so we would fetch up at Fort Pierre, on the Missouri River which was a lively place in those days. It was headquarters for a good many hunters and trappers and also people coming from the east looking for farming land and stock ranges. There were many Indians scattered through the country who claimed to be peaceable and friendly. It did not pay to take chances with them alone, though, for we would be very liable to have our stock stolen and maybe lose our hair. This was the case with a lot of smart-alecks who thought they knew it all.*
>
> *We pitched camp at Fort Pierre, my brother intending to go back to Montana to look after some mining interests in Bear Gulch, Deer Lodge County.*
>
> *At that time I was not stuck on mining and prospecting as I had gotten all I wanted of it from our Saskatchewan experience. About*

the time my brother joined a party of men that were going where he wanted to go in Montana, I met a young fellow about my age that I had known in Nebraska. He was a short, heavyset French-Canadian named Del Gue and he was quite an expert on trapping otter and beaver. Del was planning to spend the fall and winter in the Big Horn Mountains since learning that the beaver were plentiful there on some of the streams.

There were two old-timers Del had gotten acquainted with that intended to go with him to hunt, trap and poison wolves. They told him they would like to have a party of four if they could find the right one to join them. We made arrangements that I was to go with them as an equal partner.

The two old-timers were about forty-five years old or older and were very experienced in the frontier country of those days. They had been with Kit Carson, Jim Bridger and other noted men of that time. Their names were Pete Coyle and "Liver-eating" Johnson. [Secrest notes that, as in the paucity of information he found on Del Gue, "Again, no information on Pete Coyle has been discovered by the editor. It must be borne in mind that Gue, Coyle, Chris Lapp and other frontier characters noted by Anderson were not the type of men who left records behind. They were not famous, did little of note, and were merely part of an over-all, floating frontier population. Too, they spent much of their lives in the wilderness where evidence of their existence consisted of the charcoal of long-dead campfires or the bleaching bones of the Wapiti or Grizzly bear."]

Pete Coyle was one of your wild Irishmen. He did not seem to be afraid of anything and was an expert in all the requirements of pioneer life. Everyone liked him.

Liver-eating Johnson did not tell me how the Indians killed his young wife and some of his folks a good many years before I knew him. He was not much on the talk, but he said the only good Indians he knew of were dead ones, and he did the best he could to make as many good ones as possible. He was a dead shot with rifle and six-shooter and was a big, strong man with a sandy complexion and very long hair. Johnson was a hard ticket to look at, dressed in old, greasy buckskin shirt and pants. He would cut the livers out of Indians he killed and go through the motions of eating it. That is the way he got the name of Liver-eating Johnson. He was always cool and did not get excited very easily. He was well-acquainted with the lay of the land as he had followed hunting and trapping as a guide and scout for about twenty years in the wilds of the West. He seemed to know the whole layout. I was very glad that I could be a member of the party.

We had twelve pack animals and laid in a good supply of grub, traps, strychnine, and ammunition, making about two hundred pounds to the pack horse. The country where we were going was too rough for wagons and we traveled on Indian and game trails. A good deal of it was in the "Bad Land Country" which was very rough, full of canyons, and had lots of bad water. We kept north of the Black Hills, traveling quite a way up the Belle Fourche River, over to the Little Missouri and on into the Powder River country. We kept on until we struck the tributary of the Big Horn River. There we found what we were looking for—beaver and otters which were very, very plentiful. The small streams were plumb full of beaver dams and we could see the beavers working in daytime which was something very unusual. We did not see any sign of Indians anywhere. We were in the Crow Indian country, but they were supposed to be peaceful at that time.

Picking out a place to make our camp, we built a log cabin 14 by 16 feet with a good rock fireplace. It was just a few steps to a good spring of water and there was lots of dry wood handy for our fireplace. The location was in a secluded spot at the mouth of a short canyon. It ran back in the hills where there was very good bunchgrass feed for our horses.

There was plenty of deer and elk and we laid in a good supply of jerky and fresh meat. There was also lots of fish in the streams. By the time we got everything in good shape, it was September and the fur was getting prime. From that time on we were very busy tending to the traps and taking care of the pelts. We also were getting plenty of wolves and coyotes from the poison we had put out for them. From the amount of pelts we were getting, we expected to have $4,000 worth by spring, but such was not to be.

One evening I caught a mess of fish, cleaned them and put them in a gold pan filled with water. The water was cold and we had a big fire in the fireplace. It was just after dark and we were getting ready to cook supper. Pete Coyle went out to the spring to get some water and just as he was dipping it up, we heard the Indians yell. Bullets and arrows came whizzing around him pretty lively and Pete hollered for us to put out the fire in the fireplace. The light would illuminate the front of the cabin when we opened the door to let him in, and the Indians could see to shoot. The handiest thing we had to put the fire out was the gold pan full of fish and water, so I threw the whole layout on the fire and put it out. Then Pete came through the door in the dark without being hit, bringing the bucket of water with him.

We had plenty of portholes on all sides of the cabin and we kept the inside pretty dark. It was lighter outside than inside, so when we saw the shadowy form of an Indian we did our best to give him a dose of lead. The next morning we could hear them, but did not get a chance to do much shooting as they kept out of sight. The spring was so close to the cabin we could slip out in the dark at night and get what water we needed. There was quite a bunch of Indians that kept cases on our cabin for several days.

Liver-eating Johnson concluded that he would slip out in the dark with some grub, his rifle and plenty of ammunition and see if he could find our horses. He was gone two days and got back the third night. He said the Indians ran our horses off and he didn't think there was any show to get them back. He thought the best plan was for us to get out of there as soon as possible.

We didn't like the idea of leaving all our grub, pelts, blankets, saddles and everything else we had except what we could carry out on our backs. We packed about forty pounds for each one of us consisting of our rifles and six-shooters, plenty of cartridges, one pair of blankets for each one of us and the balance in grub, mostly jerky.

We had a large supply of strychnine which we used to poison wolves. When we got ready to go, Liver-eating Johnson said: "Well lads, I am going to get even with those thieving, murdering redskins.

They will think twice—those that are left alive—before they tackle another bunch of white trappers."

He went to the sacks of flour and meal and mixed several handfuls of strychnine into them. Then he took the remaining poison and dusted it very carefully over and into all the other provisions, where it would not be noticeable.

Pete Coyle said nothing, but Del Gue and I did not approve of this method of killing Indians. It seemed like murder without giving them a chance. We took several charcoal sticks and wrote on the walls of our cabin in several places: "This food is poisoned." I am quite certain that Liver-eating Johnson could not read; anyway, he said nothing about it. But the bad part about it was that very few Indians could read. I have always been certain that those who took the cabin were in a very short while writhing about on the ground. Strychnine is not good for the human system, especially in such large doses.

We hit the trail about two o'clock in the morning. I don't remember the date, but it was about the last of November. We left everything in the cabin just as it was. We would have liked to make a cache, but couldn't do it as the Indians were rather numerous around us. We left it up to Liver-eating Johnson and I believe we would never have gotten away from there if it hadn't been for him. Johnson knew just what to do, took the lead and we got away in good shape. We traveled several days and a good deal at night. We most always saw the Indians first and laid low until they got out of sight.

One morning just before daylight we came to a large stream of water and ran into a big Indian camp. As there seemed to be over a hundred dogs barking at us, we crawled back through the camp and came back to the river about sun up, just below the same Indian village. There was a good-sized boat tied to the bank—a buffalo boat made out of buffalo bull hides stretched on willow poles. It was just what we wanted and would hold a ton, but there was also a naked Indian standing on a long log that projected out into the river. Just like a flash Liver-eating Johnson shot him dead and he fell into the river. We got into the boat and shoved out into the center of the stream. By that time there was a big bunch of Indians on the bank shooting at us with bows and arrows and poor old guns. The river was very wide and we had good long-range rifles which made them hunt for cover. Liver-eating Johnson and Pete Coyle did the shooting while Del and I were busy plugging up the holes that the Indians' bullets and arrows made in the side of the boat.

In the meantime the Indian that Liver-eating Johnson shot floated down the river to where we were in the boat. Liver-eating Johnson pulled the body into the boat. He then cut the Indian's liver out and gave an unearthly yell, going through the motions of eating it. Pete Coyle told me that he had killed a good many Indians and that this was what he always did when he had a chance to do so. It seemed to me that he turned into a regular fiend when he was fighting Indians.

The river was wide and shallow so we had to watch out for snags and sand bars. We had to do most of our traveling by daytime with our long-range rifles keeping the Indians off. We were lucky not to get shot—just a few scratches. Our packs were rather bulky and were hit many times.

After going down river several days we came out into the Missouri River. The weather was cold with considerable ice in shallow places. We came to a place where the steamboats stopped for wood. There were some white men there and they said there was a steamboat coming downstream soon and it would stop and take on wood, so we concluded to wait for them. In about two days it came along and we made arrangements with the captain to take us to Omaha, Nebraska. We split up there and I boarded a train for North Platte.

If ever there was a fellow glad to get back on his old stamping ground, I was that fellow. I went to Fort McPherson and stopped for awhile with Mrs. Snell. Everything was on the quiet order there.[3]

Besides confirming the existence of Gue as one of Johnson's frequent trapping partners, Anderson hints at the camaraderie of partners working the traps and streams of the Rocky Mountain West. Over the course of his lifetime, he concluded, Johnson appeared to have teamed with numerous men, not the least notable of which was a man introduced to him as John X. Beidler.

More than a mere wandering spirit or passing character in Anderson's memoirs, Beidler was a blood-and-guts vigilante who was always on the right side of the law wherever bad men roamed. A man of action, he was instilled with the moral convictions of his parents. Merciless in the pursuit of criminals, he answered the call whenever needed, living by the frontier catchphrase "Men, do your duty."

Best exemplified by his own firsthand accounts from his memoir, *X. Beidler Vigilante*, Beidler wrote about his early life through his final days. Among the panoramic views of the growing western frontier to which he had a front-row seat were numerous brushes with the famous and the infamous. And, as in the case with his trapping partner, Liver-Eating Johnson, it all began back East.

I was born in Mount Joy, Lancaster County, Pennsylvania, August 14, 1831. Received a country school education. My mother was born in Germany and came to the U.S. when she was four years old, and my father was born in the U.S.

Moved to near Harrisburg upon a farm in 1838. The first pair of boots I got, I picked chestnuts and sold them for a "fippeny bit" [about 6 cents] a quart, and purchased the boots. I then picked hickory chips and sold them for $2.1/2 a load. Lived on the farm seven years and then wound up at Middletown, where my parents died and were buried.

On the morning of my father's death, I was coming up town to see the undertaker, and Simon Cameron asked me how father was. I told him he was dead and he told me I was shoved off the plank and would have to swim now—which I did not understand at the time.

About this time I was put to the shoemaking trade but I did not last at that business, and I got into the brick business in the summer, and broom making in the winter. I was making brick at Harrisburg and Middletown, then went to Chambersburg, Franklin County, into a hotel, as barkeeper and clerk. One summer I stayed near Get-

tysburg, at Caledonas Springs, then back to Chambersburg and made brick again the following summer.

My first and last Presidential election was at Harrisburg, in 1852, when I voted for General Scott for President. I then went to Atchison, Kansas, and made the first brick in that city.

At that time the Kansas war was going on and I had to declare myself for free state or slavery, and I went for free state. On one occasion they sent me to Kickapoo to see about illegitimate voting and to see if I could stop it. The Kickapoo Rangers were running the polls. They voted me three or four times, then told me to pull out for Atchison, and gave me ten minutes to get. I got. Reported that I could do no good.

I did not make a success at brick making. My partners running off with the proceeds, left me broke. I wintered that year at Atchison and opened a place called "The People's Saloon," and ran that a while, and in '58 I started for Pike's Peak but did not get there and came back to Atchison.

While I was in Kansas, the border ruffians threw the printing press into the river at Lawrence, and left the type in the printing office, not knowing what type was for, or what use to make of it. We sacked up the type and took it with us. We pursued the ruffians to Hickory Point blacksmith shop and being short of shot but having plenty of powder, we utilized the type by loading our howitzer with it, putting it in oyster cans and ramming it home, and turned loose, pouring the type between the chinking of the first and second leg of the building. A great quantity struck the ruffians immediately below the spinal column. Those that were not wounded in this manner, had to pick out the type from the persons of their comrades and that is the way they first learned to read. We finally dislodged them by getting a load of hay and smoking them out.

In the winter of '58 I was in Atchison, Kansas, and the U.S. Marshal from Lawrence was after John Brown. On a Sunday he sent in to Atchison for a posse to help arrest John Brown, who was running nigger slaves through from Missouri to Nebraska. Doc Hereford, William Green, a Mr. Budd and a Dutchman, were about all that could be got to help arrest John Brown. I had a very kind invitation to go along but I didn't have time. They went out and found Brown camped on a slough, and he, with his niggers, held up the Marshal and his whole posse, capturing four or five of them, and held them for trial and put a nigger guard over them, while they deliberated whether to hang, shoot, or drown them. It was left to a vote and it came to a tie and Brown had the deciding vote. He voted to let them go, then when the prisoners had been liberated, Doc Hereford got up to thank Capt. John Brown for the mercy he had extended in saving their lives.

Capt. Brown said: "Now go home boys—go to Atchison and don't hunt any more for John Brown. He is not lost."

Then Hereford and the party wanted their horses, arms, etc., when Capt. Brown says: "Why, boys, I always thought such things were spoils of war. You declared war on me and I captured you and your horses. I need horses. I will send you home on the cactus [prickly pear] line."

Doc Hereford said: "Well, Capt. Brown, let us have our weapons, then."

"You have no weapons here," answered Brown.

"Why," said Hereford, "we had our guns and pistols and you captured them and have them now."

"O!" said Brown, "when I took them they were mine and the boys'. I will not give them to you, as you will not need them on your way home. You will not meet John Brown and if you did, you would not fight him."

They came home to Atchison, glad to get back and declared they wanted no more John Brown in theirs. They looked rough but every one of them had a good word for old Capt. John Brown.[4]

In his memoir, X relays one of his legendary meetings with Brown in late fall 1858, not on the field of battle but rather in a court of law, the practical practice of which he wholeheartedly endorsed: "On the first day of November," Beidler recalled, "Capt. John Brown was brought into court to receive the sentence of death. Here is his last speech."

I have, may it please the Court, a few words to say. In the first place, I deny everything but what I have all along admitted—the design on my part to free the slaves.

I intended certainly, to have made a clear thing of that matter, as I did last winter, when I went to Missouri and there took slaves without the snapping of a gun on either side, moved them through the country and finally left them in Canada.

I designed to have done the same thing again, on a larger scale. That was all I intended. I never did intend murder, or treason, or the destruction of property, or to excite or to incite slaves to rebellion, or to make insurrection.

I have another objection; and that is, it is unjust that I should suffer such a penalty. Had I interfered in the manner in which I admit, and which I admit has been fairly proved—for I admire the truthfulness and candor of the greater portion of the witnesses who have testified in this case—had I so interfered in behalf of the rich, the powerful, the intelligent, the so-called great, or in behalf of any of their friends, either father, mother, brother, sister, wife or children—or any of that class and suffered and sacrificed what I have in this interference, it would have been all right, and every man in this Court would have deemed it an act worthy of reward rather than punishment.

This Court acknowledges, as I suppose, the validity of the Law of God. I see a book kissed here, which I suppose to be the Bible, or at least the New Testament, and teaches me that all things "whatsoever I would that men should do unto me, I should do even so to them."

I endeavored to act up to that instruction. I say that I am too young yet to understand that God is any respecter [sic] of persons. I believe that to have interfered as I have done, as I always freely admitted I have done, in behalf of His despised poor was not wrong, but right. Now if it is deemed necessary that I should forfeit my life for the furtherance of the ends of justice, and mingle my blood further with the blood of my children and with the blood of millions in this slave country, whose rights are disregarded by wicked, cruel, and unjust enactments—I submit: so let it be done.

Let me say one word further: I feel entirely satisfied with the treatment I have received at my trial. Considering all the circumstances, it has been more generous than I expected, but I feel no consciousness of guilt. I have stated from the first what was my intention and what was not. I never had any design against the life of any person nor any disposition to commit treason, or excite slaves to rebel, or make any general insurrection. I never encouraged any man to do so, but always discouraged any idea of that kind.

Let me say also, a word in regard to the statements made by some of those connected with me. I hear it has been said by some of them that I have induced them to join me. But the contrary is true. I do not say this to injure them, but as regretting their weakness. There is not one of them but joined me of his own accord and the greater part, at their own expense. A number of them I never saw and never had a word of conversation with until the day they came to me, and that was for the purpose I have stated.

Now I have done.[5]

Brown, who in 1859 had led a raid on the federal armory at Harpers Ferry, West Virginia (still Virginia at the time), hoped to start a liberation movement among the slaves, thereby seizing the armory. He had intended to arm slaves with the weapons from the arsenal, but the attack failed. Within thirty-six hours, Brown's men had either fled or been killed or captured by local farmers, militiamen, and US Marines led by Robert E. Lee. Brown was captured and tried for treason against the Commonwealth of Virginia, the murder of five men, and inciting a slave insurrection. He was found guilty on all counts and hanged.

The Harpers Ferry raid escalated tensions between the North and South, leading one short year later to the South's secession from the Union and the beginning of the Civil War.

It was a dramatic end to Beidler's staid career before upending himself and traveling west, where his partnership with Liver-Eater became legendary. A contemporary of "Bear Claw" Chris Lapp, Hatchet Jack, and other mountain men, Beidler's career preceded his notoriety, just as his notoriety exceeded his career.

Are all these men with all their accounts mere figments of Johnson's imagination? He was more honest than that, both with himself and with history. Were they mistaken identities, misremembered names, misgiven personas? Their documentation throughout history is too substantial and diverse to allow for that possibility.

More likely, they were men who—like the otters and the beavers and the wolves and the bears they stalked, trapped, skinned, and traded—had their names written on the wind but were no less real.

Not everyone, after all, could enjoy the notoriety of a Liver-Eating Johnson.

CHAPTER TEN

The Wilderness Society

THE MOUNTAIN MAN PLAYED A DISTINCT ROLE IN THE SETTLING OF THE West, more so than the colonist, settler, or frontiersman who came before him. Davy Crockett, Kit Carson, and Daniel Boone were frontiersmen whose goals were to clear a path for civilization to enter the wilderness and embrace the concept of manifest destiny: America from sea to shining sea. They were on a seriously legitimate heroic quest.

Mountain men, on the other hand, maintained no such heroic misrepresentations. Their goals were far less noble: to trap and hunt and roam the wilderness free of the restraints of a civilized world. Far from embracing manifest destiny, their enemy was society itself, with which they failed to fit in. They were the loners who weren't alone; the scouts who drew no military pay; the warriors who fought no war. That didn't mean they went through life alone, for they had their own society of loners with whom to partner. By doing so, they shared the workload and defeated the interminable boredom, as Johnson did at times by joining up with Gue, Beidler, Lapp, and others.

Historian Richard Slotkin, describing the woodsman prototype, wrote about the dissimilarities between mountain man and frontiersman: "The figure and the myth-narrative that emerged from the early Boone literature became archetypal for the American literature that followed: an American hero is the lover of the spirit of the wilderness, and his acts of love and sacred affirmation are acts of violence against that spirit and her avatars."[1]

Liver-Eating Johnson posing for a studio photograph at the age
of sixty.

For mountain men such as Liver-Eating Johnson, the concept of partnering held numerous advantages, while the disadvantages of working alone could be deadly. In a partnership, if one man was killed, that season's assets were not in vain. In the case of an attack, a companion close by could prove invaluable. When injury or illness inevitably struck, a partner could prepare food and tend to the stricken. Not even the almighty Liver-Eater could subsist in the wilderness totally without aid.

Partnerships, too, provided that while one man ran the traps or went off hunting or fishing for food, the other remained closer to home to protect the cabin from interlopers and to gather the food of the earth—plants, berries, nuts, and seeds—whenever available. Many men lived entirely on a regimen of meat with little regard for its origin, condition, or state of preparation. Consumption of vegetables was sparse, although the average mountain man had at least a rudimentary knowledge of the region's vegetation. With certain plants, herbs, and weeds in abundance, meals such as thistle soup served at minimum as a viable substitute in the absence of game.

So, the image of the solitary mountain man living in stark isolation was often far from true. Some of these men entered a new region from within the safety of large numbers—via a wagon train or some other mechanism of mobility, sometimes in groups of fifty or more, known as "brigades."[2] These brigades often included families with Indian wives and children.

As these "brigadiers" reached a likely hunting or trapping area, they broke up into smaller, more manageable groups that continued shrinking in size until two or three remained to trap on one stream together. Peter Skeve Ogden, representing the Hudson's Bay Company, traveled with a "flamboyant entourage" of more than a hundred fellow travelers, more than half of them his own relatives. While Johnson rarely partnered with more than one or two other men at a time, he occasionally traveled with small groups for safety.

Idaho author Vardis Fisher, the most well-known of the area's regional authors, was famous for his sexualized novels of the Rockies from the time of the cavemen forward. In describing the mountain man's environment, he talked about the viciousness of it and how a man had to be prepared to react to anything. As such, the realities of Johnson's life were simple: the murder of an innocent Flathead squaw living with a white man and the horrific protracted response of the husband/owner against the perpetrators were not as isolated as we might expect. The scenario was far more realistic than its alternative: a white man being murdered and his squaw allowed to go free. Things weren't done that way in the West.

One of the reasons, according to Fisher, was that the mountain wilderness had been created for and controlled by men and was entirely "antipathetic"[3] to females. The men were the drivers of intrusions into the Indian's world, not the women.

In fact, when those precious few women such as Calamity Jane came along fully prepared to grab that piece of the pie she felt belonged to her, she was regarded as an anomaly . . . a freak. Whatever concessions to females one found in the West had to be imported by the men traveling through or working in the region—from cavalry officers to trappers and settlers—and not by the women themselves.

In that regard, the standard of behavior of Johnson, Gue, Lapp, and others bore more resemblance to Indian cultures than it did to European or eastern American society. As with Native American cultures, laws broken were matters for committing to blood wherever "antisocial adventurers"[4] ran afoul of mountain norms. Extenuating circumstances or the degree of the offense rarely mattered. An insult was an insult, no matter how severe or imagined. Johnson's war against the Crow entertained no thought of equivalence to the offense: two deaths, two retributions. Instead, his campaign against his enemy was a lifelong journey to the death for not only the persons committing the crime but also the tribe that had condoned the deed. *Period.* In his mind, one and all were as guilty as sin, and it fell upon him and no one else for retribution.

That might sound like a disorderly notion of meting out justice to someone outside the realm of the mountain man's world. But Fisher emphasized that in the mid-nineteenth century the West represented *chaos*, which differs from *disorder*. Although nearly a hundred military forts had been built during the century, military protection was not available equally to everyone. Especially where the mountain man was concerned, people in the wilderness often couldn't be located unless they wanted to be. While civilized cities maintained law and order through the use of legal restraints, no semblance of law existed in the mountains. The mountain man was responsible only to himself; wilderness reality accommodated no one, and each new day constituted "a harsh lesson."[5]

As Johnson and Yellowstone Kelly learned the hard way, even the basic universal concept of marriage differed widely from the prairies back East to the mountains out West. For many mountain couples, a spouse occupied a position barely greater than that of a trapping partner and, in some respects, less so, depending upon a person's particular needs at the moment. As Fisher said, the mountain man and his colleagues were like the grizzly bear, "loners, ferocious, unafraid . . . and an opportunistic eater."[6]

Adding to a relatively unhealthy environment for most females, men were keenly aware of their isolated status and could not afford to be indecisive when responding to danger, however harsh the consequences. The most common component of justification for one's frontier mentality was to do what Johnson did: strike at anything that moved as a justifiable reflex. As a result of such cruel harshness, the "mountain-man mentality" proved frightening as much to friends as to foes—including the Indians.

THE FRONTIER MENTALITY

Thomas D. Hall, in the *New Dictionary of the History of Ideas*, discusses the concept that "frontiers are zones of intense interactions, often of several types at the same time"; these interactions can lead to *ethno genesis*, or the creation of a new ethnic group, as well as *acculturation*, or the adoption of the other group's cultural traits.[7]

Certainly, in the case of Liver-Eater, his identity shifted dramatically from what it had been back East. Such a shift could not have been avoided. A frontier is a region full of potential. Polar opposites can merge to create a new, third thing. Frederick Jackson Turner, in his seminal 1893 essay, "The Significance of the Frontier," discussed the European settler's assimilation with the Indian culture at the frontier zone:

*Before long he has gone to planting Indian corn and plowing with
a sharp stick; he shouts the war cry and takes the scalp in orthodox
Indian fashion. In short, at the frontier the environment is at first too
strong for the man. He must accept the conditions which it furnishes,
or perish, and so he fits himself into the Indian clearings and follows
the Indian trails. Little by little he transforms the wilderness, but
the outcome is not the old Europe. . . . The fact is, that here is a new
product that is [wholly] American.*[8]

Johnson's bond with nature and his respect for the Indians was filled
with conflicts and resolutions. Unlike the settlers who came later, his goal
was never to till the land but rather to trap for pelts. In those respects, the
settler and the mountain man were radically different from one another.

Slotkin differentiates between mountain man and frontiersman when
he describes mountain men as "semibarbaric figures who cut a swath in
the popular literature of the nineteenth century. They were usually viewed
by the fastidious as filthy white Indians and by the romantic as an heroic,
but only temporarily free, alternative to the money-and-status society of
the East."[9] He concludes from one study that mountain men were actually symbols of the Jacksonian desire for "upward mobility" because many
of them did not stay in the mountains through retirement but instead
returned, in the end, to civilization. Such men included X. Beidler, who
spent much of his life working with a vigilante committee before moving
to Helena after falling on hard times, and Yellowstone Kelly, who had
gotten his fill of excitement and retired to a "quieter life" in California.

But Fisher, in his introduction to his novel *Mountain Man*, portrays
just the opposite trait in those men who preferred to remain their entire
lives in the wilderness, quoting W. A. Fertis's *Life in the Rocky Mountains*:

*A strange, wild, terrible, romantic, hard, and exciting life they lead
. . . in a harsh, barren, untamed, and fearful region of desert, plain,
and mountain. Yet so attached to it do [the mountain men] become
that few ever leave it, and they deem themselves, nay are, with all
these bars against them, far happier than the in-dwellers of towns*

and cities, with all the gay and giddy whirl of fashion's mad delusions in their train.[10]

Even if Slotkin is correct, the mountain-man myth endures in the American psyche, most certainly romanticized but nevertheless based on the actual experiences of these men, one of whom was, without doubt, a peculiar partner and an unlikely foil for the enigmatic Liver-Eater.

X. Beidler was as notorious throughout the region as was Johnson, if not more so. But his notoriety came not from scourging the wilderness of red men but, rather, from clearing it of bad whites. One of the West's most notorious vigilantes, he held integrity, morality, and dignity in high stead, and, although Johnson wasn't exactly an outlaw himself, Liver-Eater was considerably less plagued by principles than his companion.

In an excerpt from *In Another Time*, author Harold Schindler references Beidler's role in the hanging of a man named Jack Slade.

Jack Slade is one of the West's many paradoxes. He was the Overland Stage Company's most feared enforcer, protecting the route from road agents and keeping the coaches on schedule. Yet, on the occasion of his death, Slade missed his connection with the Overland Stage and was fated to spend eternity in Salt Lake City. A terror to outlaws, Slade was, by all accounts, a loving husband and loyal friend, but when drunk, he became an uncontrollable, sadistic bully.

Joseph Alfred "Jack" Slade came from a respected family in Clinton County, Illinois, served in the 1846–48 Mexican War, and earned a reputation as a tough man on the frontier. His story begins in 1858 when Overland Stage hired him to superintend the Sweetwater Division of the mail line from St. Joseph, Missouri, to Salt Lake City. The division ran from the "Upper Crossing" of the South Platte River to Rocky Ridge on the east slope of the Continental Divide.

Station keeper at the Upper Crossing was Jules Beni, a sullen, bear-like French Canadian also reputed to be the leader of a band of cutthroats in the vicinity. The town of Julesburg at the Upper Crossing was founded by Beni, and it had become a rendezvous for traders, Indian fighters, buffalo hunters, adventurers, bandits, and desperadoes who rode into town to divide their loot and squander it riotously. Beni's high-handed acts with company livestock and the constant feuds arising from them brought Slade and Beni into open rupture. Jules would not submit to the authority of the division agent, and Slade would not brook Jules's interference.

Beni "sequestered" some of the livestock, and Slade recovered it for the company. That brought matters to a crisis. It was a day in the early spring of 1859 when Slade chanced to be at the Upper Crossing station. He, the hired hands, and Beni were all in the corral engaged in conversation. After a few moments Jules walked away from the group and entered his adobe quarters. Slade meanwhile headed for the bunkhouse to get something to eat.

As he was about to enter, one of the hands spotted Beni emerging from the adobe with a pistol. "Look out, he's going to shoot!" Slade, unarmed, turned at the warning and was struck by three shots from Jules's revolver. He staggered but did not fall. With a curse, Beni reached within the open door for a double-barrel shotgun. He fired both charges into Slade's slumping body. "There's an empty crate in the barn. You can bury him in it," Beni said and walked away.

But in the dramatic tradition of every wild West yarn ever spun, witnesses that day claimed a bloody, bullet-torn Jack Slade breathed through smashed lips and told would-be grave diggers not to bother, that he did not intend to die, but would live to even the score with Beni. And he did.

He was taken into the bunkhouse, his wounds treated, and in a few weeks he was removed to the family home in Carlisle, Illinois, where he eventually recovered to return to his duties on the stage line. The company hands, however, had decided to settle things their own way. While Slade was being doctored, they agreed the world would be better rid of cowards. They tossed a rope over a beam trussed between two large freight wagons, put a noose around Beni's neck, and pulled him up. It was at this moment that Ben Ficklin, general superintendent of the line, rode into the station—in time to cut Jules down before life was extinct. Hearing the story of Slade's shooting, Ficklin, because there was no legal tribunal at hand, ordered Beni to leave the country or be hanged by an informal court. He took the offer and fled. But he hadn't reckoned on Slade's terrible vengeance.

It came in August 1861, two years after the shooting scrape. Slade was riding east on the stage from Rocky Ridge to his home at Horse Shoe, some forty miles west of Fort Laramie in present Wyoming. He had heard Jules Beni was driving stock out of Denver and would be crossing the Sweetwater Division. Slade had been told, too, that if Beni saw him first, he likely would be ambushed. So Slade and a small party of Overland hands waited for Beni and in a running gunfight shot and wounded him.

There are various accounts of what took place next, Slade's friends denying them, and his enemies swearing they were true. But popular history holds that Slade ordered Beni tied to a corral fence and spent the better part of a day drinking and shooting the unfortunate captive to death by degrees. When he satisfied himself that Beni's murderous attack on him had been repaid, he put an end to it with a fatal shot, and in a final act of vengeance cut off the dead man's ears. The Overland Stage Company, which employed him, and a military tribunal at Fort Laramie, the nearest for fifteen hundred miles, exonerated Slade after he reported the shooting.

He became more troublesome than ever after that. His reputation blackened with each succeeding tale, such as how he responded to emigrant complaints seeking lost or stolen livestock by confronting a rancher he suspected of rustling and opening fire through a doorway, killing three ranch hands and wounding a fourth. Stories of hanging men and of innumerable assaults, shootings, and beatings ultimately took their toll with the Overland Company. His violent behavior—he was fond of shooting canned goods off grocery shelves—brought about his discharge from the line.

Such was the reputation he took with him to Virginia City, Idaho Territory, in the spring of 1863. There were problems in that part of the country that were to have a devastating effect on Jack Slade. A gang of desperadoes had been successful in robbing gold shipments with impunity in the region and had reached a point at which a *vigilance committee had been organized to deal with the situation. It had been discovered that the leader of the outlaws was the sheriff, Henry Hummer, himself. And the vigilantes set out to correct the matter. They began hanging men suspected of being in league with the Plummer gang. And on January 14, 1864, strung up five at once.*

After the summary executions, the vigilantes, considering their work accomplished, having freed the territory of highwaymen and murders, established a provisional court to try future offenders by judge and jury. Jack Slade found himself high on the list of community undesirables. It had become a common occurrence for him to take Virginia City by storm; he and his friends would gallop through its main streets, "shooting and yelling like red devils, firing their revolvers, riding their horses into stores and destroy the goods within," while insulting all who stood in their way. Slade had never been accused of murder or even suspected of robbery in the territory. His lawlessness while drunk and his defiance of civil authority led to the belief that as he had killed men in other places, he would, unless he was checked in his wild career, commit the same deeds in Virginia City.

After one of his all-night carouses had made the town a pandemonium—and presumably he had displayed his now infamous shriveled "Jules's ear" to patrons of the saloons he frequented—a warrant was issued for his arrest on disturbing the peace charges. Slade reacted in expected fashion. He seized the writ, tore it into bits, stamped on it in fury, and set out with a loaded Derringer in search of the judge. The vigilance committee went into emergency session.

One of its principal men was John Xavier Beidler (known simply as X. Beidler among friends), who in his own career had been a store clerk, prospector, pack train operator, freighter, deputy U.S. marshal, and stagecoach shotgun guard and was known for having backbone, despite being scarcely taller than a rifle. On one occasion in Kansas, Beidler was with a party that chased a gang of border ruffians into a blacksmith shop. For want of lead, the posse loaded a small howitzer with printer's type and fired. Those not killed, he said, "had to pick the type from the bodies of their comrades, and that is the way they first learned to read."

Of Slade, Beidler said, "We communed on many occasions as friends. He was an honest man and did not like a thief, but he was a very dangerous man when drinking." And Slade had been drinking a great deal. With him on the loose and threatening to shoot the deputy and the judge, Beidler made one last effort to avoid what he knew was coming. He asked Slade's friend Jim Kiskadden to take Slade home, that a party of miners were headed for town with the intention of carrying out the vigilance committee's order.

Slade reluctantly turned his horse around and began riding out, when he spotted his quarry near a store. With a gun in each hand, he began an insulting tirade against the judge, the deputy, and the store owner, P. S. Pfouts, who also was the president of the vigilantes. At that moment, the miners hove into view with Captain James Williams, a vigilante, at their head. The sight sobered Slade immediately; his only response, "My god!" Williams informed him he had just one hour to live, and if he had any business to attend to, "he had better do it." Beidler later remarked that if Slade had ridden out when he was told, he would not have been hanged.

A group was sent to find a place of execution and decided on an empty beef scaffold. A noose was thrown over it, and Beidler said, "When Slade's hour expired . . . he expired with it." Standing on the boxes beneath the scaffold with the rope around his neck, he pleaded for his life. The crowd responded, "Time's up." Williams ordered, "Do your duty," and the boxes were kicked away, plunging Slade into the abyss of death, for having disturbed the peace of Virginia City.

When Virginia Slade, who had been summoned from the ranch some dozen miles distant, rode into the city, she discovered to her horror she was too late. Her husband had been removed to a nearby store, his clothing arranged and prepared for burial. It was March 11, 1864. The bereaved widow cursed the town, took her husband's body home in a tin-lined coffin filled, it was said, with a keg of whiskey. She swore he would never be buried in this "damned territory," and shipped the remains to Salt Lake City with instructions for the coffin to be transferred to an eastbound stage for Illinois.

By the time the roads cleared and the stage reached Utah, it was mid-July, and Virginia Slade's instructions had become confused. Slade's body was transferred to the Salt Lake City Cemetery and buried in the Stranger's Lot, "to be removed to Illinois in the fall." But no one ever came for Jack Slade. And today his remains—and the whiskey that proved his undoing—still await the stage for Carlisle.[11]

Resentment, Repulsion, and Revenge

To varying degrees, all mountain men were fatalists who remained detached in their outlooks on virtually everything. Unlike their European and eastern American counterparts, they viewed the western wildness in its physical sense with its endless harshness pitted against its boundless potential; its lack of conventional cultures and its constant interjections of the native people of the woods with their dark skin and even darker minds—mysterious, brooding, bloody, cruel. But also they recognized the wildness in a *metaphysical* sense, with its runaway anxieties and constant challenges forcing them to look inward while staring back in time.

Before Johnson's wife was killed, Liver-Eater had succumbed to some of her civilizing influences on him; he may even have gone so far as to *like* them. As with everything in his life, the contrasts were stark and unyielding: On one hand stood the warmth and pleasantries of home and hearth while on the other raged the eternally conflicted call of the lone warrior.

But all of that vanished with her death, as did the feminine principles that might have tamed some of the wildness remaining in his soul. The devastating circumstances of his wife's murder forced the shaping of his psyche as he found himself once more alone in the wilderness except for the other "wild men."

Johnson's love-hate relationship with the Indians was obvious. It was no different than his love-hate relationship with nature itself. The Indians were symbols who evoked the very spirit of the wide-open American wilderness. Johnson coexisted with them because he had reciprocal respect, but his emotional reactions to them ranged from detachment to love, fury, resentment, and ultimately hatred. He loved The Swan and might have lived out the rest of his life satisfied with her and their child in a more subdued wildness that only a feminine touch could have brought to the landscape. That was something no bully, lout, or scrapper could hope to duplicate. But with The Swan's demise, all the promise of her influence disappeared like wisps of smoke on the horizon.

Johnson's life was changed forever.

So when twenty of the most feared and competent Crow warriors set out to run him down, he took them on, one by one in hand-to-hand combat, and, one by one, mowed through them like so much wheat before the unrelenting scythe of the farmer. Johnson sent all twenty of the tribe's fiercest warriors to the happy hunting ground. He killed each one individually over a span of fourteen years. Shortly after Johnson had destroyed the twentieth and last Crow, Del Gue—looking on in fearsome awe—allegedly turned to him.

"Good God!" said Del. "This'n air number twenty."

Johnson nodded.

"On yer trail fer ten y'ars!"

"Near fourteen," Johnson said.

Struck by the similarity of their thoughts, the partners talked about the Crows: Even more admirable than Crow brotherhood, they agreed, was Crow *tenacity*. For a warrior to spend so many years away from his family on such a trail of death was incomprehensible. The partners spoke of how many times a warrior must have hidden near his own village to spy upon his family and watch his children grow. They considered, too, how as "one by one the others of the chosen twenty died, loneliness must have come upon him like the dark converges to cover the prairie grass until nothing more remains of it."

"I'm shore glad that's over," Del said.

Johnson merely nodded, for he respected the Indians, and they respected him. Crows believed that the stronger one's enemy, the stronger the tribe. A strong enemy forced them to fight well. And Johnson's ferocity in battle and success as a warrior reflected well upon them even in defeat.[12]

Although Johnson displayed his overall animosity for the Indians, he simultaneously fostered a genuine admiration for the warriors of many different tribes. Even as he earned his reputation as the Killer of Crows, the time arrived when through his own sheer admiration for the Crow's benevolence he stopped his vengeance and became the tribe's brother-in-arms.

In his treatise "The Mountain Man as Literary Hero," University of Utah's Don D. Walker proposed the West as a "vast unsettled wilderness, a region, real or imaginary, 'out there' in the mountains, forests, plains, and deserts."[13] In such a scenario, the mountain man would have become America's first true western hero. Explorers such as Hernando de Soto, Ponce de Leon, and, later, Lewis and Clark may have arrived on the scene earlier and "penetrated the geographical unknowns well before the mountain man loaded his traps and pushed up along the rivers; but the mountain man was the first to make the wilderness his own, or, better, to recognize that he belonged to the wilderness."[14]

But for those more conventional shopkeepers and homemakers and bank tellers back East, what more thrilling investment in time than to covet the unbridled pride of discovery that drove each western hero from his very doorstep into the vast uncertainty of the unknown, the "black abyss" of the future?

Even before the end of the eighteenth century, Americans had followed and idolized the skills, savvy, and daring of men such as Daniel Boone and Davy Crockett. Even back to James Fenimore Cooper's Natty Bumppo and the Leatherstocking Tales, Americans read with awe and horror about every hidden danger that lurked behind each foreboding boulder or turn of the trail. We didn't merely read about Chingachgook in *The Last of the Mohicans*, we wished we had *been* him, to have lived in those days when courage meant everything and integrity took a backseat to nothing.

Even today, with the wilderness mostly gone and the days of the intrepid explorer long ended, we relive those memories in modern dreams—exploring the vastness of the ocean or the emptiness of space. And, perhaps, to relive the excitement, danger, and wild and lonely life of the last of the mountain men.

Walker explains:

For the mountain man's often solitary venture into Western space, there is, I think, no 20th century equivalent. It is true that we have made heroes of the men who have pioneered into outer space, but there is no real similarity between a trapper and an astronaut. However dangerous his task may be, the spaceman is never alone, is never wholly dependent upon his courage and ingenuity. Even if he is the sole occupant of a capsule orbiting two hundred miles out in space, his very heartbeat is pulsing visibly on earth; a whole array of electronic systems watches and guides him. He is backed up, as we say in the language of our time, by a vast technological organization of men and machines. The mountain man had no back-up systems. If his reflexes failed, if he erred, he was dead and his hair was gone. And he found the final solitude of an unknown grave. If John Glenn had been attacked by the Blackfeet of outer space, the whole world would have known almost as the arrows were beginning to fall. But if John Colter had stumbled or run out of breath, no one would have known but the Blackfeet, and they kept no books. At best some historian of the fur trade could later have noted obscurely: John Colter, who had been with Lewis and Clark, went trapping in the Blackfoot country and was never heard of again.[15]

It's an interesting philosophy and one with merit. If the mountain man has no modern-day equivalent in terms of unmatched physical courage, primitive ingenuity, and dogged self-determination, we have no one upon whom to pin our hopes and dreams. That's why we read, examine, study, and dig into the roots of history, to turn the soil of the past so that we can relive at least figuratively our forebear's life. The mountain man endured not only the day-to-day practical problems of nature such as the freezing cold, drenching rains, roaring rivers, and deadly animals but also the most life-threatening forces of hunger, thirst, disease, injury, and hostile Indians.

"Out of the raw stuff of his history," Walker writes, "came some great examples of heroic survival. . . . Besides men such as Colter and Glass, history offered *other* heroes. All must have been physically tough, with nerves tempered by isolation and danger, but a few are remembered not for crawling, running, or fighting but for a special intensity of purpose. If they were not perhaps typical mountain men, they may nevertheless represent other facets of heroism to be found in the fur trade, and they may suggest other possibilities to the imaginative writer. The extremes of contrast can be marked here by the names of two men, John Johnson (or Johnston) and Jedediah Smith."[16]

The legend of Liver-Eating Johnson spread like cholera through a crowded schoolyard. Before his vengeance had run its course and he had become a brother of the same enemies he had long pursued, he was rumored to have killed three hundred Crows in total, including twenty of the tribe's bravest warriors, scalping each one and eating their livers raw.

Cruel? Perhaps. Inhuman? Possibly. Insane? Some might conclude so. But in reality, had he been *only* those things, his legend would never have spanned more than a century and continued to grow with every passing year, causing creative writers to take note. Some of them managed to create similar stories. Among the most popular is Robert Montgomery Bird, whose Bloody Nathan in *Nick of the Woods*, published in 1841, vowed death to the last Shawnee warrior standing. But Walker points out a more appropriate theme from still another writer:

In a story which is otherwise melodramatic and highly sentimental, C. W. Webber dealt with a hunter's monomania of vengeance. Old Bill Smith, the titular character in Old Bill Smith, The Silent Hunter, *published in 1852, has taken his family west with Boone in 1784. Coming back from a trip for supplies, he finds his wife and children dead, killed by Shawnees. He buries them, then disappears on the trail of their murderers. After a long silence the people of Boone's Fort hear from a captured Shawnee the story of an Evil Demon that has been haunting the war-path of his tribe for nearly two years. More than thirty of their best braves, including several chiefs, have disappeared. When Smith does come in to the forts, he is regarded, like Johnson, with awe. "He was never heard to speak to any one—he came without a greeting and went without farewell. He was regarded with a curi- ous feeling of dread and respect by the Border people, none of whom ever ventured to address a word to him." At the story's end he is found dead in his cabin.*

His face in death alone had lost that still and fearful expression of astonied ferocity, which was said never to have left it from the time of the death of Mattie and his children. Monomaniacs are proverbially known for the frequently marvelous cunning displayed by them in bringing about the accomplishment of the one object, which is the single thought of their lives.

Though Webber does little more than suggest it, here at least is the right note, the right emphasis. A fictional Crow Killer will be a solitaire, or as Melville would put it, an isolato, not because he goes his revengeful way alone, nor because he is never surrounded by other people, but because his monomania, however understandable it may be, has removed him, as Hawthorne would put it, from the moral community of men.[17]

Might Liver-Eater have read C. W. Webber's book of "astonied ferocity"? Johnson was able to read and write since early childhood and certainly could have stumbled across the book at some point in his life. Or perhaps he read Bird's *Nick of the Woods.* As a young man of seventeen when the book was released, Johnson most certainly would have had access to it at some point. By then, he was most likely serving on a whaler out of New Bedford and had plenty of time on his hands between pulse-racing sightings and the frantic cry of *Thar she blows!*

Could that be what put the notion of indulging in a lifelong vendetta against the mighty Crow Nation into the mountain man's head? Or was it something developed spontaneously, autonomous of any outside influence, a gut reaction that sprang more from his innate sense of justice, of knowing right from wrong, than from a chance encounter with literary license?

Only one man on earth ever knew the answer to that question.

And he's not talking.

CHAPTER ELEVEN

Putting Down Roots

By 1877, following the winter campaign of 1876–77, the power of the Indians of the Northwest began its slow, steady decline. The victory of General Miles with the aid of Johnson, Kelly, and the others at Wolf Mountain had broken the spirit of Crazy Horse and his allies. With the passing of the mighty Sioux Nation, too, began the inevitable decline of the lifestyle Johnson and his compatriots had long known and loved.

But the rounding up of the last of the hostile tribes would not take place for many more months. In the meantime, the occasional uprisings and massacres—although increasingly rare—continued for another fifteen years. In between, settlers and gold hunters and even cattlemen with sprawling herds of beeves driven up from Texas swarmed into what had been a wilderness only moments before. These new arrivals found the endless plains and spiraling peaks of the Rocky Mountain West frightening in their vastness. But, as authors Raymond W. Thorp and Robert Bunker described in their book *Crow Killer*, "for old-time trappers the old-time feeling of their country had gone."[1]

As had happened earlier in the eastern and then central United States, the frontiers of the Rockies had all dried up, and the frontiersmen who needed the open spaces like a human body craves oxygen withered and died. Not from generations run afoul of life's natural finite mortality, for very few mountain men lived to die of old age, but rather they met their callings at the hands of fever and boredom and apoplexy and despair. They passed on from starvation and exposure, from too little water . . . or too much. They didn't outlive their time so much as time outlived them.

In the fall of 1878, Del Gue and Hatchet Jack Ireland found Liver-Eating Johnson camped at Pryor's Fork on the Yellowstone. The three talked over their prospects for the future. Fur was scarce, and scalps even scarcer. Good equipment was hard to come by: Jack, replacing a worn-out hatchet, could find only a replacement better suited for driving nails than for "choppin' Injuns."

But with richly lived lives come never-ending dreams, so the three men, with three muscular packhorses in tow, left camp for the Little Rockies below the Milk River not far from Bear Claw Lapp's canyon. Crossing the Yellowstone and the four forks of the Musselshell and finally the Missouri near the locale of Johnson's old wood yard, the trio arrived at their chosen site without incident. Sometime before spring, they promised one another, they would go learn whether Bear Claw was in his winter retreat as usual, and they looked forward to exchanging stories with him. But first, they had to make preparations of their own for the coming winter.

Del, who had been the first to come upon the campsite with Old Mizzou years earlier, set about choosing a suitable clearing near a cold, fast-running spring in the rocks on the southern edge of the range. They began felling straight, tall pine trees and dragging them by horse to the homesite, where they shaved off the stubble and prepared the ends for business. When they had assembled several large piles of freshly fallen timber, they set about laying the footprint of the cabin. It was still only mid-October but light snow had already fallen, and while that made working uncomfortable, they took heart in the fact that an early winter meant good trapping and thick, luxurious skins. Sure enough, when Johnson and Jack ventured off to test their luck, they returned a few days later with an impressive catch, which they promptly turned over to Gue for skinning.

According to Thorp and Bunker, all went well at their new site with no sign of Indians to worry about through mid-December. Then one evening Del reported that, while returning from his day's hunt with the shoulder of an elk, he had heard the discharge of a gun at a distance. Likely Bear Claw, he speculated, although Johnson thought it would be wise to investigate come morning.

The next day, with the stars still twinkling overhead, Johnson and Hatchet Jack left Gue to run their traps. They followed Del's well-beaten trail from the previous evening back into the hills until they found where, the day before, Lapp had broken a path across the wind-packed snow. They followed in his steps before stumbling upon the carcass of an elk that the old-timer had shot and cached in a tree. Johnson pointed out the obvious: More than one shoulder of the beast had been cut and both of its hams removed.

"Three red coons on foot, Jack," he most likely said, reading between the signs. He knelt to study further. "Blackfoots," he added. The Indians had apparently heard Bear Claw's shot and arrived after he had already treed the elk. Lucky for Lapp.

Realizing that the Blackfeet had most likely followed Lapp's tracks back to his cabin, the two set off along the hardened trail, the packed snow cracking and crunching beneath their moccasins. At last they came upon a broad, shallow canyon. Rounding one of the many turns leading down to the valley floor, they spied Lapp's cabin set into a natural niche in the rock wall. The front door was open. As they approached, they watched for signs of danger. Edging slowly up to the door's threshold, they stopped. Johnson peeked in.

Nothing. No pole bunk bed, no crudely fashioned chair or small table, not even any of its occupant's personal belongings hanging from the pegs on the cabin walls. All had been stripped of the cabin save one thing.

Bear Claw!

The two men rushed in to find Lapp on the hard-packed earthen floor. Blood covered his head, face, and shoulders. One hand clutched a partially finished necklace of bear claws, with several other claws scattered across the floor. He had never known what hit him; he had never heard the danger coming.

Until it was too late.

Johnson, looking around the walls, found a crack where the chinks had fallen from between the logs; Lapp's failure to repair the crack had led to his demise. One of the three Indians had raised his rifle barrel to the crack, threaded it through, and—as he spied the crusty old mountain man with his back to the wall—opened fire. Johnson walked around to the outside, found the crack, and lifted his own rifle up. He sighted through the crack, along the route leading toward the dead man's head, and to the far wall just inches aside a small window. Johnson returned to the cabin, checked around until he found the hole, and fished out the ball with the tip of his bowie knife.

"Needle gun," he said.

Hatchet Jack cursed, vowing then and there to hunt down the white coons who had sold the rifles to the Indians down by Fort Peck and "pole their heads."

The men examined their fallen compadre's body. Although cold, it wasn't yet solidly frozen. Some of the coagulating blood hadn't fully dried. From that, they deduced that Lapp had been killed only that morning. Johnson and Jack pieced the clues together. They knew without uttering a word what had happened.

The Blackfeet trail to the cabin led in only one direction; they had come upon Bear Claw's cabin after his previous day's hunt. They had come into the same woods where Del had been hunting and heard Lapp's shot the night before. The Blackfeet lay in darkness to ambush him, but he never showed. When they gave up hope, they stumbled across Lapp's elk and cut off a shoulder and two hams before heading back to their camp.

Lapp might still be alive had they not stumbled across his cabin by accident. They stayed all night, hoping that its occupant would open the door so they could rush him. Knowing that other trappers were nearby, they were too smart to set fire to the cabin. But in the early morning, before sunrise, a light from inside the cabin shone through the crack in the log wall, betraying their quarry. One of the Indians peeked through, saw Lapp, and shot him. Then the braves broke down the door. They scalped Bear Claw and stripped the cabin nearly clean.

Johnson looked around for anything else the Indians might have taken, and then he noticed it. Bear Claw's "pretties"—the finest of the necklaces he had made—were gone.

Johnson shook his head. The Blackfeet had gotten his best in more ways than one. He lifted Lapp's head once more and nodded toward the bloody clot where his scalp had been taken. A surge of anger boiled up to replace the sorrow he'd felt earlier. Now, with the morning sun only beginning to threaten the peaks, the time was right.

Hurrying from the cabin, the two men traced the Blackfeet's trail—three sets of hoofprints from the horses they'd stolen from Lapp. They had made no attempt to cover their tracks. Suddenly Johnson pulled up short with Jack right behind him. The mountain man sniffed the air. He motioned his partner on, cautiously, as they approached the rim of another canyon. When they arrived, they snuck to the edge and looked down into a clearing. There they spied the three Blackfeet.

Having finished breakfast, two of the warriors wrestled with a large, heavy trunk while the third held the bridle of Bear Claw's skittish packhorse.

The trappers sank down onto their bellies, sighting along their heavy rifle barrels. Johnson whispered for Jack to shoot them in their shoulders to put them out of commission. As their shots bellowed out, the sounds bouncing around the canyon walls, the packhorse that the third Indian was holding broke loose, knocking the Blackfoot to the ground. When he looked up, he was horrified to see that his two companions had their right shoulders blown away. As the packhorse whirled around and ran off in the direction of the trees, the box fell on the Blackfoot who had been holding the horse. Johnson quickly slipped a long, heavy cartridge into his rifle, dropped the breechblock, and fired.

With all three Indians disabled, the trappers took their time in working their way carefully down the jagged rocks to the canyon floor. Once they arrived, they approached the chest, and Jack broke the box open with one swift blow of his hatchet. Chris Lapp's lifetime of work spilled out before their eyes—all of his finished pieces made up of carefully matched claws.

Jack put up his hatchet and drew his knife. The Blackfeet, knowing they would soon bleed to death, began singing their death songs. Jack stepped up to one of them, ran his blade into his eye socket, and popped out the eyeball, sending it rolling across the ground. His victim flinched but never yelled.

Sheathing the knife and grabbing his hatchet, he lifted each of the Indians' heads by its topknot and, whacking off one scalp after another—

close to their skulls—with the heavy blade, muttered something about "That's for Mad Mose." When he'd finished that, he removed the remaining eyes. Johnson came up and severed the three heads at the neck and wrapped them in a burlap sack.

Retrieving the horse that had run at the sound of the shots, Johnson lifted Lapp's trunk and, while Jack held tight the bridle, lashed it onto the animal's back. Then, each man grabbed a saddled horse and, with the pack animal in tow, picked their way slowly up and out of the canyon back toward Bear Claw's cabin.

Once they arrived and dismounted, Jack threw the three heads on the ground before following Johnson into the hut. They carefully lifted Lapp and carried him out. Gathering up huge armfuls of brush and dry saplings, they mounded the fuel around the cabin's interior and set it on fire, waiting hours for the flames to burn themselves out and the smoke to turn gray. When the ground had cooled to a point where they could scrape the thawed earth away, they dug Bear Claw's grave.

Jack went down to cut some stakes from a stand of box elders and returned to help wrap their companion in his own blankets, leaving only his face exposed before setting him into the hole. For thirty-five years, Johnson had known the "coon." Thirty-five long, useful, productive, informative years. Thirty-five years of friendship, camaraderie, aid, and comfort. There was nothing Bear Claw wouldn't have done for another trapper. And as Johnson reflected upon the three-and-a-half decades that had passed in the blink of an eye since he had stumbled across the man very near to where they stood, Jack reached into the trunk for a handful of necklaces. Pulling them out, he scattered them around the hole before Johnson lifted the heavy crate and emptied the remainder of its contents onto the ground.

The necklaces tumbled out, followed by a passel of scalps. Nearly a hundred of them, Johnson estimated. Bear Claw had kept each and every one, braided, oiled, and hooped, instead of selling them at the station the way most trappers did. Johnson threw them into the grave as well before shoveling the loose dirt from Bear Claw's cabin floor and sprinkling it over the man. When at last he lay completely covered, the men raised a monument of stones to mark his resting place. Then Jack dug three holes with his hatchet, one each at the head, foot, and side of the grave, and planted each of his sharpened box elder stakes. Finally, he jammed the three Blackfoot heads onto the tops of the stakes. He and Johnson marveled at how quickly and decisively Mountain Justice had reared its unrelenting head. It was not the first time; certainly, it wouldn't be the last.

Back at their own cabin, Del had just finished running the last of the two men's trap lines. He had a gnawing feeling that his partners had run into trouble of some sort and hurried back to the cabin in case they needed him. When he finally returned, it was already dark. He found his partners inside. They had lighted the whale-oil lamp and had elk steaks on a hot pan over the fire, with skillet biscuits as only Liver-Eater could brown them.

After the three men retired for the night, a blizzard swept through, shaking the newly built cabin to its stone foundations, but the oversize fireplace glowed, and the men were relieved to have made it through another day alive. Along with their tales of Bear Claw, they recounted their remembrances of the worst winters they could recall. Johnson said he remembered a much colder Christmas season when Portuguese Phillips rode to Fort Laramie. Del said that the roughest winter he had ever survived was the one in which Johnson had trekked back after his escape from captivity from the Blackfeet.

True to his promise, several days later, Hatchet Jack performed one final act of retribution for Bear Claw's death, as well as for the deaths of *all* the mountain men whom Indians had shot with white men's rifles. He sought out the traders who had sold the needle guns to the three Blackfeet, killed them, and poled their heads above Fort Peck.

ON TO LEADVILLE

With Bear Claw dead and Liver-Eating Johnson and Del Gue growing "old"—at least for trappers—Johnson began giving some serious thought to his future. Even though he still had all the strength and vigor of a man in his prime, he was in his middle sixties. And not without pain. His joints ached constantly, and his shoulder where he had been shot during the war had begun to atrophy seriously.

Gue, like Johnson, was in fine physical condition and, like his partner, in constant pain. The mountains can be your friend for only so long, and then they become your enemy.

Finally, after several more weeks had passed and an extraordinarily good winter's catch was just about put to bed, Liver-Eating Johnson made a decision: He would leave his pards and move away from his old haunts. And the next day, he did just that.

He headed north toward Leadville, Colorado, stopping off just long enough to report to White Eye Anderson what he'd been up to.

Leadville, high up against Colorado's Rocky Mountains on the eastern slope, won its fame almost overnight as a place where fortunes could be made and lost in the turn of a hand—or a shovel. It was inhabited largely by Welsh miners and other European immigrants willing to dig away their lives underground in the hopes of striking it rich. Most didn't, but some did. Their successes brought pouring into town the gamblers and confidence men from out East and the central United States, as well as desperadoes and hired killers who roamed the streets day and night, looking for easy prey. And then, of course, the prostitutes, always on the lookout for the next big strike, arrived on every stage. Highwaymen sold their booty and ambushers sold their services, all right in the center of town.

From such older strikes as those at Alder Gulch and Deadwood came a new host of swindlers, for in Leadville they could win their fast bucks even faster. As the gamblers and con men flooded the town, buckskin leggings and moccasins gave way grudgingly to woolen slacks and patent leather shoes.

Of course, there were honest men in Leadville, too, including investors, lawyers, and bankers (well, *mostly* honest, in any event), just as there were mountain men who dropped in to see the diggings and watch with amusement the action—quiet, bearded men in deerskin or buffalo robes, "disturbed because disturbance had come to their mountains but competent to look out for themselves," according to Thorp and Bunker.[2] Although mere wisps in the willows of a more raucous, untamed past, the new breed of genteel killers made sure to walk past these mountains of men cautiously so as not to arouse the fury that allegedly brewed just below the surface. A six-gun, even in the hands of a skilled shootist, was no match for scalping knives and tomahawks thrown with a vengeance and Hawken rifles that could blow a hole in a man as large as a dinner plate.

White Eye "Jack" Anderson and his longtime trapping partner, Yankee Judd, had joined forces in Leadville to work first as foremen and then as guards in the Bullseye Mine. White Eye recalled their time there:

I had a job waiting for me at the Silver Iron mine. The Silver Iron was about one mile above Leadville, on Iron Hill. They owned about a mile of the contact, or croppings, of a very rich vein of carbonate silver ore. Bill Godfrey had mentioned my name when he was talking to some of the people at the mine and one of them turned out to be my old partner, Yankee Judd. He was one of the guards employed to guard the Bull's Eye Mine, which was very rich. The company had eighteen guards, six on a shift in eight hours. Judd had charge of one shift. As soon as he heard I was in Leadville, he told the superintendent of the company about me. As a result I was offered the job of taking charge of one of the shifts at one hundred dollars per month, with board and lodging.

I was very glad to accept the offer and to be with my old partner again. Those eighteen guards were supposed to be good, reliable men for that kind of business. They had to be on the alert all the time, always looking for trouble, quick on the trigger, cool, and deliberate. The country was full of tough men willing to do most anything for money and they were the ones we had to look out for.

One evening when the miners were changing shifts, a gang of toughs attempted to make a raid on the mine as there was over one hundred thousand dollars of very rich ore in the bins. The gang planted two hundred pounds of dynamite in an old shaft that was right over the main working incline of the Bull's Eye Mine, then touched it off. It happened to be on my shift, but we knew what was coming and were ready for them. There were several heavy iron ore cars on the dump and the six of us who were on duty turned them over and got under them as quickly as possible. After the blast had gone off, we were ready for them.

As soon as the big rocks stopped coming down . . . the gang rushed to the dump and ore bins to take possession. We had the drop on them, however, and made them surrender. We held them until our twelve relief guards came and took the whole outfit off to jail. There were twelve or fifteen men, with two or three ore sleds hauled by big, strong horses in the outfit. The ore was about ninety percent pure silver, so you can see that a ton of that ore was quite valuable.

There were about fifteen hundred men on the payroll at the Silver Iron mine and payday was a big day. A good many of the boys would take in the town that night. They would spend their money drinking, dancing and gambling and the next morning lots of them would be broke. When our crowd would go I generally went with them, but the boys called me "the old man" because I did not drink to get drunk. If I did it would make me very sick and sometimes it would take me a week to get over it. When the others got full and went to the "cooler," I generally was on hand to get them back to the mine.

One evening after payday, about a dozen of us went downtown to see the sights. Jim Jones was with us and when he would get about half-full he was full of fun. About eleven o'clock we went into a big dance hall called the Red Light. One of the main characters in the place was a very large woman, weighing more than two hundred pounds. They called her "The Great Eastern." She came up to Jim and asked if he was going to treat, and Jim said, "Sure, let's have some beer." The Great Eastern said, "No, I want champagne." Jim told her to go to hell for her champagne. She was big and strong and she hit him a hard lick on his head. Then a big man behind the bar jumped on Jim and knocked him down and our fellows just about paralyzed that bartender which started a general fight.

We had private signals that all understood, and when the signal was given, every light in the dance hall was shot out with our six-guns. You can bet there was some excitement in that dance hall when all the lights went out. Hundreds of people were in the hall and it sounded like hell had broken out with men cursing and women

*screaming. Our boys all got out and met at a place agreed on previ-
ously in case we got into trouble.*

*Yankee Judd and I planned to go prospecting in the spring, about
the first of April, so we were saving our money instead of spending it
like the other fellows did.*

*"Chicken Bill," who got his name from stealing a lot of chickens,
salted a claim he had on Fryer Hill. He put sand carbonates of silver
in the bottom of a forty foot shaft he had dug where he had not found
anything. He sold the claim to Governor Tabor for a few thousand
dollars, but Tabor dug the salt out and went down twenty feet further
and struck it very rich. This was before Tabor was governor and before
he was very rich. In a few months he was worth over ten million dollars. Mr. Tabor called the mine "The New Discovery," and it turned
out to be one of the richest mines in Leadville.*

*Governor Tabor was a good friend of mine and very generous
with his money. He was always ready, willing and even anxious to
grubstake anyone who would go into the hills and prospect. There
was nothing strange about that; he had made his money from just
such arrangements. Many times I have had him stop me on the street
and try to interest me in a grubstake from him. The amount of the
stake did not interest him. If you felt that you wanted to take a year
or so at it and needed one thousand dollars or so, that was perfectly
all right with him. He had the money to do with as he pleased and
he was always ready to take a long chance. He grubstaked scores of
men, some of them two, and a few three or four times. He knew
of my claim in Arizona and was always asking me if I wanted to
"work it a little." His checkbook was as good as gold, but I was not
in a position to take him up on the several occasions that he made
me a proposition.*

*I saw in the daily Leadville papers that "Texas Jack," or Jack
Omohundro, was a leading character in a drama being played in
Tabor's Opera House. He married an actress named Madam Malacki
[sic] who played an Indian princess in the play and seemed like a very
good woman. Jack put Yankee Judd and I on the deadhead list to take
in the show whenever we wanted to go, free of charge. The worst trou-*

ble with Jack was that he had so many friends he kept busy drinking with them and finally got so he could not let up.

Texas Jack was a better government scout in the Indian wars than Buffalo Bill or Wild Bill ever was. Cody was a big hero in the newspapers and dime novels, but when it came down to the real thing, he could not measure up to the other fellows.

Texas Jack's wife wanted me to do my best to get him sobered up, so we took him over to the soda springs to drink the water. It was all right while he was there, but when he came back he was as bad as ever and he died before the spring of 1880. I helped to bury him the same as I did Wild Bill in 1876.[3]

While Anderson and Judd were guards, they sometimes shared the same shift and occupied a double room above the saloon of Rowdy Joe Lowe, an occasional gunman and former saloonkeeper from Newton, Kansas. He had resettled in Colorado after killing a man back home. Lowe came highly recommended via his acquaintance with a mutual friend, the late Wild Bill.

Rowdy Joe had been a familiar character in the Southwest for nearly fifty years. Born in Texas, he went into government service as a scout at a young age. He arrived in Leadville in 1878 and ran a variety show for a short time. He spent time in the mining community before making the fatal decision to travel on to Denver, where he met his untimely death. He was killed there on February 11, 1882, after getting into a heated row with a Denver police officer who pulled a gun and fired several shots into him.

One day, as White Eye looked out the window of their Leadville room, he counted twenty Cheyenne warriors occupying a hastily erected camp just down the street. They had supposedly come to town to buy provisions but actually were there to "acquire" arms and ammunition. Black Kettle, their chief, was resplendently garbed in his customary buckskin, beads, and feathered headdress.

Several days later, just off their shift at the mine, White Eye and Judd were cleaning up in their room when they heard a ruckus coming from the street. Peering out the window, they noticed that the Cheyenne had

John Baker "Texas Jack" Omohundro, 1846–1880, served in the Confederacy before traveling west to work as a military scout, where his path crossed that of Liver-Eating Johnson.

deserted their camp, and a crowd of passersby had assembled. The two miners, strapping on their guns, hurried down to see what was happening.

Pushing their way through the hard-packed crowd, White Eye and Judd found Liver-Eating Johnson and, lying at his feet, two burly but comatose miners. White Eye knew them as Lavery and Morgan, two scrappy troublemakers from his own shift.

Johnson stood silhouetted against the buffalo-hide tepees of the Cheyenne, glaring at Bill Greiner, the Eagle County sheriff. Del Gue, with his back against the crowd, stood off to one side, leaning on his own rifle and Johnson's with a half-grin on his leathery face.

Greiner was a powerful man renowned for his toughness. Shy ten pounds, he was as big as Johnson. Rumor had it that he rarely used his Colt pistol because he seldom needed to. He could subdue half a dozen ordinary men with one cuff of his bear-size paw. His sheriff's star shone sharply in the morning sun as he looked Johnson squarely in the eyes.

"We can't have our citizens knocked around like this, stranger," Greiner said sternly.

Johnson replied that he had better keep those two coons off him then because he hadn't killed anybody there . . . *yet*. The two tenderfeet, he explained, had jostled up against him, so he knocked their heads together.

A dozen mountain men in the audience roared their approval, and the sheriff was thinking about telling them that the two weren't tenderfeet but miners.

"All town pilgrims air tenderfoots," Johnson said, reading his mind.

Del Gue chuckled again. White Eye, alongside him, wondered if perhaps he might head off trouble by telling the sheriff who Johnson was, when suddenly a staid, older Cheyenne pushed his way through the crowd. Yankee Judd whispered to Del that it was Chief Black Kettle.

Johnson turned to greet the old man. The chief craned his neck to see who had recognized him. "*Dah-pih-ehk Absaroka*," he said, nodding to Johnson. Then the chief turned to Greiner: "This is the killer of Crows. He is the Great White Chief of the Shoshoni. His victims are strewn in all the mountains and the plains. My grandsons, great warriors, were not born when he took the trail of the Crows, and my sons were still but boys."

Greiner seemed unimpressed. The chief continued.

"*Dah-pih-ehk* will kill you with one hand. White lawman, you are only a papoose."

For once, Greiner's eyes flashed. He turned from the chief who had just disparaged his authority back to the mountain man who had knocked the "town tenderfoots" to the ground.

"So," Greiner growled at last, "you are Liver-Eating Johnson."

Johnson nodded once. Then, looking Greiner over with some grudging admiration, he said, "You're about the biggest papoose this child ever seen. Are we going to hug?" For a moment, the sheriff thought about fighting him, but soon enough, the anger melted from his face, and he extended his hand. "I don't think we'll hug," he said. "Welcome to Leadville, Johnson." The two waylaid miners, finally regaining consciousness, groaned as Johnson reached down and wrapped his powerful hands around the neck of each. Lifting them up that way, he dropped them down onto wobbly legs and sent them scurrying down the street.[4]

Johnson enjoyed the three weeks he and Del spent in Leadville. They looked in on former mountain men, including White Eye, Texas Jack Omohundro, and Colorado Charley Utter, who had quit trapping and become one of the town "tenderfoots." Johnson, as Bill Greiner's guest, watched with admiration as the sheriff handled the roughest of the rowdies in town. Meanwhile, Del, eyeing each new stagecoach arrival, was amazed to see all the eyeglasses and canes and tan shoes, the waistcoated big bellies of investors and the painted cheeks of dance-hall girls with each new influx. But the investors looked through Del as if he weren't there, and the girls looked at him more intently than he liked.

"If I wanted a woman, I'd grab me one," he said, "but I'm danged if I'll let any of 'em grab *me*!" Del, fed up with town life, urged Johnson to accompany him back into whatever wilderness still existed, and Johnson finally agreed.[5]

But after several weeks of hunting and trapping had passed, Johnson grew restless, so the partners packed up camp and rode north into Wyoming. There, Del shook his head at a herd of long-horned cattle on their way along the Bozeman Trail up above Fort Laramie. If he'd had his way, he said, he would have fed the entire bunch of them strychnine.

"They'll be wanting us to milk 'em next," he said. "Wasn't nobody on the Bozeman Trail when the Sioux was here. Nobody but me and Portygee Phillips."[6]

The tenderfoots and cattle weren't all that drew the wrath of Liver-Eater and Gue. The Northern Pacific Railroad, too—stretching out toward the Yellowstone River and beyond—also generated a fair amount of ire. The mountain men agreed that life would not be worth living once no one was needed to defend it anymore.

John Johnston, Justice of the Peace

Tiring once more of their wanderings, the men again decided to go their separate ways. Del took off for parts unknown while Johnson moved on to Miles City, Montana, to catch up with some old friends, including former army scout turned Custer County sheriff, Tom Irvine, who pointed out that the county was in need of a reliable lawman, news that caught Johnson's ear.

Johnson indicated he might be so inclined to accept the position "for a while," and the deal was consummated. According to Dr. Lorman L. Hoopes's book, *This Last West*, the Custer County Board of Commissioners appointed Johnson justice of the peace for Custer County on December 24, 1881. He was living at the time in Miles City with Irvine.

But Johnson's stint as a lawman lasted less than a year before he was bored again. When Del showed up and suggested they ride over to Fort Keogh to see what sort of mischief they could get into, Johnson jumped at the chance.

Setting off on horseback, the two turned right at the Powder River to trace its course. After several days in the saddle, they arrived at the fort, where a frontiersman caught up with them and gave Johnson a message. Del considered it yet another sign of the West's changing for the worst: The Northern Pacific Railroad had rolled into the Billings-Coulson area on August 22, 1882. Sheriff Tom Irvine needed a "firm hand" to keep the rowdy railroad crews in line. With the quick growth and frontier atmosphere that sprang up overnight, it didn't take long for Coulson to gain a reputation as a wild place.

"In its saloons and sod-roofed gambling houses they drank, gambled, caroused and fought," wrote Kathryn Wright in her 1953 book, *Billings:*

The Magic City and How It Grew. "It was a quiet night, indeed, when there was no one to bury in the nearby Boothill Cemetery."[7]

A December 17, 1905, article in the *Anaconda Standard* recalled the wildness of the town, saying that at least seven or eight murders had occurred, but there were very few, if any, arrests or convictions, partly because there was no jail.

Johnson and Gue knew all this firsthand, so when Liver-Eater agreed to accept Irvine's offer, Del merely shook his head. He wanted nothing to do with "that railroad town's desperadoes," but Johnson insisted that what Greiner could do at Leadville with two hands, he could do at Coulson with one. He told his partner to "rest up" for a day or two before getting ready for their next big adventure.

"But suppose you're called on to kill a white man? What would you do then?" Del asked. "You know that's against your mettle."

Johnson replied that he figured he could keep those galoots in line without killing them.

Del shook his head. "I don't know. I don't think it sounds like something you should get yourself into."

But Johnson had already made up his mind: He accepted the appointment as Coulson's deputy sheriff. Gue, determined to steer clear, wanted no part of the adventure, so the two parted ways once more. Johnson set off for the Platte River and, before long, had reached Coulson, where he settled into his new position as if he'd been born to it.

Coulson had been founded on the north bank of the Yellowstone River. With the opening of a general store in 1879 followed in short order by a hotel, post office, saloon, and ferry crossing, the town had become a welcomed stopover for frontiersmen passing through and a hub of regional activity.

In their history of the Billings area, *Billings: The City and the People*, Roger Clawson and Katherine A. Shandera wrote that Coulson's central placement between Minneapolis and Seattle, along the trail from Fort Custer to cattle country in the north, brought in a wide, wild range of characters. "Coulson's muddy streets thronged with cattle buyers, saddle tramps, prospectors lured by rumors of gold on the Upper Yellowstone, bison hunters, railroad surveyors, soldiers and the army of civilians (farmers, freighters, guides, scouts and others) serving the military in this area at the close of the Indian Wars," they wrote. "Coulson's bustle drew preachers, gamblers, prostitutes and Midwestern business people ready to invest their life savings."[8]

Another one of the people it drew was Liver-Eating Johnson, and the locals were thrilled to have him—at least those who wanted someone to maintain the peace. The hardened desperadoes ran from town like rabbits at the sound of a twelve-gauge the moment he moved in, leaving Johnson little more than the occasional barroom brawl and card-game shenanigans to handle. His reputation took care of most everything else. As Johnson's friend Packsaddle Ben Greenough wrote, people believed Johnson was "the strongest man in Montana Territory"[9] and wanted no part of him.

It showed. Within weeks, Johnson had everything moving along smoothly until, one day, Sheriff Irvine stepped down off the stage from Miles City, where he held jurisdiction. Johnson was surprised to see him in Coulson. Irvine said he was surprised to be there, but someone had brought to his attention the question of why his new deputy sheriff had made so few arrests. That paucity had resulted in a steep drop in fines collected for the county! Johnson explained that the men he disciplined weren't bad ones, merely "likkered up." He said that all it took for a meeting of the minds was to grab their two heads and bounce them off one another. That, he concluded, was that.

Irvine explained to Johnson that all lawbreakers were expected to be arrested and sent to Miles City for trial, but Johnson held to his own ways: He couldn't see throwing someone in jail if he could help resolve their differences "amicably."

Tom Irvine must have stared at him slack-jawed before finally recognizing defeat and conceding that, as long as Johnson was his deputy, he'd have to accept the man's unorthodox methods of enforcement. Irvine took the next stage home.

A local newspaper republished the original story of the showdown several years after its occurrence, albeit with a few embellishments added along the way:

> *Tom Irvine, of Miles City, Deputy collector of internal revenue, paid Billings a visit last week. In relating some old time reminiscences for*

which he is famed, he said that in the early days of Coulson while Tom was sheriff of Custer county, Liver-Eating Johnson was his deputy at that lively village. Repeated rumors of fights, assaults and affrays in Coulson floated down the Yellowstone and reached Tom at Miles City, but no persons were brought down to Miles nor apparently any arrests made. On visiting Coulson he interrogated Mr. Johnson on the subject and enquired why more of the numerous law breakers had not been apprehended. Calmly chewing a handful of Climax, Johnson said:

"Well, there is no jail here and I didn't think there was any use in makin' arrests. When a man breaks the peace I lick him, and in that way I manage to keep the town pretty orderly." This form of general return of legal business transacted satisfied Sheriff Irvine, who could appreciate a good thing, [even] if he did lose a lot of fees by it.

The writer well remembers when "Liver-Eating" was deputy at Coulson. On one occasion a six-foot cowboy got drunk and started in to paint the town the redest kind of red. "Liver-Eating" remonstrated, when the fellow suddenly hit him just the aft right ear. With an oath, Johnson turned, picked the man up as if he were a child and raising him above his head flung him to the floor. Bystanders supposed that every bone in the drunken man's body was broken, but after laying for a few minutes he picked himself up and disappeared. Johnson is over six feet tall and has a muscular frame, and boasts of having killed more Indians than any other man in Montana.[10]

No matter how exactly the matter transpired, the townspeople certainly appreciated Johnson's effective, if somewhat heavy-handed, methods of law enforcement nearly as much as they enjoyed gawking at the giant's well-worn buckskins. An article written in 1889 described Johnson's preference for wearing his traditional mountain man clothing while walking the streets of the towns for which he served as justice of the peace and county deputy sheriff:

[I]n dress, looks, and general outline, he [Johnson] is the typical character of the early hunter and trapper, and glories in the fact that the onward march of civilization has failed to make any impression on his frontier modes and habits of life. His hair and beard are still long

*and shaggy, and for wearing apparel he still clings with the greatest
tenacity to the skins of wild beasts, like the untutored savage.*[11]

No matter what his apparel, his methodology for keeping the peace
usually ran along the same line. "Well, boys," he'd tell the principals of
a skirmish as he yanked them apart, "this has gone far enough. And
whichever coon don't like it can meet me now, here on the spot, with fists,
knives, clubs, or guns."[12]

Some men, intent upon fighting regardless of the odds against it,
simply took their grievances out of town and beyond the long arm of the
law. Johnson didn't mind. Irvine had told him to keep the town's streets
safe. He'd said nothing about the outlying communities.

Of course, there were occasionally more serious matters with which
Johnson had to deal. A June 16, 1882, article in the *Coulson-Billings Post*
tells of one of them when "Deputy Sheriff Johnson passed through on
the stage en route to Deer Lodge with six sentenced prisoners in charge,
one of whom has engaged board and room for 30 years, his crime being
murder in the second degree. This trip of one deputy with six prisoners
from Miles City to Deer Lodge sounded like quite a feat, until it dawned
upon the compiler, that the super-officer was none but the redoubtable
'Liver Eating' Johnson."[13]

So, the town was happy with Johnson, Johnson was happy with the
town, and Irvine was stoic about the whole thing. And then it happened.

Ironically, Johnson may never have accepted the job as sheriff but for
the incident when Henry Lumph had gotten drunk and shot and killed
Johnson's predecessor and close friend, Deputy "Muggins" Taylor, after
Taylor had gone after Lumph for beating his wife at a local laundry in
Billings. Taylor had earlier won a reputation as an eyewitness to Custer's
Little Bighorn massacre and was one of the first to relay the details of
the battle to government officials. Before that, he'd been known as a crack
shot during battles with the Sioux at Fort Pease, a trading and trapping
station located on the Yellowstone River near where the Bighorn empties
into it.

As one story of Muggins's adventure goes, thirty hunters, trappers,
and wolfers had found themselves huddled inside the walls of the fort.

These included Muggins, X. Beidler, the McCormack brothers, and Liver-Eating Johnson. It was the winter of 1875, and the Sioux were angry partly because the wolfers had resorted to using strychnine to kill wolves to get their pelts, and, coincidentally, they killed more than an occasional pet dog or two of the Sioux.

Although there were thirty men at Fort Pease that day, they were armed with only fourteen rifles. The rest had been lost when a boat capsized on the Yellowstone. More men than rifles spelled trouble.

While waiting for reinforcements from a town located near present-day Billings, Muggins was peering out on a rise above the fort, observing the animated antics of a particular Sioux warrior. Raising his rifle, aiming, and holding his breath as he squeezed the trigger, Muggins let loose his volley. The Indian—more surprised even than Muggins—leaped into the air, clutched his chest, and fell without a word to the ground. Although Muggins later protested that the shot was "jest a fluke," and that "it couldn't be done agin' on a thousand trials," the others in the group attributed it to the sharpshooter's twenty-twenty eyesight and outstanding marksmanship:

> *Muggins was armed with a Colt repeating rifle, which had been given to him by a wealthy Eastern sportsmen who he had guided through Yellowstone Park on a hunting trip. . . . For several successive days, an Indian had appeared on an eminence at a considerable distance from the stockade, where he had gone through mocking antics and derisive gestures. . . . Rushing to one of the portholes, where he could get a careful rest, Taylor "drew down" on the defiant figure. "Crr-rack! W-h-a-m!" and as a cloud of smoke breezed away from the muzzle of his rifle, the interested watchers saw the Indian reel unsteadily and dizzily. Several within the stockade had field glasses trained on the distant redskin, and noted that he sank to the ground."*[14]

When years later Henry Lumph got the drop on Muggins Taylor in a bar in Coulson, everybody knew it was murder. If Johnson had been there, he might have faced a dilemma: Could Liver-Eater have killed another white man? Even one who had just killed his friend? As it was,

Johnson was out of town when Taylor was killed, and a local bartender arrested the intoxicated Lumph and had him sent off to neighboring Billings for trial.

Whether or not that incident played a part in Johnson's decision to take the position vacated by Taylor is unknown. Regardless, days after accepting the job of deputy sheriff, Johnson recalled that he had been in a black mood that day, wondering what he was doing living away from his beloved wilderness. When he spied his old pard Wind River Jake come riding down the street, Johnson's eyes lit up, and he rushed out to greet him. He was shocked to see how Jake's back was no longer erect in the saddle. He saw that his hair, which "nary an Injun" ever touched, had gone long and scraggly in the twenty years since they had seen one another last, and how the wrinkles converged upon his face.

Jake reined in his horse next to Johnson. Despite his age, he jumped down from his mount like a twenty-year-old. After hugging and patting his longtime friend on the back, Jake said that he'd just come from the Platte River with a message from Del Gue. Johnson asked what Jake was doing so far north with winter nipping at their heels. "Do you recall just how tough winter can be?" he asked the old man.

"Up on the Milk!" the trapper blurted out. "Toughest winter o' my life." That, he said, was what brought him to town. *Winter*. He had just begun laying in for the coming season when Del rode up and asked him to deliver a message to Liver-Eater the next time Jake went to town.

Arkansas Pete, Del told him, was on the Milk River across into Canada getting set for the winter's trapping. Pete was building a large cabin, and he wanted Johnson to share it with him. "You're a mountain man, not a tenderfoot!" Jake said, shaking his head. "Del says fer you to meet him on the Milk."

Jake had delivered his message in the shade of the feed store where he had originally met Johnson years before. Johnson led him to his shack of an office—a one-room cabin behind the store—and poured them each a hot cup of joe. Suddenly the older man spotted the faces on the wanted posters hanging on the wall. Sensing Johnson wavering in his resolve, Jake brought up a more persuasive point: All the men on the posters had either been captured or killed. It was clear: "They don't need no officer here!"

Johnson asked if Del would be on the Milk with Pete, too. Jake replied only if the Liver-Eater agreed to join them. The two men puffed on their pipes for several minutes before Johnson invited Jake to the stable to see his new horse. In the livery, Jake turned to his old pard. "Where'd you get this one?" he asked. Johnson replied that a rancher had given him the horse because Johnson had admired it so.

"And just like that, he up and give it to you?"

Johnson had to admit the story was a little more convoluted than that. The deputy sheriff had helped the rancher out of a poker-playing fracas with a notorious card shark. Johnson "convinced" the gambler to leave the money on the table and catch the next stage out of town. The horse, the rancher reckoned, was the least he could offer in appreciation.

The next day, when Jake headed off on the long return trip back up the Platte, he was confident that by the time Del reached Arkansas Pete's place, he'd find Johnson already there. He wasn't far wrong. Shortly after Jake left town, Johnson tendered his resignation. He re-leathered his horse's saddle for another season's use and laid in a good supply of rifle and revolver cartridges. He honed the blade of his bowie. And then, on one fine, crisp fall morning just twelve months after he had arrived in Coulson, he mounted his big black, took the reins of his packhorse in hand, and set off into the wild free winds blowing down from the mountains to the northwest—and into heaven.

At sixty-eight years of age, Johnson realized this might be his last foray into the wilderness.

He didn't know it yet, but he had just entered the last phase.

CHAPTER TWELVE

One Last Play

In an October 1965 article in *True West* magazine, Raymond W. Thorp retells the tale of a mountain of a man in the graying years of his life. After resigning from the office of deputy sheriff in October 1882, Johnson made good his plans to leave the citified confines to which he'd assigned himself and return to the wilderness.

"The big man who closed the door of his office in Coulson, Montana, in October, 1882," wrote Thorp, "had been the deputy sheriff of Custer County—later Yellowstone County. John Johnston had sent in his resignation to Tom Irvine, the sheriff, who lived in Miles City."[1]

Swinging from Johnson's waist was one of Mr. Colt's Peacemakers and a bowie knife with a foot-long blade. As he prepared to light out of town, he packed aboard a high-strung, muscular, midnight-black stallion some four years old and as powerful as its master. It was a good thing because Johnson, who normally weighed north of 220 pounds, had gained an extra 10 pounds or so since settling down to his more placid lifestyle. "The color of the animal," Thorp commented, "was traditional with Johnston, who had started out with a black pony in 1843 and would not use any other color in a mount."[2]

Old Joe Robidoux had sold Johnson his first horse when the easterner originally entered the western mountains with John Hatcher, a famous trailblazer who had spent time mentoring the younger man. The saddle had previously belonged to Big Anton Sepulveda, who had been killed by the Nez Perce Indians. Johnson had the saddle recovered and added a new boot to hold his needle gun, a deadly accurate .56-caliber buffalo rifle that he had carried for years.

Mounting up after checking his bedroll and supply of sugar, salt, coffee, and pipe tobacco, he set off on his last great adventure, his saddlebags ripe with ammunition for his rifle and the Colt revolver he used for close-in fighting.

Heading due north from the Yellowstone to the Musselshell, he had time to think about something Jake had told him. Del Gue, Johnson's frequent trading partner, was down on the Platte and would likely jump at the chance to join them again. It had been some time, and Liver-Eater looked forward to their reunion.

After several days on the trail, Johnson broke upon some timber in the Big Bend of the Musselshell, where lay the scarred remains of a burnt-out cabin he had helped rebuild for a crazed white widow. Her family had been killed by the Blackfeet, and she starved to death not long after during one especially frigid winter. The Crows, who hated the Blackfeet, believed the woman to be possessed by spirits and so interred her remains in a grave covered with stones.

Johnson looked out over the site, where not much remained other than three of the four poles that he had erected for the Crazy Woman after the Blackfeet had struck. She had burst in on the Indians raping and killing her daughter. A brutally swung ax dispatched four of them, and when Johnson stumbled upon the scene, he helped jam their heads atop the poles as a warning for others to stay clear.

The slaughter had taken place near sundown, and rumors persisted that the woman's plaintive wails rang out every night hence. Johnson was far from superstitious, but he nonetheless goaded his stallion around the eerie site until they were out of the tall timbers again.

Nosing his horse west toward Fort McKenzie, Johnson passed near the Little Rockies where his partner Bear Claw Lapp had been murdered by the Blackfeet while he sat in his cabin. As Thorp recalled,

"When Johnson and Hatchet Jack Ireland came across Lapp's body, they tracked and caught up with the murderers. Jack is said to have scalped them with his hatchet before plucking out their eyes with his bowie knife and finally killing them."[3]

As Johnson continued on, he stumbled upon a small settlement of a couple dozen families that had only recently been founded and, noticing a small store there, dismounted to buy some tobacco and salt. Before long, several young boys and a few curious adults had wandered over. The bravest of the boys asked if Johnson was a trapper, according to Thorp, to which he replied, "Yes, laddie, fer a long time." His bearlike size and flaming-red beard had intimidated most of those gazing upon the beast until one man worked up the courage to ask, "Ye air Liver-Eatin' Johnson, ain't ye? I useter live down at Taos when I war a young feller, an' heerd about ye from Bill Bent."

Johnson looked him over carefully before replying. "I knowed Bill Bent. Took in a ketch thar now an' then. Ol' John Hatcher war my pardner then."

Johnson paid for his goods, walked out, and mounted the black before riding off. The man who had confronted him turned out to be Ed Johnson, from whose biography the character of "The Virginian" was molded years later. The man went on to admit, "I guess he knew I was lyin'. I never knew Bill Bent—jest wanted to make talk an' look him [Johnson] over."[4]

Johnson proceeded west past old Fort McKenzie, stopping when necessary to kill game. Once he came across a large mountain lion and brought him down with a single shot between the eyes. The predatory animals were a delicacy to most mountain folks, Johnson included.

Sitting around the campfire that night, he recollected a hunting party of Piegans he had met along the trail north of the fort. He immediately recognized one of their maids as Waving Grass, who had earlier traveled with him during the Indian Wars and may have actually saved his life. When she left him to return to the stockade at Knife River, Johnson loaded two packhorses with gifts that he gave to her and her tribe. The Indians were so appreciative that they warned him of the Assiniboine who were warring with the whites.

By the time Johnson reached the Canadian border, travel had become rougher, but his big black mount had been bred to endure the hardships of winter and actually thrived in the bitter weather. As Johnson approached the Milk, he spied Pete's cabin set below a low bluff. With the warnings of the Assiniboine still resonating in his head, he proceeded cautiously, moving his horse around to the rear of the cabin, where it was disguised by a thick band of willows.

The sun was already low in the sky, and Johnson thought it peculiar that no smoke snaked out of Pete's chimney. He saw that the corral was empty as well—another suspicious sign. Convinced finally that the cabin was clear, he nosed his horse around to the front and dismounted when he heard the call of a kettle of vultures circling the bluff behind him.

Cautiously, he entered the cabin to find it had been ransacked. Pete had done a good job in building it. The crude homemade furniture included a pair of straw bunks. Beyond the main room sat another smaller area for storing the season's catch. Johnson went back outside, remounted, and rode up to the top of the bluff. There he found the scattered remains of a dismembered corpse. Taking a closer look, he recognized the grimaced face with one missing tooth up front as Pete's.

Looking around, he spotted an old Bible near the body. He knew the story of that Bible: Mormon Jake had once stolen two Bibles from a church and given one to Pete, and since neither Jake nor Pete could read, they asked a more educated companion to mark the passages that they had come to memorize. He guessed that the Arkansan had been "reading" it when he was ambushed and killed.

Johnson examined the body: Pete's chest had been smashed to bits by a large-caliber shell. "Needle gun," he whispered, recalling how Hatchet Jack had once captured and hanged two white traders who had sold such guns to the Indians who had killed Chris Lapp.

As Johnson walked around the site, he noticed a thick stand of willows nearby that might have concealed the murderer. He looked further, stumbling across signs that pointed in one direction: "Assiniboine!" He judged from the condition of the body that Pete had been killed the day before. He would need to avenge his old pard's death, without saying. He was relieved that the murderer hadn't been part of an entire war party.

Returning to the cabin, Johnson unsaddled and unpacked his horse, turning it loose with some dried oats he found in Pete's stockade. Back inside, he felt a sense of remorse that all of Pete's hard work and good intentions—not to mention Johnson's own long journey—had come to nothing. He built a small fire, chewed on some pemmican (dried meat pounded into bits and mixed with fat, an Indian staple) he had brought with him, and wolfed down a few of Pete's biscuits that the Assiniboine had overlooked. All the while, he was devising a plan. Later that evening, he knocked the ashes from the bowl of his pipe, lay flat on his back on the floor, and fell asleep.

"He was up long before daybreak," according to Thorp, "and went to the top of the bluff where he gathered up Pete's body parts and skull, placed them in a feedbag, and brought them back to the cabin. Setting them off in one corner, he said, 'I'll bury ye when I git yer scalp an' the topknot frum thet Injun.' He knew that Pete would rest better knowing that. He did not take food along with him since the Assiniboine was well fixed in that respect. When the red ball of the sun shone through the haze on the river, the Liver-Eater was on the trail. Nothing but an act of God could save the murdering redskin now."[5]

Johnson knew from experience that the main camp of the Assiniboine was on the Saskatchewan River; it made sense that his quarry would head for that. He had no trouble following the Indian's trail. He had five horses with him, carving out a path wide enough for even a tenderfoot to follow. And, since the Indian had come upon Pete alone, he'd never suspect that anyone would be trailing him. But he would learn. All in good time.

That night brought the first bone-rattling cold of the season. The geese overhead signaled their flight south. The following morning, according to Thorp, "the Indian fired into a V-shaped flock with his needle-gun and scored a hit."[6]

On his second night out, the Assiniboine appeared to have camped on the banks of a small stream. He had brushed away the snow to form a clearing and staked out his remuda of animals before chopping a hole in the ice to get water. He built a roaring fire from seasoned driftwood, smashed some of the stolen coffee beans on a rock, and made a pot of java. He had skewered the legs of the goose on a spit and mixed Pete's flour with water to make browned biscuits in Pete's bread pan. As he went to wash the sticky dough from his hands, he heard a voice behind him and froze. The brave looked over his shoulder to find Johnson casually rubbing his hands over the far side of the fire.

Johnson eyed the Indian suspiciously. The brave considered his situation for a moment. His rifle leaned against a tree closer to the intruder than to himself. His tomahawk lay ten feet away where he'd pounded the beans into grounds. His knife was in his belt, but he hesitated to draw it because of the slick dough on his hands.

Johnson asked if the Assiniboine minded some company for dinner before the Indian flipped the dough from his right hand and reached for his knife. Before he could pull it from its sheath, Johnson leaped across the fire, grabbed the Indian's arm, and snapped it at the wrist before unleashing a mule kick to the man's groin. He grabbed a burning stick and shoved it into the brave's eyes. Screaming in agony, the Indian staggered back, and Johnson landed a blow to his neck that broke the man's jaw. He quickly pulled his knife and scalped the Indian before settling down to a steaming hot meal of two goose legs and freshly brewed coffee. He rounded up the horses and, gathering the big black in with the others, hobbled them in the creek bank, then served out some of the shelled oats that the Assiniboine had taken from Pete's cabin.

Later that night, Johnson cut out the Indian's liver and lifted it up to the heavens. He thought for several seconds about biting into it before deciding otherwise. He had no truck with the Assiniboine, and until he could think of some other use for the memento, he placed it in the crotch of a tree. After emptying one last pipe of tobacco, he stoked the fire, rolled himself up in his buffalo robe, and fell off into a light sleep.

By morning, the snow that had begun falling during the night was so thick he could hardly tell the time of day. He reopened the hole in the ice for the horses to drink and gave them more oats before packing up for the trip back to Pete's cabin. Before he left, he retrieved the Indian's liver—by then frozen solid—and mounted the black. He would decide what to do next once he arrived back at the cabin.

On the morning of the fifth day out—he had figured the remainder of the goose would last that long—he saw the long, snowy stretch that was the Milk River. When he came toward Pete's bluff, he stopped and circled around. Leaving his little horse herd on the bank near the thick stand of shrubs from which Pete's killer had operated, he crawled to the top of the bluff and looked down. Smoke poured from the cabin's chimney. When he had taken off after the murderous redskin, he had brought along only his knife, knowing that the Indian would have plenty of guns, including Pete's rifle and revolver. Now, looking over the bluff, he had the Assiniboine's needle gun at the ready.

He nested the stock against his shoulder and waited until he saw some movement inside. Within seconds, the front door opened. The three sharp clicks from cocking the weapon caused the occupant to hesitate a split second before leaping back to safety.

As Johnson evaluated the situation, his eyes fell on a single jug-headed horse inside the corral. Only one man in the entire Rocky Mountain West rode a jug-headed mount like that. He let out a sigh, retrieved the remuda, and led the animals down off the bluff to the cabin where he called out to his old trapping *compañero*, Del Gue.

REUNITED

After catching up on one another's lives, Del and Liver-Eater set about the task of daily life, salvaging whatever of old Pete's things they found around the cabin and in the shed. The two men stayed the entire winter, running Pete's trap lines and hunting. Pete had selected all the best sites long before the snows had come, and it was easy for the mountain men to find them by the crude map he had drawn up before his death.

One day, Del—his troubled look betraying an overactive mind—approached Johnson about his having cut out the liver from the Indian he'd killed. He had never appreciated the stories about Johnson and the birth of his moniker, which made him "queasy." Johnson took a long hard look at his partner and told him he'd wondered when Del was going to spit out what was grinding on him. Johnson told him he had only taken the liver to make the Assiniboine *think* he had cut it out and eaten it. Del, not quite sure if that story was true, nonetheless knew when not to press the mountain man and let the matter drop. For the time being.

The partners continued their trapping through March. Their catch consisted mostly of marten, otter, and beaver mixed in with the occasional wolf and fox. The back room was filled with valuable furs.

On those nights when the winds howled—barking their warnings to mere mortal men—and the thermometer plummeted to 45°F below, Gue and Johnson worked on their pelts and their equipment in the comparative warmth of the cabin, retelling old tales and occasionally fabricating new ones. One of Johnson's favorites involved being captured by the Blackfeet but escaping after knocking the guard out and cutting off his leg. Naked to the waist, Johnson had walked a distance of two hundred miles to Gue's cabin, nibbling on the leg for sustenance as he went. Gue, as Thorp recalled, said he would never forget the sight that frigid winter's night:

> "When ye opened the door . . . ye pretty nigh scared me to death," Del said.
>
> "Aw, thet wuzn't no cold winter," replied Johnston. "When I rode wi' Portygee Phillips ter Laramie Fort, thet war ther coldest."
>
> They wrangled back and forth, straining their memories, until Del changed the subject. "Member Leadville," he asked, "an' ol' Ben Raymond? He kilt thet Cheyenne whut ambushed Yankee Judd, a likely lad."
>
> "Yas, Wil' Ben, we called him," replied Johnston, "an' the lad wuz a partner o' White Eye. Wonder whar thet coon went?"
>
> "He's down in Arizony," volunteered Del. "He's got him a gol' mine thar." They both agreed that a gold mine was a good thing to own.
>
> "Beats trappin'," said Johnston, filling, tamping, and lighting his pipe.[7]

With the dawning of the first spring thaw, the two partners packed up their baled pelts and prepared for the trip south. The last thing Johnson did before leaving had become his calling card. Extracting a burning brand from the fireplace, he set fire to Pete's cabin. Gue knew what that meant: They would never be back that way again. He had watched many a cabin burn to the ground when Johnson was through and ready to move on. He had seen Hatcher's home on the Little Snake River go up in flames. It was where Johnson's wife had been killed and scalped by the Crows, the event that had started the Crow Killer's bloody vendetta.

Before mounting his black stallion, Johnson tied a sack to the saddle horn. Inside were Arkansas Pete Arnold's skull and bones, his old gray scalp, and the topknot of the Assiniboine who had done him in. Johnson planned on burying it all in the country Pete had roamed all his adult life, down on the Yellowstone. As Gue looked at the sack, he thought of that old mausoleum on the Little Snake where Liver-Eater had buried the bones of his wife and child with the scalp of the brave who had killed them, accompanied by a few body ornaments and other mementos.

Johnson rattled the sack and nodded toward Del, saying he guessed they'd take care of "this ol' coon back home." And, with the stallion leading the small train southward, they rode off, neither man looking back at the blazing flames. Mountain men, once pointed right, never look back.

HEADED HOME

When the partners finally arrived back home on the Yellowstone, they constructed a small cabin from which to fish and hunt. But once again, something was gnawing at Gue, and Johnson saw it right off. He asked him outright.

The shorter man stroked his frizzy beard for several moments before blurting it out, according to Thorp:

> "Ye did eat that Injun's liver, didn't ye?"
>
> "So thet's whut is botherin' ye?" Johnson grinned. "Look hyar, son."
>
> Reaching up, he took his possibles sack from a peg on the cabin wall. Gue's eyes bugged out when he pulled out a beautiful otter skin he'd never seen before. Johnson said he'd saved it while they sold all the other pelts. Johnson laid it across his knees. "I traded thet thar Injun liver fer this," he said, stroking the pelt casually.

"Hell-a-mighty," the bewhiskered trapper said. "Ye baited a trap wi' [that]?"

"Done it fer ol' Pete's sake," Johnson replied as they took turns admiring the trophy.[8]

That fall, after a successful year of trapping, Gue saddled his mount and prepared to move on. Johnson asked where he was going, and Gue said somewhere off toward the Gila River. He asked if Johnson wanted to ride along. The man thought for several seconds before shaking his head, saying he guessed he'd spend his days right where they were.

Gue mounted up and reached down to shake the bearlike paw of his close friend. Both had seen partners die, burned at the stake, mauled to death by wild animals, frozen solid with the life ripped from their bodies, and succumbed to the hatchets and knives of crazed red men. Both had lived an eternity, marching in and out of one another's lives. But on this day, the parting was quick and casual, as befit the lives of two mountain men. Perhaps that was because they never expected this to be the last time they would lay eyes on one another. Or perhaps it was because forty years to some were like forty *minutes* to them.

As Johnson retreated into the cabin to get some more tobacco, Del sidled his mount down the riverbank veering south. He never looked back. He knew that behind his longhorn whiskers lay secrets about his companion that no one else knew—or could possibly even imagine. He knew, too, that the day would dawn when he would spill those secrets like bears' claws from a leather sack. And Liver-Eating Johnson would live again.

As for Johnson, he remained at the cabin to hunt and trap until, in time, wanderlust got the better of him once more. He moved on to Red Lodge, Montana, where he obtained a section of land near the town in Montana Territory—a full 160 acres—and built yet another cabin on Rock Creek.

Red Lodge, which was founded as a mining town in 1887 with the establishment of the Rocky Fork Coal Mine, became a stopover for the Northern Pacific Railroad to take on coal for its engines. As the town's prosperity grew, so too did its population. The locals soon realized they needed a lawman, and Johnson's arrival seemed propitious. They offered him the position of town marshal, and he accepted it. Even four years following Gue's departure, X. Beidler, the Vigilante Chief of Virginia City, said of the Liver-Eater, "He's of magnificent physique, and fit to take a hand with anyone that wishes to collide with him."[9]

A studio photograph of Johnson taken in 1889 shows the officer posing with a Winchester rifle and wearing a pistol, or "short arm" as Johnson called it, at his side—although in his police action, he rarely used either. His friend Ben Greenough detailed the method used most often by Johnson in keeping the peace in Red Lodge:

> *Liver-Eating Johnston was . . . over six feet tall, weighed 220 pounds, wore size 12 shoes. I remember one time, I was in an old saloon (George Howard's) near where Red Lodge high school is now. I was playing Pin Pool with an old timer called Jack the Ripper. There was two little old Scotch miners, drunk and fighting on the floor. Johnston happened to pass by, looked in and saw them. He came in and picked them both off the floor, one under each arm. There was only plank sidewalks and a hitch pole, where they tied their saddled horses and teams in front of saloons and stores. Johnston walked out with those two men under his arms, fighting and cussing, laid them across the hitch post, banged their heads together, dropped them both down in the dirt, walked off and left them lying there. I thought he had killed them. They laid there for a few moments, then both got up and put their arms around each other—fight all out of them both, sober by that time.*[10]

Johnson wasn't so formidable a foe to *all* the residents of Red Lodge, though. To the small boys of the town, he was a hero, albeit one about whom dreadful tales were told. He had nevertheless by the sheer positive aspect of his nature managed to befriend them. One local, Ralph Lumley, recalled a typical incident sixty years later:

> *I was a small boy at the time he was town marshal here, and he was sure kind to the kids. A road show would be put on in town. The show*

hall as it was called had a large window in the back, and at that time money was scarce with children. There was a saloon adjoining the show hall and they used to throw out the empty beer barrels, and by placing a couple of these barrels alongside of the window we could see the show in progress.

One time four kids was standing on two barrels when we heard a booming voice say "Get down off them barrels" and he pulled us down by the seats of the pants. I was in one of those seats. Two boys got away and we thought they were sure lucky not to have to go to jail. The marshal was a big man and he had on a bigger overcoat as it was winter. He took us to the front of the show, slapped his overcoat open and put it around us, one on each side, and walked right in without the ticket taker knowing what had been done. He sure liked the kids and sure had a kind heart toward them. The other boys were sorry they had run away.[11]

CHAPTER THIRTEEN

The Great Rocky Mountain Wild West Show

FRONTIERSMAN THOMAS WILBUR HARDWICK WAS BORN IN CARROLL-ton, Missouri, in 1844, at a spot that was less than forty miles from where he died in 1901. His father had been a slave owner, and when the Civil War broke out, the son enlisted in the Confederate army. Failing to see action, he mustered out at war's end and became a buffalo hunter and plainsman. Roaming throughout the Midwest, he learned the topography of the country so well that he soon became an invaluable scout for the US Army. His quests for buffalo, wolves, and other large game took him as far north as Montana and the Dakotas and along the boundary of "British America," Canada, where he frequently encountered and clashed with warring Indian tribes.

Growing up with his parents, Hardwick traveled to California in 1850, and that, along with his later travels, made him a reliable source of information for nearly every state west of the Mississippi River. His knowledge of the country, along with his abilities as an interpreter (he spoke several Indian languages and also understood and used sign language), made him valuable to the US Department of War as a scout and a guide on numerous expeditions.

Along the paths of his many journeys, he met and became close friends with Colonel William Cody ("Buffalo Bill"), James Butler Hickok ("Wild Bill"), W. F. "Doc" Carver, and other great frontiersmen, as well as with General George Armstrong Custer and other military fig-

James Butler "Wild Bill" Hickok, 1837–1876, earned national fame as a drover, teamster, soldier, spy, scout, lawman, gunfighter, gambler, showman, and—finally—an actor whose path crossed that of Liver-Eating Johnson late in life.
COURTESY LIBRARY OF CONGRESS

ures scattered across the West. He was only fourteen miles from the scene of the Custer massacre and must have heard the echoes of the powder shots. After the battle ended, Hardwick swore to avenge his comrades by killing as many Indians as possible, but he killed most by his hands either in self-defense or to prevent thievery.

While working as a scout, according to rumor, Hardwick never slept under one roof. He was in the saddle and on the trail continually. An expert horseman, he once claimed he was never thrown from an animal—not even the wildest of stallions.

Before long, his reputation spread. Tom Hardwick was known throughout the West, particularly in South Dakota, where he made his home in his later years, and at Fort Benton on the Yellowstone River, where he lived for several years more. Although a brave man and one who had experienced more than his share of thrilling and bloody battles with the wildest of men of all creeds and colors, he was reticent, rarely speaking of his own exploits or achievements without a fair amount of prompting.

Hardwick spent a good deal of time in Montana, where he raised horses and achieved considerable notoriety after Indians from Canada crossed the border and stole some of his best broncos. Hardwick and some friends tracked them down across the border, where they attacked the Indian camp—a less than judicious thing to do. Although Hardwick recovered his stolen horses, he ended up serving nearly two years in prison in Helena for violating border agreements.[1]

On another occasion, according to legend, Hardwick erected a fortification on the Yellowstone River to be used as a trading station. Leaving it in charge of nine men, he went off on one of his usual journeys. When word reached him that the fort was under siege by a band of more than 150 warring Indians, he took out. One of the men assigned to the fort had been out fishing when the attack occurred, and he wisely lay low while trying to decide what to do next. His men had nearly exhausted their ammunition and were just about out of food and water. Hardwick and fifteen of his followers closed in on the besieged garrison. He drove away the troop of Indians ten times their number, saving the lives of the white men in the fort.

When the rescue party found the man who had been hiding in the bushes, his hair and beard, which formerly had been coal black, had mysteriously turned white. Hardwick took that as an omen of a prosperous future.

Returning to Deadwood, he convinced William Skeigle to partner with him in gathering together a number of friends, cronies, and peaceful Indians to begin touring the country with the Hardwick Great Wild West Show, as it was originally billed. He hoped to capitalize on the phenomenal success of the dozens of similar shows that had already popped up across the West, beating even the best-known of all western extravaganzas—Buffalo Bill's Wild West show—to the punch.

Among the "pards" Hardwick engaged for the tour was a fellow associate from the Black Hills, where he had once been appointed deputy sheriff. She was the raucous frontierswoman named Martha Jane Can-nary, better known as Calamity Jane. Calamity had already developed a remarkable dime-novel reputation that proved an asset both to herself and to Hardwick as he prepared to tour the Midwest in 1884.

Calamity had previously appeared in a theatrical show called, surprisingly enough, Calamity Jane, which offered a combination of talent featuring former army scouts and a party of Crow Indians. The newspapers reported that the Indians would "be arrayed in feather costumes and . . . carry with them their ponies, tepees and everything necessary to furnish a true picture of savage life and customs"[2] on the plains.

This article appeared on September 7, 1883, in Kansas's Atchison Daily Champion:

> Calamity Jane *is a wild and wooly show, replete with the most thrilling scenes and startling sensation that ever froze the blood or chilled the heart. The public had been, to some extent, prepared for the horrors of the entertainment, by the street parade, which commenced early in the forenoon and let up at sundown. It was a grand spectacular parade, consisting principally of a bear, a nigger and a jackass, led on by Calamity Jane herself and a tuneful brass band. The audience at the show was not up to the manager's highest hopes, but it was enthusiastic all the same, and frequently whooped and laughed when the other thing was expected. Men were killed right and left and re-appeared and were slaughtered again with a brutality that tasted of the real Wild Bill sort of border life. In the last scene Calamity Jane got in her work beautifully, made all the villains bite the dust, and married her "best man."*

Hardwick's Great Rocky Mountain Wild West Show, as the showman rechristened it, was one of several early efforts to assemble an authentic cast of western characters to tour eastern cities. Within a short period of time, several dozen touring companies were crisscrossing the nation, including the Buffalo Bill, Pawnee Bill, and Doc Carver shows that dominated the scene. Hardwick's troupe faced stiff competition from the likes of Sitting Bull and Buffalo Bill, whose carefully scripted, professionally presented shows had been choreographed by none other than T. N. Newson, who had written a popular drama about Calamity Jane in 1878.

Not to be left behind in the Halls of Yellow Journalism, Liver-Eating Johnson stumbled onto his fifteen minutes of show-biz fame when the Great Rocky Mountain Wild West Show began its tour of Bismarck in May 1884. "The band of Crow Indians who under the lead of Liver Eating Johnson are starting out for a starring trip in the east, showed in Bismarck a few nights ago," reported one Montana newspaper. It went on to write that the legendary John Liver-Eating Johnson, one of the show's featured attractions, had reportedly eaten the livers of the Crow Indians he killed after they murdered his family.[3]

On May 22, 1884, the Lewistown, Montana, Fergus County Argus memorialized the troupe's departure for parts east, writing:

> *Among the band of Crow Indians that recently went east were Old Crow, Curley, Liver Eating Johnson, and others. They carried with them Icheg, a horse that survived the Custer massacre, and White-head's famous bucking pony. The troupe will be exhibited under the management of F.R.N. Rogers, an enterprising Englishman of Custer [South Dakota].*

The legends of both Calam and Liver-Eater notwithstanding, the real star of Hardwick's show was Curley, the Indian scout billed as the only survivor of Custer's Last Stand. The crowds always yelled and cheered the loudest when he survived the reenacted Little Bighorn massacre time and again.

After finishing up their performances in Bismarck, the troupe's itinerary appears to have continued through Minnesota and Wisconsin before finally reaching Chicago. Apparently, the show had begun that leg of its tour without Calamity. As the caravan progressed eastward, however, Hardwick returned to Montana "to purchase more ponies and secure the services of several cowboys" as added attractions. According to the Billings Post, "The erratic female, known as Calamity Jane, who was one of the first stampeders into the Black Hills country, left on Monday's train to join the Liver Eating Johnson troupe." The newspaper rather ungraciously noted that "Calamity is not so attractive in appearance as she was in the early days of Deadwood."[4] Subsequently, Montana newspapers referred to Hardwick's Great Rocky Mountain Wild West Show as the "Calamity Jane–Liver Eating Johnson Combination," in deference to their celebrity performers.

By late June, shortly after Calamity Jane had rejoined the show, Hardwick began encountering problems. Several Crow Indians had folded up their tents and returned home. "Old Crow, String Leg, and one who couldn't give his English name" stopped at the office of the St. Paul newspaper, according to local reports, and said they were stranded. They hoped to find work "to earn their way back to Fort Custer, Montana, their home." When Hardwick was asked about the situation, he denied the show was in any kind of financial trouble.[5]

But the enterprise was actually mired in dire straits. Newspapers detailed both the show's performances and its increasingly desperate financial situation. Advertisements preceding the June 3, 1884, arrival of the Great Rocky Mountain Wild West Show at Janesville, Wisconsin, described it as "a vivid and thrilling illustration of wild western life" and claimed that at least "one thousand men, women, Indians, squaws and animals are connected with this show." Highlighted in the publicity was Curley, "the only survivor of the Custer massacre." The newspaper observed: "If half that is advertised is performed, it will afford amusement enough for anyone."[6]

The Janesville festivities began with a parade to the fairgrounds— standard fare for such performances, designed to whet the appetites of the locals. That was highlighted by afternoon and evening performances. About a hundred Crow Indians, cowboys, and animals performed "quite a number of lively and startling acts which kept the audience awake at least," the newspaper reported, "and made some of them take a good care that they did not lose their heads." The reporter seemed most impressed by the presentation of "Custer's last battle, showing the position of the troops and of the Indians, and how Curley, one of Custer's scouts, made his escape."[7]

The enactment proved hugely popular, and the troupe departed for nearby Milwaukee on July 4, where they repeated their skits. According to several Milwaukee newspapers, between seven and ten thousand people attended the afternoon performance. One reporter, describing the attack on the emigrant train and stagecoach, said, "When the red devils bound their unfortunate captives to the stake, preparatory to burning them alive, the excitement of the vast crowd became intense; and when the daring scouts came gallantly to the rescue, dispersing the Indians and releasing the captives, they were greeted with a round of applause." Another reporter rated the show "fully equal" to the more famous "Buffalo Bill combination," and commented that the stage passengers recruited from the audience were robbed "in a manner that would do Jesse James credit."[8]

Despite large crowds and positive reviews, financial conditions worsened due to increased competition and poor management. Soon, newspapers reported that the exhibition was "temporarily stranded in Milwaukee." In fact, the show remained in Milwaukee for the balance of that week, charging 10 cents for a visit to the Indian camp and an admission fee of 25 cents for adults (10 cents for children).[9] By July 18, the troupe had finally earned enough money to enable them to leave for Chicago, where they hoped to make a killing.

Calamity Jane is not mentioned in the midwestern shows' billings, although she should have arrived before the performances in Janesville and Milwaukee. She may have failed to catch up with the troupe in time to be featured in the publicity. Although Curley continued to receive most of the attention from the press, Hardwick was considered the "chief attraction," giving "a graphic illustration of how he once saved a family of emigrants from being burned at the stake, after being captured by hostile redskins." The only other performer to receive individual mention was Liver-Eating Johnson, misidentified by the Chicago Times as "Lion-Eating Johnson," who "appeared in the scene of the rescue of the treasure-coach from the road-agents."[10]

Only in America.

Despite all best efforts, the show's financial problems grew. The cowboys added to Hardwick's headaches, going on a drunken shooting spree one night in downtown Chicago. The police confiscated "twelve large navy revolvers and a knife" from them after they were arrested. The culprits were fined $3 each for disorderly conduct and $5 for carrying deadly weapons. Calamity may have been among them, although it's unlikely that Johnson was sociable enough to have invited himself along. That afternoon, the troupe "gave their usual exhibition to a crowd of 12,000 people."[11]

Shortly afterward, the cowboys approached the proprietors for their wages, which they hadn't received for some time. The local papers said that "hot words were exchanged and revolvers drawn." Once again, proprietors T. W. Hardwick and William Skeigle were unable to make payment, and the partnership collapsed.[12] The Decatur *(IL)* Daily Republican covered the incident in this way in its July 24, 1884, edition:

> *A number of the attaches of the Rocky Mountain show exhibiting in this city invaded "the levee" Saturday night, and put in practice the tactics with which they sometimes clean out Western towns. Pistol shots were fired as the party passed Fourth avenue and Clark street, and a small-sized reign of terror was inaugurated by the frontier tactics of the drunken scouts. Their pastime was stopped, however, by Detectives Granger and Jones, who took ten of them to the Armory and booked them for disorderly conduct. One of the party gave the name of "Slow-Trail Jack." The whole party was dressed in regulation border costumes, and each had a large revolver and bowie-knife slung at his belt. They, at least, looked dangerous.*

The Chicago newspaper Inter Ocean had yet a slightly different take on the story in its July 30, 1884, issue:

> *T. W. Hartwick and William Skakle [sic], the late proprietors of the Rocky Mountain Show, were fined in Justice Rees' Court at Hyde Park yesterday. While camp was being broke Monday night the cowboys approached the proprietors for money, when warm words were exchanged, revolvers were flourished, and a cowboy came out of the fracas with a decorated eye.*

The return to Montana of the Crow Indians with "their ponies, buffaloes and other paraphernalia" was reported by the Livingston Daily Enterprise on August 8.

The next week, "the portly form of John Johnson, better known as Liver Eating Johnson," was again seen on the streets of Billings. "He had a good time," the Enterprise said, "but we understand that the company did not make a financial success of their exhibition."

Calamity Jane's return to Montana was not mentioned, but the New North-West newspaper of Deer Lodge, Montana, reported on August 22 that "the Calamity Jane–Liver Eating Johnson–Crow Indian–Cowboy Combination called Hardwick's show, busted in Chicago. The members of the circus were not paid by the manager, and were forced to sell their ponies in order to get back to Montana."

After Hardwick's performers had all returned home, newspapers announced that Calamity was leaving Montana for Wyoming, apparently spurred on by reports of a gold discovery near Buffalo. And Johnson, ever bonded to his beloved Montana, returned to his former job as a deputy sheriff in Coulson.

Which at least was a bit more reliable than show biz.

Chapter Fourteen

Peace at Last

On January 21, 1892, Liver-Eater paid a call on Judge McAnnelly in Red Lodge, where Johnson was in the midst of serving a seven-year stint as the town's constable. A reporter for Montana's *Helena Independent*, present at the time, reported the sheriff's comments:

> *"Liver-Eating Johnson" was in Judge McAnnelly's office, down in Red Lodge, the other day, and he entertained the boys for an hour or more by detailing some of his experiences in the early days. It is probable he did not intend they should be printed, but Harry H. Howe was present. In the current issue of the* Bozeman Courier *the latter had one story published.*
>
> *"When I struck Bozeman," said Johnson, "many years ago, I was dead broke, and as the place had only a name and nothing else to speak of, you bet it looked a little rocky to a man with my attenuated exchequer. However, Tracy had a tater patch just about where the heart of the town now is, and I struck him for a job. It was the harvest time for taters, so he gave me a contract by the day to yank out the tubers. Folks didn't work for nothing those days, so when the job was finished I had some dust in my buckskin purse.*
>
> *"Winter came early that year, so I made up my mind to get out on the trail and hunt game for the camp. Sam Turner, of the East Gallatin, and some others wanted me to go with them, and, as they claimed to be old mountain men from way back, I concluded to join my forces with theirs. Well, we started and had just got fairly into the*

mountains when on come the biggest snowstorm I ever saw. We had only one sack of flour, and I tell you that went mighty fast. We was on Twenty-five Yard creek when our flour gave out, and I made up my mind to strike back for the settlements. We were three days without anything to eat, and on the evening of the fourth made camp in a big quaking aspen grove. I got the boys started to make a fire, when I told them I would go out and get some game if there was a hoof left in the country.

"Now, I did not expect to get any big game, for they were all snowed under, but I traveled around about twenty miles and brought back six of the biggest jack rabbits I ever saw. Of course, I was a little tired, for the snow was breast high and I couldn't keep my usual gait. When I got back to camp, you ought to have seen that fire! It wasn't big enough to cover the bottom of a small frying pan, and the boys were huddled over it with their hands touching. They would have frozen to death, sure, in twenty minutes, if I had not come. I put them to work skinning the rabbits, while I put on four or five cords of wood, and you bet I had a fire. I cooked the rabbits and let them have every bit of them, for I knew how to live for a while without cooked grub. That night while they were sleeping in the grove, I went to work to keep the fire going, and also to get a little exercise and I was never more surprised in my life when morning came and I saw that I had cleaned up all the trees in a nine acre grove, just to keep one camp fire burning.

"You bet, when I make a fire it is a fire.

"Well, for two weeks I kept the boys in rabbits and the fires a-going, and never eat a bit of cooked grub. How did I live? Why, as I walked along I would just grab pine boughs right and left and eat them on the jump. The great objection to this kind of fodder is the general sameness of flavor, and then, too, a fellow has to keep up a continual munch, but it's somewhat fillin' and keeps one spry on his feet. However, I can't say I pine for this sort of fodder.

"Did I experience any bad effects, Judge, from these rations of Mother Nature? None that I can recall at this late date, only that Dutch John, who kept the restaurant at Bozeman, charged me for *five meals when I had only taken one, and, oh yes, it seems that I ate more of those boughs than I imagined for when I changed my toggery I found that my shirt, from its northernmost point to its southernmost extremity, was the loveliest and loudest green ever seen on canvas or in nature."*

The always gruff, often feisty, fearless, and imaginative Liver-Eating Johnson couldn't have resisted relaying that story to the judge. Mountain men, even after they'd become "tenderfeets," couldn't help but exaggerate their wilderness exploits while sitting around the campfire or, apparently, some magistrate's office. Johnson was no exception. Nor did he shrink from any opportunity to express his true feelings about any subject that happened to stagger across the open range of his mind, as was the case in this open letter he wrote the following spring to the *Red Lodge Picket*, dated May 27, 1893:

To THE EDITOR OF THE PICKET: I now take the opportunity of writing you so that people can know of the whereabouts of Liver Eating Johnson. At present he is living on a ranch and hopes to continue doing so. He has done all that he can to assist in opening the country. He is not one of the three mouths men who wear their hair long and hunt up a crowd in order to tell of their experience. As to what he has been, it amounts to naught. He has never done any very marvelous deeds, but what he has done was done with a will. Such men as many people are looking for nowadays, like Frank Miles and Yellowstone Kelly, are plenty. The latter man is one of the long haired scouts. I have been with him a great deal and failed to see any of good qualities. He got a great name by drawing figures on the trees and telling the officers that the Indians had done it, and that he laid behind the hills and watched them. Anyone who is acquainted with the ways of the Indian knows that they do not do such things. No one ever saw long hair on my head, or did I ever tell tales. I hope that Frank Miles will do well and all of the rest of them. – Yours truly, John Johnson.

It's not apparent why Johnson had such a low opinion of Kelly. The two had spent time scouting together during the Indian Wars, when Kelly had only good things to say about the veteran. But once Liver-Eater made up his mind, he never shied away from speaking it.

One of Johnson's last acts as constable of Red Lodge unfolded on June 21, 1894. He was by then sixty-nine years of age, soon to turn seventy. But he was still spry enough to get around—and to stay one jump ahead of an angry mob, as evidenced by this article appearing in the *Butte Miner* on June 21, 1894:

> *Freund [sic] Ladhoff, who murdered Patrick Cannon at Red Lodge Tuesday morning, was brought here this morning by Constable Johnson and placed in the county jail. The murder seems to have been an unprovoked and cold-blooded affair. The men are reported to have had no quarrel and no reason can be assigned for the awful deed. They had been drinking during the night in Martin Johnson's saloon, and about 2 o'clock in the morning Ladhoff called Cannon to the bar and just as Cannon stepped to the bar Ladhoff pulled a revolver and placed it close to Cannon's head and pulled the trigger. Cannon fell over dead and Ladhoff walked out of the saloon and coolly remarked to the spectators that he had shot Pat Cannon in self defense. Cannon was employed as a miner at Red Lodge and is said to have been a quiet and good natured man even if under the influence of liquor. Ladhoff is a married man and has a family of three children who reside on a ranch near Red Lodge. He was seen at the jail, but refused to make any statement other than that he had committed the deed in self defense.[1]*

Frank Ladhoff, as his name turned out to be, was eventually convicted of manslaughter and sentenced to ten years in the state penitentiary at Livingston. His request for a retrial was denied.

The following year, in 1895, with Johnson's tenure as constable due to expire, he decided to run for the position of marshal one more time. But his health had been steadily failing, and his age was beginning to show. The ravages of a lifetime of physical and mental hardships, of his battle wounds, injuries, and illnesses, caught up with his rugged lifestyle. Bent over from rheumatism and spinal scoliosis and suffering the effects of a dogged skin disease, heart disease, the loss of vision in one eye, and the slow deterioration of his hearing, he appeared to be anything but suited for another stint as lawman. At the end of the day when all the votes had been cast and all the ballots counted, Johnson lost.

Undeterred, he decided to make the best of what remained of his life by returning to the wilderness. To help with his infirmities, he increasingly relied upon the "healing waters" of the nearby sulfur hot springs. Occasionally, he spent several weeks there at a time, camping out nearby in the evenings and taking the "cure" during the days. One such venture had Johnson and a friend, Cass Prudhomme, heading out to the springs when they ran into trouble. An article in the *Red Lodge Picket*, July 25, 1896, ran a short mention of the event:

Cass Prudhomme and "Liver Eating" Johnson started out with a team and camp outfit yesterday intending to go to the Big Horn hot springs for a month's outing. Out at Grove creek the team became frightened and ran away with the result that the wagon was overturned and Mr. Prudhomme suffered a compound fracture of the right leg above the knee. He was brought into town this morning and is a now under a surgeon's care where he will make the best of the situation and an accident insurance policy.

A follow-up article on August 1 confirmed that Johnson made the trip to the Big Horn Hot Springs at present-day Thermopolous regardless. The story emphasized that Johnson visited the springs as often as possible to help ease his chronic pain from a "lifetime of hard living." The article continued:

"Liver Eating" Johnson did not give up his trip to the Bighorn hot springs after the runaway accident on Grove creek which resulted in Cass Prudhomme getting his leg broken. Mr. Johnson left the following day by way of John Chapman's where he will endeavor to get Frank Roberts to join him.

Following several days at the springs, Liver-Eater returned to his cabin near Red Lodge none the worse for wear, but not much for the better either. The *magical waters* provided little more than a few hours' relief upon any given dip, after which Johnson was forced to endure his pain and other maladies once more.

Interestingly, Johnson realized his internal clock was winding down and turned to friends to join him in things he would have tackled alone only a few years earlier. As he found himself less able to perform those tasks that he had always undertaken so easily in the past—fishing, hunting, trapping, cooking, chopping wood—he spent "more time in town than at his cabin," according to author Dennis McLelland. "While in Red Lodge, he stayed with friends who took care of him. Being penniless (except for his monthly twelve-dollar pension), he relied upon the good will of friends and neighbors. Johnson was a proud man who hated having to depend on charity; but by that point, he had little choice."[2]

By that time, Liver-Eater had become a prisoner to the passage of time. Although his spirit remained strong, his body was quickly failing him. In time, he became virtually immobile. His friends and neighbors occasionally came to visit, as did some gawkers intent upon seeing one of the last great western frontiersmen before he would be gone forever.

Before long, Johnson's pain had become so bad that he couldn't lie down to sleep and had to have an attendant prop him up in a chair to get any rest at all. Alone with no family in Red Lodge—no wife, no children, no brothers or sisters—he endured what must have been a veritable hell on earth.

But even with his body wracked by pain and slowly withering away, he still had his memories to keep him moving forward. He had his thoughts of brighter days, and he must have thanked God for his ability to look back upon his boyhood in Little York, New Jersey, and to recall those good times and the bad. He thought about those thrilling days after running away from home only to chase the behemoths of the ocean up and down the seaboard. He thought back, too, to the life-altering decision he had made to desert ship and walk away from his service in the navy—to when he set out for a life on the run.

No doubt he recalled atoning for that sin and then some by enlisting in the army during the waning days of the Civil War and later serving as an army scout in the Indian Wars. Certainly, he recalled the wound to his shoulder that had plagued him forever after.

He remembered every single day of his life on the move, roaming from one mountain range to the next, from one stand of trees to another. He remembered every fight, every one of the Indians he had killed. He recalled the beautiful young Flathead squaw he had married and somehow come to love despite himself—so much so that her premature death altered his life forever.

He thought back about all his old pards—those that came and went from his life along with the ones he helped to bury. And even those few who remained to that day—Del Gue, Buffalo Bill Cody, White Eye Anderson, and others to whom one "determined old coon" had entrusted his life's story.

And as he looked around the room in which he had become a prisoner, the only acquaintance he could rely upon was the one he had never welcomed the thought of before: *pain.*

As Johnson's time on earth closed in upon him, he made one final claim for an increase in his military pension. A medical report dated November 15, 1899, detailed the eroding physical condition of Liver-Eating Johnson:

> *A progressive spinal scoliosis causes loss of power in limbs to the extent that he is unable to arise or lie down and requires the aid of attendant day and night. Also, arterial sclerosis and disease of the heart, and swelling of extremities. The disability is permanent.*[3]

Shortly after filing the claim, an article appeared in the *Yellowstone Journal* detailing Johnson's worsening condition:

> *One of the most famous characters of eastern Montana and the hero of many hairbreadth escapes during the days of Indian warfare on the northwestern frontier, is about to leave the scenes of his exploits*

forever. Liver-Eating Johnson has at last been compelled to yield to advancing age and cumulative effects of his years of exposure and hardship, and seeks rest and care in the national soldiers home in California, entrance to which he gained by various service in the Army. For weeks the old scout and Indian fighter has been bedridden at his home near Red Lodge and being without means has made application for admission to the home. The county in which he resides has agreed to defray the expenses of the trip and has also furnished an attendant. Gradually the ranks of the man who was the advance guard of civilization of the erstwhile wilderness and desert, which marked the boundary of what has grown into a prosperous and grand state are thinning and soon only their names will remain to be recalled by the story teller and the historian.[4]

On December 7, 1899, the *Anaconda Standard* ran a follow-up article regarding Johnson's application for admission to the old soldiers' home. The piece was originally published by the *Harlem Enterprise* and subsequently republished.

Taking the case of "Liver Eating" Johnson, a well-known character in Anaconda, for a text, the Harlem Enterprise *makes a plea for the pioneers as follows:*

"'Liver Eating' Johnson, one of the pioneer frontiersmen and scouts of the state, is bedridden at his home near Red Lodge and has made application to be sent to the National Soldiers home in California, he being entitled to entrance there by reason of having served in the regular army.

"It seems to us that the people of the state should take some steps towards raising a fund for the purpose of erecting a home for the indigent ones of those men who blazed the pathway leading to the El Dorado which has brought wealth in almost Monte Cristo-like quantities to many of its citizens. If the millionaires alone in this state were each to subscribe a comparatively insignificant sum the amount realized would be more than enough to endow such a place. Many are not like Johnson, who has a home to go to, but are dependent

upon charitably inclined people for their support, or else become county charges. If they had a home to go to where, surrounded by the congenial atmosphere of old-time companionship, these worthy old fellows could with peace and happiness await the time when they shall be called to cross the unknown river 'from whose bourne no traveler returns.'"[5]

Less than a week later, a complement to that article appeared in the *Carbon County Democrat*:

"Liver-Eating Johnson" has been a well known man in Montana for more than a decade, his last years being spent in Yellowstone and Carbon counties. Several residents of Fergus county were in the fight with the Indians on the lower Musselshell where the hero is reputed to have earned his title. Among these is Col. G. I. Norris of Judith.

The Carbon County Democrat *of the 13th inst. contained the following: John (Liver Eating) Johnson departed Saturday for California where he has permission to enter the soldiers home. The health of the old scout has been failing very rapidly for the past year, and his once powerful physique is not recognized now in the feeble and broken-down old man, who boarded Saturday's train. Yet there was a time when the name of Liver Eating Johnson was a terror to the Montana Indians, many of whom his trusty rifle has assisted in their research for a land where snow is at a premium.*

It was chiefly as a raconteur of the brave deeds of the past that the present generation knows the Liver Eater and his reminiscences were told with becoming modesty. From the commencement of this town Johnson has made his home here. And it was plain to see that he was most reluctant to leave it, even when his better judgment convinced him against his will that it was the part of wisdom to accept the provision made for the nation's heroes. Indeed it is not a two to one bet that Old Johnson will not turn around in his tracks and come back to Red Lodge, to spend his few remaining days among the friends he loves and it would not be an unwelcome sight for a good many of our best citizens to see old Liver Eater arrive at the Red Lodge station.[6]

So the man once called "irrepressible" had arrived at the point in life when his vulnerability had reached its pinnacle. Stripped of his dignity, his health, and his pride, he had little of the Liver-Eating Johnson spirit remaining within him. He departed by train for California on December 13, 1899. Some say, as Liver-Eater stood hunched over on the station platform waiting for his attendant to help him board the coach for his final journey into the sunset, he cried.

CHAPTER FIFTEEN

Final Farewell

JOHN LIVER-EATING JOHNSON PASSED AWAY AT THE NATIONAL SOL-
diers Home in Los Angeles, California, on January 21, 1900, little more
than one month after arriving there. The *Red Lodge Picket* memorialized
the event in an article dated February 2, 1900.

*"Liver-Eating Johnson" of Red Lodge Passes Away at National Sol-
dier's Home in California.*

BLAZED MONTANA TRAILS

*He Was Brave as a Lion and Death to Indians—How He Got
His Uncouth Name*

*John Johnston, known the country over as "Liver-Eating John-
son," died at the National Soldiers home at Santa Monica, Cal., on
Sunday, Jan. 22 [sic], and thus came to an end the earthly career
of a trail blazer and intrepid pioneer whose heroic exploits on the
western plains are inseparably connected with the early history of the
commonwealth of Montana. The announcement of his death was last
Saturday received by* The Picket *in a letter written to this office by
Sargeant [sic] Whitehead, who penned this brief note:*

*"National Soldiers Home, Los Angeles county, Cal., Jan. 22,
1900—To the Editor Red Lodge Picket—Dear Sir: Thinking some
of his friends might be interested and like to know, I write to inform
you and them that John Johnston, better known there as 'Liver-Eating Johnson,' died at this home yesterday and was buried here today."*

This simple announcement will produce a pang of pain in the hearts of those of his companions of early days who are still in the land of the living and will be received with feelings of genuine sorrow by his legion of old-time friends throughout Montana. For the past twelve years Mr. Johnston had made Red Lodge his home, coming here from Billings and taking up a ranch, which he disposed of last summer to C.W. Savage of Hunter's Hot Springs. Before Billings had a place on the map, Mr. Johnston was deputy sheriff of Custer county, with headquarters at the town of Coulson, and was on duty there in the early eighties at the time his bosom companion, "Muggins" Taylor, himself an officer of the law, was shot and killed in the discharge of his duties by Henry Lump [sic], a drunken galoot whose wife supported him by taking in washing. Mr. Johnston was the first constable of Red Lodge and served several terms in that capacity. Though a powerful man physically, exposure in camp and on the trail brought its inevitable result, and his iron constitution finally gave way. Wrecked in health and in purse, he was forced to accept financial assistance from his friends, and this worried him considerably. Though disliking to leave the scenes of his former exploits, with the attendant associations, his aversion to being made an object of public charity overcame his prejudices against becoming an inmate of the home for disabled veterans and so he reluctantly consented to enter the California Soldiers home. Upon leaving Red Lodge, less than two months' ago, the old man broke down and wept like a child as the train whirled him away from his friends, and it is fair to presume that his last thoughts as he lay dying in a strange land, among strange people in that home by the side of the sea, were of those generous friends and exciting scenes of former days. "Liver-Eating Johnson" was a man among men. Brave and loyal and true, he never shirked a duty, never betrayed a friend, never gave quarter to a foe. Born in New Jersey three-quarters of a century ago, he came to Montana in 1862 and remained a few months in Alder gulch. Then he went to Colorado and enlisted in the war for the preservation of the union. He served under General Price of Missouri and was in several fierce engagements. He was wounded in the battle of Newtonia and discharged from further service.

HEALTH DEPARTMENT

LOS ANGELES COUNTY

January 21 1900

" It shall be the duty of all physicians practicing in this County to report on postal cards provided for such purpose, to the Health Officer in whose district the same may occur, all births at which he may attend, all deaths for which he is entitled to sign death certificates, and the number of cases of contagious disease."—*Sec. 15 County Health Ordinance.*

CERTIFICATE OF DEATH.

THIS CERTIFICATE MUST BE LEGALLY FILLED OUT IN PLAIN ENGLISH AND IN INK.

Name John Johnston

Age 76 *years* *months* *days.*

Sex M

Color W

Married or Single Single

Occupation Farmer

Place of Birth New Jersey

Place of Death Pac. Br. N.H.D.V.S.

Date of Death Jan 21ª 1900

Cause of Death Peritonitis

Medical Attendant D H E Hane

Death certificate of John Johnston issued by the L.A. County Health Department on January 21, 1900.

A year later found him back in Montana and from that time until the capture of Sitting Bull he camped on the trails of hostile Indians and saved the lives of hundreds of early-day settlers. He served as chief of scouts under General Miles in 1877 and participated in more raids against the red-skins than any Indian fighter of the west. It is related of him that he took more scalps in those eventful days than anybody. It was during one of these Indian-killing expeditious that he got the uncouth name that he took to his grave. This was at the heart of the Musselshell in 1868. The story is that he killed an Indian, cut out the savage's liver and actually ate with great relish. But the story is only partly true. The circumstance is perhaps best related in his own words as he told the story at Hunter's Hot Springs less than a year ago. He said:

"We was attacked by Injuns, and we licked 'em—licked 'em good. There was fifteen of us and we killed thirty-six of them and wounded sixty. It was toward the close of the fight that I got my name. I was just gettin' my blood up and feelin' like fightin'. We was short of ammunition and as I saw an Injun running toward the cover I threw my gun to Bill Martin and took Bill's knife. I wasn't going to waste no good cartridges on him, for I could lick any Injun I could lay my paws on. I was considered the best shot with a rifle in Montana at that time, but I wanted to save my cartridges. We had a 300-yard run to the bushes and I caught the Injun by the hair of the head and threw him down just at the edge of the brush. I danced and sang on the Injun's body, for that's what they done to a party of whites a few days before. Then I scalped him and then I danced and sang some more. Then I ran my knife into him and killed him and part of his liver came out with the knife. Just then a sort of a squeamish old fellow named Ross came running up. I waved the knife with the liver on it in the air and I cried out:

"'Come on, and have a piece! It'll stay yer stomach 'till you get home to dinner.'

"'Don't want none,' sez he.

"'Come on,' sez I, dancing around; 'I've cut some and it's just as good as antelope's liver. Have a bite!' and I kind of made believe take

a bite. Then Ross he threw up his guts. And he always swore after that that he seen me tear a liver out of a dying Injun and eat it. But that ain't so. I was all over blood and I had the liver on my knife, but I didn't eat none of it. The liver coming out was unintentional on my part. But Ross he vowed 'twas so and I never got rid of the name."

Epilogue

IN 1973, THE STUDENTS AT PARK VIEW MIDDLE SCHOOL IN LANCASTER, California, were studying American history, but, according to teacher Tri Robinson, they weren't responding the way he'd hoped. Robinson tried every trick in the books to inspire them to get more engaged with their studies. Finally, in frustration, he began relaying riveting tales of the Old West. Not even *that* worked . . . until he stumbled upon the character of John "Liver-Eating" Johnson.

He told the students about the mountain man who had spent his life as a soldier, hunter, trapper, whiskey peddler, scout, deputy sheriff, and town marshal in the Big Sky country of Montana. He told of the "Crow Killer" and his twenty-five-year vendetta against the Indians who had killed his Flathead wife and unborn child in 1847. He explained how Johnson got his nickname and how old age and not Indians finally forced him to leave his home in Red Lodge for a veterans' hospital in California, where he died in 1900 and was buried in a military cemetery a few hundred feet from a bustling freeway.

"Up until that point," Robinson recalled, "none of my stories had gotten a rise out of my students, but they were outraged that [Johnson] was buried by the freeway. They acted like it was a total injustice."[1]

Robinson's wife offered a suggestion: If they don't like it, tell them to move him.

Impossible, Robinson thought before realizing that such a venture might just spur his students on to civic action. So, a "committee" was born, and the kids began writing letters. They petitioned governors, chambers of commerce, historical societies, and even Congress. The Montana town of Red Lodge wrote off the students' request, stating disinterest in the venture because Johnson had been an "Indian killer" and was, therefore, an "undesirable."

But a friend of Robinson's who lived in the Wyoming town of Cody, named after the famed frontiersman Buffalo Bill Cody, responded more positively. Bob Edgar told Robinson that, if his students could get permission to disinter the body, he would pay to have it moved from California to Wyoming and reburied at Edgar's "Old Trail Town."

The students petitioned Congress, whose members declared them to be Johnson's "next-to-kin" proxy to legalize his reburial. The kids even convinced actor Robert Redford, who played the main character of 1972's hit film *Jeremiah Johnson*, to come to Cody to serve as one of Johnson's pallbearers!

At the last minute, town representatives of Red Lodge realized what a mistake they had made by refusing to rebury Johnson there, but they were too late. Liver-Eating Johnson was exhumed in California and moved to Cody, Wyoming, where he was reburied in June 1974.

"The ceremony had something of a circus atmosphere," wrote Gary Svee, a reporter at the time for the *Billings Gazette*.[2]

But not everyone enjoyed the show. Red Lodge resident Fred Longmore, who as a child had held Johnson's hand on the railroad platform before the train arrived to trundle the old warrior off to the Golden State, recalled the event three-quarters of a century earlier: "[Johnson] looked at the Beartooth Mountains, and tears rolled out of his eyes. . . . I said, 'Don't feel sad, Mr. Johnston, because you'll come back. They won't keep you down there long.' Johnston replied, 'Oh, Freddy boy, I'll never see them mountains again.'"[3]

Red Lodge historian Harry J. Owens lamented the truth of Johnson's last words: "He would have abhorred the reburial at a tourist stop [Old Trail Town] near some warehouses in a Wyoming town. Nowhere can be seen his beloved Beartooths. Liver Eating Johnston would enjoy the last laugh, however, as all that was left of his earthly remains when the grave was opened [in California] was a large leg bone and a few fragments of the cedar coffin he had been buried in. And, although this tourist stop now claims his remains, they did not capture his spirit. The spirit of John Johnston still roams wild and free over his Beartooths and, in the final reckoning, that is what really counts."[4]

No Regrets

By the time Johnson had left Red Lodge for good and been enrolled in the National Soldiers Home, he was listed in official government records as standing under six feet tall. Some friends claimed he'd "nearly overnight got old." True, he was diminished in physical size . . . but not in legend.

Throughout his lifetime, Liver-Eating Johnson had worked as a farmer, sailor, scout, soldier, gold seeker, hunter, trapper, whiskey peddler, guide, deputy, justice of the peace, sheriff, log-cabin builder, and just about any other job he could find to hold him over yet one more bitter, hard Rocky Mountain winter.

He could have escaped at any time of his life and moved to town, to the warm climes of Arizona or southern New Mexico—anywhere his old bones would have welcomed the warmth of the sun. But the truth is that he never wanted to live anywhere else. From the moment he first laid his eyes on the spiraling majesty of the Rocky Mountains and reveled in the clean, sweet air blowing down off the wildflower-covered slopes, he was home.

Whether in Red Lodge, Montana, or in Cody, Wyoming, he was finally at peace in one of his favorite stomping grounds—a scant sixty-five miles from his hometown of Red Lodge and his beloved Beartooth Mountains where, to this day, backwoodsmen claim they can still smell his pipe tobacco drifting into camp and see the ghostly figure of Johnson leading a pack string down an ancient trail in the moonlight.

He had lived a long and satisfying life, and the stories of his violent adventures were passed on through generations. While some of the events from his life are verifiable, many of the stories are no doubt improved upon from over a century of retelling and embellishment. But one fact is beyond reproach.

When it came to the world of hard-working, hard-living, hard-driving mountain men, no one on earth matched the physical prowess or the will to survive of John "Liver-Eating" Johnson.

Or made a better "pard."

Notes

INTRODUCTION
1. "Charles Astor Parker Writes of Persons and Things He Has Seen and Found in the Western City," *Star Tribune* (Minneapolis, MN), December 17, 1899.
2. Ibid.

CHAPTER 1
1. John X. Beidler, *X. Beidler: Vigilante* (Norman: University of Oklahoma Press, 1969), 137–39.

CHAPTER 2
1. "How Liver-Eatin' Johnson Got His Uncouth Name," *Anaconda Standard*, July 18, 1899.

CHAPTER 3
1. Don D. Walker, "The Mountain Man as Literary Hero," *Western American Literature* 1, no. 1 (Spring 1966): 20.
2. Ibid.
3. Michael Schaubs, "The Mountain Men," Mountain Men and Life in the Rocky Mountain West, accessed August 22, 2018, http://www.mman.us/mountainman.htm.

CHAPTER 4
1. Raymond W. Thorp, "Revenge of Liver-Eating Johnson," *The Best of the West, 1971 Annual*, February 1971, 64.

CHAPTER 5

1. Alan Bellows, "Liver-Eating Johnson, Damn Interesting," last modified January 26, 2017, https://www.damninteresting.com/liver-eating-johnson.
2. Ibid.
3. Ibid.
4. Ibid.

CHAPTER 6

1. Genealogy records search, Genealogy.com, accessed December 10, 2018, https://www.genealogy.com/lp/genealogy-records?s_kwcid=genealo-gy+sites&o_xid=57495&o_lid=57495&o_sch=Paid+Search+Non+Brand.

CHAPTER 7

1. Ella Lonn, *Desertion during the Civil War* (Lincoln: University of Nebraska Press, 1998), vi.
2. "How Liver-Eating Johnson Got His Strange Nickname," *Flathead Courier*, December 21, 1939.
3. Will Carpenter, "Liver-Eating Johnson," *Westerner Magazine*, November/December 1971, 36–37.
4. Ibid., 62.
5. Joe DeBarthe, *The Life and Adventures of Frank Grouard* (St. Joseph, MO: Combe Printing Company, 1894), 18.
6. Ibid., 69.
7. Ibid.
8. Ibid., 69–72.
9. "Chapple–Rixon–Panton," Yellowstone County Miscellaneous, MTGen-Web Project, revised May 8, 2002, http://www.mtgenweb.com/yellowstone/misc/chapple.htm.
10. J. W. Reddington, *Way Out West: Remembrances and Tales* (New York: Lewis Publishing Co., 1923), 37.
11. Joseph Foster (White Eye) Anderson, *I Buried Hickok: The Memoirs of White Eye Anderson*, ed. William B. Secrest (College Station, TX: Creative Publishing Company, 1980), 152.
12. Edward S. Bernard, ed., *Story of the Great American West* (Pleasantville, NY: Readers Digest Association, 1977), 236.
13. Luther S. Kelly, *Yellowstone Kelly: The Memoirs of Luther S. Kelly*, ed. M. M. Quaife (New Haven, CT: Yale University Press, 1926), 167.

14. John D. McDermott, *Forlorn Hope* (Boise: Idaho State Historical Society, 1978), 12, 54.

15. Elliott West, *The Last Indian War: The Nez Perce Story* (Oxford: Oxford University Press, 2009), 5–6.

16. Michael P. Malone, Richard B. Roeder, and William L. Lang, *Montana: A History of Two Centuries* (Seattle and London: University of Washington Press, 1991), 135.

17. Charles Erskine Scott Wood, "The Pursuit and Capture of Chief Joseph," New Perspectives on the West, PBS, accessed August 12, 2018, www.pbs.org/weta/thewest/resources/archives/six/joseph.htm.

18. Merrill D. Beal, *I Will Fight No More Forever: Chief Joseph and the Nez Perce War* (Seattle: University of Washington Press, 1963), 130.

19. Wood, "The Pursuit and Capture of Chief Joseph."

20. Ibid.

21. Ibid.

22. Beal, *I Will Fight No More Forever*, 130.

23. Alvin M. Josephy Jr., *The Nez Perce Indians and the Opening of the Northwest* (New Haven, CT: Yale University Press, 1965), 632–33.

24. Jerome A. Greene and Alvin M. Josephy, *Nez Perce Summer, 1877: The US Army and the Nee-Me-Poo Crisis* (Helena: Montana Historical Society Press, 2001), xi.

25. Robert Leckie, *The Wars of America* (New York: Castle Books, 1998), 537.

26. Dennis McLelland, *The Avenging Fury of the Plains, Liver-Eating Johnson* (West Conshohocken, PA: Infinity Publishing, 2008), 2.

27. "The Scout's Life," *Bismarck Tri-Weekly Tribune*, February 7, 1878.

28. George Booth, *Frontier Folk* (New York: A. S. Barnes, 1880), 21–22.

CHAPTER 8

1. Kelly, *Yellowstone Kelly*, 1.

2. Ibid., 6.

3. Ibid.

4. Ibid., 21.

5. Ibid., 23–24.

6. Jerry Keenan, "Yellowstone Kelly: From New York to Paradise," *Montana: The Magazine of Western History* 40, no. 3 (1990): 6, http://www.jstor.org/stable/4519312.

7. Joseph Mills Hanson, *The Conquest of the Missouri: Being the Story of the Life and Exploits of Captain Grant Marsh* (New York: Murray Hill Books, 1909), 102–3.

8. Clay Fisher, *Yellowstone Kelly* (New York: Pocket Books, 1965), 133.

9. Ibid., 134.

10. Ibid., 134–35.

11. Ibid., 135–36.

12. Anderson, *I Buried Hickok*, 147.

CHAPTER 9

1. Mick McAllister, "You Can't Go Home: Jeremiah Johnson and the Wilderness," *Western American Literature* 13, no. 1 (Spring 1978): 46.

2. John Liver Eating Johnston (website), home page, accessed December 10, 2018, http://johnlivereatingjohnston.com.

3. Anderson, *I Buried Hickok*, 152.

4. Beidler, *X. Beidler: Vigilante*, 5.

5. Ibid., 7.

CHAPTER 10

1. Richard Slotkin, *Regeneration through Violence: The Mythology of the American Frontier, 1600–1860* (New York: Harper Perennial, 1973), 22.

2. Schaubs, "The Mountain Men."

3. McAllister, "You Can't Go Home," 37.

4. Ibid.

5. Ibid., 45.

6. Ibid.

7. "Borderlands, Borders and Global Frontiers: Borderlands and Frontiers as Zones of Ethnic Change," JRank Science Encyclopedia, Net Industries, 2018, http://science.jrank.org/pages/8487/Borders-Borderlands-Frontiers-Global-Borderlands-Frontiers-Zones-Ethnic-Change.html.

8. Frederick Jackson Turner, *The Significance of the Frontier in American History* (London: Penguin Books, 2008), chap. 1, Kindle, https://www.amazon.com/Significance-Frontier-American-History-Penguin-ebook/dp/B003P9X-CCQ/ref=sr_1_1_twi_kin_2?s=books&ie=UTF8&qid=1544054894&s-r=1-1&keywords=turner+%22the+significance+of+the+frontier%22.

9. Slotkin, *Regeneration through Violence*, 22–23.

10. Vardis Fisher, *Mountain Man* (New York: Pocket Books, 1972), viii.

11. Harold Schindler, "Here Lies Joseph Slade," in *In Another Time* (Boulder: University Press of Colorado, 1998), 115–17.

12. "The Saga of Liver-Eating Johnson," *homelessphilosopher* (blog), December 8, 2015, https://homelessphilosopher.wordpress.com/2015/12/08/the-saga-of-liver-eating-johnson.

13. Walker, "The Mountain Man as Literary Hero," 15.
14. Ibid.
15. Ibid., 16.
16. Ibid., 20.
17. Ibid., 22.

CHAPTER 11

1. Raymond W. Thorp and Robert Bunker, *Crow Killer: The Saga of Liver-Eating Johnson* (Bloomington: Indiana University Press, 1958), 145.
2. Ibid., 152.
3. Anderson, *I Buried Hickok*, 164–65.
4. Thorp and Bunker, *Crow Killer*, 153.
5. Ibid., 154.
6. Ibid.
7. Zach Benoit, "Born by the River, Killed by the Railroad: Town of Coulson Laid the Foundation for Billings," *Billings Gazette*, September 13, 2014, https://www.questia.com/newspaper/1P3-3435454011/born-by-the-river-killed-by-the-railroad-town-of.
8. Ibid.
9. McLelland, *The Avenging Fury of the Plains*, 151.
10. "Liver-Eating Johnson," *Bozeman (MT) Weekly Chronicle*, May 13, 1885, http://chroniclingamerica.loc.gov/lccn/sn86075108/1885-05-13/ed-1/seq-1.
11. "Liver-Eating Johnson: The Career of a Yellowstone County Man as Pictured in a Leading Eastern Journal," *Billings Weekly Gazette*, January 24, 1899.
12. Raymond W. Thorp, "Liver-Eating Johnson's Last Trail," *True West*, October 1965, 156.
13. "As It Was in Billings 45 Years Ago," *Billings Gazette*, June 16, 1927.
14. E. A. Brinstool, *Fighting Indian Warriors* (New York: Indian Head Books, 1953), 289–90.

CHAPTER 12

1. Thorp, "Liver-Eating Johnson's Last Trail," 18.
2. Ibid.
3. Ibid., 19.
4. Ibid.
5. Ibid., 20.
6. Ibid.
7. Ibid., 49.
8. Ibid.

9. Ibid., 50.

10. Harry Owens, "The Saga of Liver Eating Johnston: He Never Ate Crow," *Old West* 19 (1983): 16.

11. Ralph Lumley: Letter from Red Lodge, Montana, May 1, 1950, in Thorp and Bunker, *Crow Killer*, xxxi.

CHAPTER 13

1. "Tom Hardwick Is Dying," *Deadwood Daily Pioneer-Times*, February 16, 1901.

2. "Calamity Jane," *Atchison Daily Champion*, September 7, 1883.

3. "Liver-Eating Johnson," *Fergus County Argus*, May 22, 1884.

4. "Montana Matters," *Daily Independent*, July 2, 1884.

5. "Well Guyed," *Yellowstone Journal*, June 28, 1884.

6. *Janesville Gazette*, July 2, 1884.

7. "Liver-Eating Johnson," *Janesville Gazette*, July 4, 1844.

8. *Milwaukee Sentinel*, July 3, 1884.

9. *Deadwood Black Hills Daily Times*, July 13, 1884.

10. *Chicago Times*, July 19, 1884.

11. *Chicago Times*, July 22, 1884.

12. *Billings Post*, August 7, 1884.

CHAPTER 14

1. "Was the Killing of Patrick Cannon at Red Lodge by Freud Ladhoff," *Butte (MT) Miner*, June 21, 1894.

2. McLelland, *The Avenging Fury of the Plains*, 180.

3. Ibid., 184.

4. "Liver-Eating Johnson: A Tribute from Col. Sam Gates of Miles City," *Carbon County Democrat*, November 29, 1899.

5. "Plea for the Pioneer," *Anaconda Standard*, December 7, 1899.

6. "Liver-Eating Johnson: Goes to the California Soldiers Home To Spend the Remainder of His Days," *Fergus County Argus*, December 27, 1899.

EPILOGUE

1. Jana Bommersbach, "Freedom from the Freeway," *True West Magazine*, May 4, 2016, https://truewestmagazine.com/freedom-freeway.

2. "Keeping Memory Alive: The Legend of Liver-Eating Johnston Keeps Getting Taller," *Montana Standard* (Butte, MT), August 27, 2017.

3. Ibid.

4. Ibid.

Index

H
Hairy Bear (Sioux chief), 12
Hardwick Great Wild West Show.
  See Great Rocky Mountain
  Wild West Show
Hardwick, Thomas Wilbur, 197
Harpers Ferry, West Virginia,
  140
Hatcher, John (Jack), 36, 46, 185
Hawley, Jennie, 14
Helena, Montana, 18, 23
Hickok, James Butler "Wild Bill,"
  2, 172, 197
House, James, 76
Houston, George, 90
Howard, Otis, 89, 92
Hubble (mountain man), 2, 6
Huffman, L. A., 109

I
Indian Wars, 86, 107, 126
Ireland, Hatchet Jack, 140, 162
Irvine, Tom, 176, 178, 185

J
Jackson, Bob, 88
Janesville, Wisconsin, 202
Jeremiah Johnson (film), 4, 129,
  224
Johnson, Ed, 187
Johnson, George, 88
Johnson, John "Liver-Eating"
  army scout, 86, 96, 107, 117,
    122, 125, 128

Beidler partnership, 77, 82, 136,
  143
boxing match, 83
burial, 223
caretaking, 81
childhood, 29
death, 8, 217
deputy sheriff (Coulson,
  Montana), 177, 185
gold prospecting, 34
Gue partnership, 37, 129, 143,
  162, 191
Hatcher partnership, 36
illness and decline, 210
Indian vendetta, 11, 19, 40, 42,
  47, 49, 50, 53, 59, 131, 146,
  155, 165, 189
Indians, attitude toward, 3, 47,
  154
justice of the peace (Custer
  County, Montana), 176
Lapp partnership, 143
Leadville, 168, 174
legend of, 1, 11, 22, 27, 51, 158
"Liver-Eater" moniker, 11, 13,
  16, 19, 20, 51, 69, 77, 79, 84,
  100, 132, 191, 193
marriage, 37
National Soldiers Home (Los
  Angeles), 8, 24, 214, 217
pack guide, 86
petrified man (Antelope
  Charlie) attraction, 23
Sims partnership, 75

About the Author

Born and raised in Chicago, **D. J. Herda** worked for years at the *Chicago Tribune*, as well as at numerous other Chicago-area newspapers and magazines, before becoming an internationally syndicated columnist. Herda's interest in western Americana goes back to his childhood. He has published biographies of Calamity Jane, Doc Holliday, Frank and Jesse James, Billy the Kid, Butch Cassidy and the Wild Bunch, Wyatt Earp, and other western legends. He has written "Forts of the American West" and other articles for *American West, Arizona Highways*, and other magazines. D. J. Herda has lived in the Rocky Mountains of the southwestern United States for nearly three decades.